SATAN

He felt the firs
ripped up into
knew that it was happening all over again, tried to scream but couldn't. It was worse than last time, sheer malevolence behind each lash. Laughter in the darkness all around. He writhed and struggled, prayed again for death. It was denied him.

He knew the wooden steps were there but it was impossible to negotiate them. Rolling. Falling. Every bone jarred with each step until he hit the snow-covered rock surface below.

For one brief moment he could see. He was lying in the snow beneath the huge front door with the brass plate on it. A tiny flower stood erect only inches from him. A snowdrop; the same one that he had studied from his hiding place in the bushes. And the red stain surrounded it again, strawberry sauce poured haphazardly over a vanilla ice-cream.

Only this time Pierre Lautrec knew what the colouring was. *It was blood, seeping up from the ground below.*

Also by Guy N. Smith
in Hamlyn Paperbacks

LOCUSTS

DEATHBELL

SATAN'S SNOWDROP

GUY N. SMITH

Hamlyn Paperbacks

SATAN'S SNOWDROP

ISBN 0 600 20171 6

First published in Great Britain 1980
by Hamlyn Paperbacks

Hamlyn Paperbacks are published by
The Hamlyn Publishing Group Ltd,
Astronaut House,
Feltham,
Middlesex, England
(Paperback Division: Hamlyn Paperbacks,
Banda House, Cambridge Grove,
Hammersmith, London W6 0LE)

Made and printed by
Hunt Barnard Printing Ltd., Aylesbury, Bucks.

For Father Francis Hertzberg,
a good friend.

PROLOGUE

The dance of death.
All that go to and fro must look upon it,
Mindful of what they shall be; while beneath,
Among the wooden piles, the turbulent river
Rushes impetuous as the river of Life.

The tall man standing in the snow-laden bushes had read the words on the brass plaque above the door of the house countless times during the day with a kind of morbid fascination. He knew them off by heart. He tried to remember who had written them. He thought it was Longfellow. It didn't really matter.

Beneath the scarf which covered the lower half of his face he smiled. Or it may have been a scowl. The features moved, the lips stretching out to a gaping slit, the mouth extending across the sallow cheeks, the vivid scar opening up, nostrils flaring. The beret was pulled down almost to his eyebrows, hiding the zigzags of badly healed flesh on his bald head, a detailed map of inter-city roads, crossing, joining up again, some wide, others narrow, a few petering out.

His fists clenched in the pockets of the ill-fitting raincoat, the eyes which stared across at the huge ornate wooden house remembered. Hate boiled inside him, a cauldron that had simmered for twenty years.

With an effort he checked himself. He would have the opportunity to give vent to his feelings shortly. Darkness was less than an hour away. Once night cast its mantle over these snow-powdered Swiss mountainsides he could make his move. But first he had to be certain that the man he sought was indeed here. For hours there had been no sign of life inside the building. It could well be empty, in which case the relentless pursuing hound had drawn yet another blank covert. It was always the same; some clue would send him to yet another destination. Another house, another country, across the continent and back, and then start all over again. But one day, some time, some place . . .

The man closed his lips in a slitted expression of determination. That was it. It *had* to be. He had almost phoned Deydier in Paris from Interlaken. 'It is him at last, Deydier. The name of his hiding place should have led us here years ago. The Reichenbach Falls. Where else for the infamous Reichenbach to skulk like a Swiss mountain fox that has outrun the hunters over the first chase and now lies breathless, waiting for them to catch up with him? Come at once. Bring Legros with you. We must make sure this time. He must not escape us.'

But he hadn't phoned. The delay whilst Deydier and Legros travelled to Switzerland could have meant yet another reprieve for Reichenbach. That was what he told himself but he knew the real reason; he did not want to share his revenge. Instead he would send them a cable from Basel tomorrow. Just three words. *It is finished.* They would be angry that he had carried out the task alone but that did not matter. The three of them would never meet again. The tall stooping man with the slashed cheeks and scarred head would vanish as completely as Reichenbach had done.

It had been a long day, the frustration building up in the hunter, knowing that his prey was so close and yet might still elude him. The long wait in Interlaken for the train that would take him to Meiringen. On to Rosenlaui. Nietzsche had booked in at the hotel there at the end of the last century. The place had also been used in fiction. It seemed a fitting refuge for Reichenbach, a veritable fortress built within sight of the infamous falls. Men had perished there, frail bodies bouncing and smashing on the jagged rocks in the chasm below, lost in the flying spume as the current took them. Unrecognisable pulped flesh and bone was washed up a mile or so further downstream. That was where they would find what was left of Reichenbach.

The watcher studied the house again. He remembered where he had last read those lines. On the Spreuerbrucke down the Reuss. There had been a seventeenth-century painting of the Dance of Death, too. It *was* Longfellow; taken from the conversation between Prince Henry and Elsie in *The Golden Legend.*

The house seemed somehow out of place up here. There was a date over the door: 1643. The weathered timbers bore evidence of three centuries of battling with the elements, dignified and preserved yet battle-scarred. Four storeys without a brick to be seen on any of them. The scores of carvings bore the hallmark of the same Swiss craftsman, a life's work that had begun in youth and ended in old age, the style of that row of totem-like faces beneath the high gable depicting the boyish enthusiasm that finally waned with frailty and weariness.

The designs beneath the mullioned windows represented flowers which grew wild in the mountains, yet every so often a lone snowdrop seemed to dominate in harsh contrast, almost as if it had been fashioned by a different wood-carver who sought to inflict his own style.

Strangest of all were the stilts on which the house stood: massive wooden beams that jutted up and supported the building fully six feet above the ground. There was no reason for them, except that the builders were unable to dig foundations out of the rocky ground . . . or else, and it seemed more likely, the house had, at some stage, been transported here from another place. The Frenchman shivered. In his imagination he saw it in its former setting, perched over an area of treacherous marshland, shifting quicksands gurgling beneath it, enshrouded in mist. Cold and uninviting. *Evil!*

But *why?* Why build it on marshes that would suck down without trace an unwary traveller? And why, then, bring it here to totally contrasting terrain? There had to be a reason. Possibly it was better not to seek it. It did not matter. All that mattered was the man who hid behind the ornate walls.

The shadows were lengthening across the uneven garden which separated the thick shrubbery from the house. Snow lay in patches, a cake that had been sparsely iced by a careless housewife.

The man stared at one of the lower windows, felt the blood course through his veins and his pulses quicken, as he detected a movement. Somebody had passed across the room and disappeared from sight. Only a brief glimpse, but it was enough. *Reichenbach was here!*

The watcher glanced upwards in to the pale blue sky, the shades of evening in the west turning to a deeper red hue as the sun sank further beyond the snow-capped mountain peaks. It was not time to move yet. He must be patient. What was another hour after twenty years of waiting?

Something else caught his eye, a patch of bright crimson at the foot of the wooden steps which led up to the front door, stark against the whiteness of the snow and the small flower which swayed gently in the breeze in the centre of it. A patch of late evening sunlight around a lone snowdrop? But no, it was impossible. The mountains had already cut out the sun's rays. A reflection? Something inside the house shining out through the windows? The windows were dull and dark, facing eastwards. No light shone from within.

A trick of the light? He tried to find a solution but could not, and when he looked again the snow around the flower was virgin white. The tip of his tongue licked a full course around those disfigured lips. It was uncanny. Almost frightening. It was also very stupid of him to pay such attention to irrelevant details. All that he was concerned with was Reichenbach.

The weight of the Luger in the pocket of his raincoat was comforting. He had walked through both French and Swiss customs with it just like that. A risk, but he knew they would not search him. They did not trouble themselves with vagrants.

The pistol was useful, but he would not use it to kill Reichenbach. It was too quick. The German had to be made to suffer. He had to experience the suffering of three thousand people, dragged to the ultimate of human endurance, praying that death would come quickly.

A light shone from one of the downstairs windows, a pale yellow glow that turned the snow outside golden. Somebody had lit an oil lamp in the room beyond, leaving the intersecting door open. The Frenchman stared, but there was no movement to be seen within. He glanced up at the sky again, made an attempt to purse his disfigured lips, and came to a decision. Moving slowly, half-crouching, he followed a course along the thick shrubbery which would bring him in a half-circle to the door. The Luger was clutched in his right hand, the fourth and fifth fingers of which were no more than stumps protruding above the whiteness of the knuckles. Yet neither speed nor marksmanship would be impaired if the occasion demanded. But that would be a last resort.

He took his time, moving slowly, stopping to look and listen every yard or so. It was ten minutes before he was at the foot of the wooden steps. Something prompted him to glance down. That snowdrop was virtually indiscernible against the snow. There was no crimson surround. It *had* been a trick of the light.

He began to mount the steps, testing each one before putting his full weight on it. They did not creak. They were strong and well-made, the work of a master craftsman that three centuries of wear had not spoiled.

He was almost at the door, his left hand stretching out for the huge brass knob, when the stench first hit him, a sudden wave of vile odours that caught him like a hammer blow and forced him to turn his head away, gasping for the pure mountain air which lay behind.

'God in heaven!' He turned once more for the door, striving not to retch.

The smell was one of putrefaction, the ultimate in rotting matter. Mingled in with it was a vaguely familiar aroma, one that had been so common in the Nazi prison camps twenty years before: *the unmistakable stench of death.*

The fingers of his intact hand closed over the knob and turned. He was surprised when the door swung silently inwards on well-oiled hinges, a stygian blackness yawning beyond, that stench, stronger and more putrid, coming at him like some monster of weird fantasy out of a pit of slime.

He hesitated, and then stepped inside, closing the door silently behind him. The foul air was thicker here as though he had stepped on to a battlefield where thousands of corpses were decomposing, the dead rotting into a mountain of flesh as the maggots squirmed and wriggled higher and higher.

He pulled the scarf tighter around his face, and with his

left arm at full stretch, moved forward. The blackness was complete. Somewhere in the house he knew that a light burned, but it did not penetrate the hall.

His fingers brushed carved oak, invisible wooden features that leered at him in the darkness. The stench seemed to have lessened somewhat, or perhaps he had become accustomed to it. Fear gripped him, rising up with the bile into his throat. The atmosphere was colder in here than it had been outside during his long vigil in the shrubbery. He sensed the evil, felt invisible fingers clawing at him, heard voices that were probably inside his own brain.

Find Reichenbach and destroy him. The order came from his conscience, a reminder of his mission. *You owe it to three thousand people.*

Eventually he found a doorway leading off the hall, a heavy oaken one which swung silently back into an adjoining room. The walls were hung with rich tapestries, and in the wide fireplace flames were beginning to crackle, licking hungrily and noisily at a pile of dry wood.

And before the fire a man was seated. The intruder stared, believing that perhaps he had made a mistake and this was not the man he sought. Briefly his mind went back to that prison camp; the tall thickset man with the shaven head, eyes that glinted cruelly behind rimless spectacles, thin lips that were almost invisible, just a bloodless slit where the mouth was, the low laugh as he stepped forward to inflict the atrocities conceived in his warped brain upon yet another hapless victim.

Here, twenty years later, there was barely any physical resemblance between this man and the Nazi torturer from Nuremberg. Those same rimless spectacles, the eyes behind them staring sightlessly. The body seemed to have shrunk to a skeletal sparseness on which the ragged suit hung limply. Lips that were a mass of sores. Ulcers. Growths that wept their stinking pus, which ran down the wasted chin like an old man's tobacco juice. The face was a mass of tiny cancers, resembling a photograph of some alien planet, the crust of which was covered with craters and molten streams which gave off their vile gases. It was from here, this diseased but still living body, that the smell of putrefaction came.

'Guten Abend.' The voice was a hoarse croak, the sightless eyes turned towards the door. *'Was wünschen Sie? Wie heissen Sie?'*

'Lautrec,' the tall man answered. 'Pierre Lautrec. And I have followed your trail for twenty years, Reichenbach. To kill you!'

'Ich verstehe nicht.'

'There must be many like myself. A good many of them died from your tortures, Reichenbach. A few lived. Like myself. And Deydier . . . and Legros. Just three of us. But you remember me, surely? Lautrec of the French Resistance movement, taken by the Gestapo in Paris and brought to you at Nuremberg. And what you did to me!'

Silence. Just a slight twitching of the lower festering lip.

'So you do remember, eh? Then look at this!' The scarf was flung to the floor, the beret following it, revealing the hideous scars, the mouth that had been extended by two or three inches at each side where the razor blade had cut a path right up into the cheeks, a gash that had never knitted.

'Well?' Lautrec bowed his head so that his cranium disfigurements glinted in the light of the oil lamp which hung from a beam directly above him. 'What have you got to say for yourself now, Reichenbach?'

'I cannot see,' the dull eyes had a kind of cataract over them, a thick opaque film. 'My sight has gone.'

'Then let me refresh your memory, Reichenbach. You wanted me to name two men and their whereabouts, the men who were responsible for organising the Resistance in Paris. Deydier and Legros. But you didn't really want me to give the information until you had finished with me. I'll never forget that time. How long I was kept in your torture-chamber at Nuremberg, I'll never know. Time meant nothing to me. Just pain. Pain that threatened to rob me of my sanity. But, most of all, I hate you for what you did to my wife. D'you think any woman would want a man who had had done to him what you did to me?'

Silence. Just another slight tremble from the German's thin lips. Lautrec wondered if the other remembered. It was doubtful. There had been so many.

'Let me refresh your memory some more. That bullwhip.

You could sever a matchstick at five paces. I was stripped and hung from the ceiling by my wrists, my ankles tied back to the wall so that I was virtually doing the splits. Six lashes, so perfectly placed that they shredded my testicles without even touching any other part of my body! The next day you scalped me, just like some heathen Red Indian! Well, d'you remember now?'

'Ich weiss nicht.'

'Maybe, and maybe not. The following day you cut off a finger. Another the next. You were getting desperate. You had to have the names, otherwise the Gestapo would lose faith in you. You were going to sever one of my limbs each day until I told you what you wanted to know, but I cheated you. I went into a fever, then a coma.' Pierre Lautrec laughed harshly. 'They had to keep me alive. They were scared that if I died they'd never find out what they wanted. But the war ended and the Allies got to me before the Nazis could finish me off. I spent the next twenty years, financed by Deydier and Legros, on your trail. Why didn't I think of it before? The Reichenbach Falls, the ideal cover for you. Maybe you're even trying to claim that your ancestors owned this land, that it is your heritage.'

The German licked his lips. Even his tongue was yellow and blistered.

'I'm going to kill you, Reichenbach, even if you are an old man riddled with cancer.'

Lautrec paused. He wished that it hadn't ended like this. The huntsmen had pursued their fox over a long chase only to come upon it sitting meekly, diseased with mange, waiting to be put out of its misery. In a way he was doing the other a kindness. Possibly it would be better to leave Reichenbach to die a lingering death, a rat suffering its last agonies in a solitary warren.

'You would do best to leave this house whilst you can, my friend,' the Nazi said tonelessly, 'before it is too late.'

'You're in no position to make threats, Reichenbach.'

Lautrec turned and stared at the wall behind him. It resembled a museum, a section of some ancient castle with the torture instruments of past centuries on display. He stepped closer, and spat. The stench of death was magnified a thousand times in this room, the putrid smell of a diseased man whose flesh was decaying whilst he still lived. 'My God, you didn't mean to forget, did you?' His eyes flicked over an assortment of thumb screws and various other instruments of pain fashioned out of iron. 'A genuine scavenger's daughter, I see. The opposite to the rack. Screw it up and the victim's body is compressed into a bloody ball. Bilboes, too. Iron collars. Ah, a bullwhip with a steel cap on the end of the lash. Is this the one you used on me?'

'Ich weiss nicht.'

'Of course you don't know. But it'll do for my purpose. Now, let's strip those clothes off your vile stinking body.'

Reichenbach's resistance was feeble, merely a token protest as the Frenchman tore the garments off. He was surprised how light the other was, as though most of the skin had already rotted away. The putrid weeping sores had spread all over his body, the thick matter saturating the clothing. Lautrec heaved. He should have been relishing this moment. Instead, he was loathing it, repulsed by the sight and smell of the naked German.

Reichenbach allowed himself to be led across the room, and then his hands were lifted and secured in a pair of manacles amidst the grisly collection. He faced the wall, still wearing his spectacles.

'Ich verstehe nicht.'

'You soon will.' Pierre Lautrec stood back, and slipped off his raincoat. He ran the leather thong between his fingers, feeling the worn smoothness. Hate welled up inside him, not just because of what had happened to himself, but on account of thousands of others who had flinched beneath its force . . . those who had died.

The crack was deafening inside the room, biting deep into the emaciated shoulders of the victim, cutting, leaving a red weal as it fell away. Yellowish rivulets oozed their way downwards.

Crack . . . crack . . . crack.

Blind fury gripped Lautrec and he struck with the venom of an enraged cobra. He wanted to hear the other scream, plead for mercy.

But not a sound came from Reichenbach. His back was an

area of raw meat, blood running down to his buttocks, dripping to the floor.

Crack . . . crack.

The German's head fell forward. His body sagged, only the steel manacles holding him upright. Sweat glistened on Lautrec's distorted face, and he swung the whip with even greater force. It was some time before he realised that the man whom he had pursued for two decades was dead.

It was an anticlimax. The Frenchman tossed the whip into a corner and buried his face in his hands. Oh, God, it seemed such a waste. Twenty years of hate just for this, to kill an old man who would have died anyway. And now . . . nothing.

He didn't know why he unlocked the manacles and let the corpse slide to the floor, rolling over and staring up at the ceiling with sightless eyes. Expressionless. That was the worst part. If there had been fear, even hate, in those dead eyes then it would have been worth it. But there was nothing.

Lautrec turned away. He wondered how long it had taken, what time it was. The fire in the grate had burned low; a pile of embers glowed faintly. The oil lamp hanging from the beam seemed to have dimmed. Above all, it was bitterly cold. As he picked up his raincoat he shivered uncontrollably, and then the fear which he had experienced earlier in the pitch darkness of the hall returned. Sheer terror.

He stepped back, looking about him wildly. The light dimmed still further, the flame flickering as though a gale was tearing at it.

And Pierre Lautrec knew that he was not alone in the house.

He had to get out . . . out into the freedom of the mountains, and run all the way back down to the safety of Meiringen. He moved, and then stopped. The door leading from the room had swung wide open and the blackness of the hall was the most terrifying aspect of all. The density of the darkness was alive with forces incomprehensible to the human mind.

The Frenchman panicked and tugged the Luger from his pocket. It bucked in his hand and flame stabbed from the barrel. Somewhere in that awful hallway woodwork splintered.

Blindly he fired again. And again. He heard the bullets ploughing into oak panelling, glass breaking. Still he kept firing. And then the gun in his hand was clicking on an empty chamber and he knew that no way was he going to be able to summon up the courage to pass through that hall.

He backed away, mouthing curses and trying to remember how to pray. He hadn't prayed since before Nuremberg. He'd left it too late, a meaningless gibbering that he hoped his Maker might understand. No words would come.

With a final flicker the lamp went out and the darkness closed in on him. He felt it touching his skin, cold and clammy, fingers around his throat, his wrists, his legs. Helpless. And then the stench hit him with its full force of putrefaction, suffocating in its vileness. He was retching, vomiting.

Reichenbach! Oh, Jesus God, he could hear him getting up off the floor and shuffling about. Unintelligible grunts, others moving about in obedience to those inarticulate orders.

Lautrec tried to close his eyes but it was impossible. The lids refused to move. He was compelled to stare sightlessly into the blackness around him. He whimpered and managed a silent prayer. *Oh, God, don't let me set eyes on . . . on them. Let me die, quickly.*

He didn't see them. Neither did he die quickly. He heard them, felt them . . . *smelled them.*

They were taking him somewhere. It was impossible but it was happening. His initial sensation was one of his mind being dragged forcibly from his body.

The room was changing, too. He couldn't see it but he could sense it, timber turning into damp, slime-covered, rough stone. Shrinking. A cell. He was being hoisted upwards, wrists lashed to a ring in the ceiling, legs splayed and tied open.

The cell at Nuremberg!

They can't hurt me. My body's in Switzerland. No matter what they do, they can't . . .

He felt the first lash, searing pain that ripped up into the

2

pit of his stomach, knew that it was happening all over again, tried to scream but couldn't. It was worse than last time, sheer malevolence behind each lash. Laughter in the darkness all around. He writhed and struggled, prayed again for death. It was denied him.

Oblivion. Floating. The house on the Reichenbach Falls again. Blackness everywhere, that stench dominating everything. Mind and body joined again. Crawling. The cold, but this time not the cold of psychic forces but mountain air on his face.

He knew the wooden steps were there but it was impossible to negotiate them. Rolling. Falling. Every bone jarred with each step until he hit the snow-covered rock surface below.

For one brief moment he could see. He was lying in the snow beneath the huge front door with the brass plate on it. A tiny flower stood erect only inches from him. A snowdrop; the same one that he had studied from his hiding place in the bushes. And the red stain surrounded it again, strawberry sauce poured haphazardly over a vanilla ice-cream.

Only this time Pierre Lautrec knew what the colouring was. *It was blood, seeping up from the ground below.*

Even as he wrestled with the problem he was aware of consciousness starting to slip from him. He laughed softly. His garbled prayers had been answered. He was going to die.

A few weeks later when the mountain snows began to melt, the raging torrent that came down from the Reichenbach Falls brought with it the mangled remains of a human body. The features were totally unrecognisable, and there was no means of identification. Just a torn raincoat clinging to the sparse form, and two fingers missing from the right hand. This brief description was circulated by the authorities in the hope that the relatives of some missing mountaineer might come forward. None did. Another 'missing persons' case was put on file and forgotten.

And over the years the untenanted house by the Reichenbach Falls began to show signs of decay.

PART ONE:

TOD

1

LA MAISON DES FLEURS

'*La Maison des Fleurs.*' Tallien, the property agent from Luçerne, smiled benignly, perhaps nervously, beneath his heavy moustache, and waved a hand vaguely in the direction of the large wooden house which stood close to the Reichenbach Falls. 'The House of Flowers.'

Arrogant bastard, Al Pennant thought as he carefully selected a Rossli from the silver case which he carried in the inside pocket of his Savile Row sports-jacket. He wished to hell the other didn't speak English. A conversation in French would have been much more satisfying. That was the trouble with two-thirds of these continentals: they spoke fluent English. Gave them an air of superiority, particularly if one had not progressed beyond written French at school.

'A bargain,' Tallien went on. 'Half a million dollars for a quick sale.'

'And you want to sell it quick.' Pennant watched him carefully, noting the nervousness which Tallien was doing his best to hide, the way he averted his gaze, concentrated on trivial details, kept up a banter as though he was trying to cover something up and hoped too many questions would not be asked. Maybe this was the biggest thing he'd ever handled. Mountain chalets were his usual line. Or villas for tax exiles.

'Those flowers' – it was the first time that Veronica Pennant had spoken since the journey up from Meiringen – 'they're sure intriguing. Look, there's *Hypericum coris, Asperula taurina, Helianthemum fumana,* but the most predominant are those snowdrops. Just like they've been put in as an afterthought. Some of the original carvings might have been removed to make way for them.'

Tallien stared blankly at the tall girl with long flowing auburn hair. On the face of it she looked just another dumb American girl in her late twenties, the sort that a guy like Pennant would marry as a second or third wife whilst he was looking around for a more permanent one. Good in bed, but once you'd exhausted her sexual repertoire she'd become boring. For once he'd misjudged a fellow human and it annoyed him. Still, maybe flowers were her particular hobby in life and she didn't know anything about anything else. Pennant was smart, though. He had a reputation for shrewd dealings. Honest, too. And he'd made a few million dollars on the level. Hell, they should have put the asking price up to $750,000. Pennant would still have bought it; he was ambitious and still under forty. But Stotenburg wanted the place sold fast. He didn't want it hanging on, and people who hadn't bought it at the first throw asking why it hadn't been sold.

'A marvellous example of seventeenth-century Swiss craftsmanship.' Tallien puffed out his chest and tried to keep his spreading waistline from spilling over the top of his trousers.

'Crap,' Pennant was examining the flight of wooden steps leading up to the front door.

'Oh, most certainly it is. The date . . .'

'Yeah' – Pennant drew on his Rossli – 'the date is carved in the woodwork by some joker, probably at the end of the last century when those snowdrops were substituted for whatever was there originally. There's a lot you haven't told me, Tallien, but maybe you don't know yourself.'

'Like what?' The agent experienced an acute uneasiness. Why couldn't some easygoing Yank speculator have come along with a wad of dollar bills who didn't give a damn whether the place was seventeenth or nineteenth century. The best scenery in Switzerland. Double its value in five years . . .

'Like it wasn't built here on the Falls in the first place.' Pennant removed the cigar from his mouth and noted with annoyance that he had chewed the end. 'And its history. The Reichenbach legend. How many bodies have they fished out of the river below the falls? And the last Reichenbach, what happened to him? He was a Gestapo torturer, in case you didn't know . . .'

Tallien looked down at the ground and then up at the deep blue summer sky above. Pennant had shaken him. He needed a few seconds to get control of himself. He hadn't expected anyone from New York to have heard of the legend of the House of Flowers. Or of the Reichenbachs.

'This Nazi . . . yes, he did live here for a time. About ten years ago. No never troubled anybody, and Switzerland has always maintained her neutrality . . .'

'What happened to him?'

'I . . . I couldn't say. Maybe he went away and died in another country.'

'Who is the owner of this house, then?'

'Nobody. All efforts have been made to trace the relatives of the Reichenbachs, but as far as we can ascertain there is none living. The property was put into the hands of our company by the authorities. It is to be sold and the money placed in a bank deposit account until such time that it is proved that there are no living kin of the Reichenbachs left. This house is not listed as a building of antiquity, for some reason.'

'Doubtless because, as I said, it was brought here from elsewhere. Probably only the locals knew of its existence until tourist interest was shown in the Reichenbach Falls.'

'I know nothing of that.' Tallien was sweating. Too many people knew the stories attached to this place. The sooner it was sold and the matter concluded, the better.

'A lot of people have died here,' Pennant was mounting the steps, his wife close behind him. The boy, their son, who had been roaming in the garden ever since their arrival, came running across to join them. Tallien tried to conceal his annoyance. He didn't like children. Particularly ten-year-old boys who looked as though they might indulge in any kind of mischief they came across.

'Dad,' the youngster pulled up at the foot of the steps, an expression of bewilderment on his freckled face. Blond hair ruffled in the breeze, and there was mud on his trousers.

'What is it, Tod?' Veronica Pennant turned sharply, reprimand in her tone. 'Just look at your trousers. Whatever have you been doing?'

'Dad,' Tod ignored her, his gaze going over her head to where his father stood at the top of the steps.

'Yes, son.'

'Dad, I don't like this place. We're not going to live here, are we?'

Tallien flinched visibly. It would be just like this kid to go and ruin the whole deal.

'What don't you like about it, Tod?' Al Pennant removed the inch or so of cigar from his mouth and flicked the ash into the air, watching the wind take it, carry it, dash it to powder on the rocky ground.

'It's . . . it's creepy, Dad.'

'All old places look creepy, son. Until you get to know them. Then they take on a warmth and character of their own.'

'Like that place you shipped back from England. That Elizabethan cottage you bought off Mr Parlane?'

'Yeah. Just like that.' Pennant turned the brass door knob and stepped through into the hall. Why the hell did kids always bring up things like that at the most inconvenient time? The less Tallien and Statenburg knew about his importation of old buildings into the United States, the better. He was just a dealer. He didn't want to go into details.

'Of course, there's no guarantee that you'd be able to export this place immediately, Mr Pennant.' Tallien seemed to read his mind.

'I've nothing definite in mind,' Pennant lied.

'I just mention it in passing. There's a clause in the contract. Just in case one of the Reichenbach family turns up. Of course, they couldn't buy it back from you unless you wanted to sell, but it would be rather unfair to allow their family home to be shipped out of the country, wouldn't it?'

'I suppose so. Just for the record, how long would I have to leave it in Switzerland?'

Tallien smiled glibly. This time he had judged right. Another property was bound for the States.

'Oh, no more than six months. A holiday house, eh? And

when your holiday's over you leave for home and take the place with you.'

Al Pennant stepped into the hallway. Then he stopped, almost backed away but just checked himself in time. The smell hit him as though an addled egg had just smashed at his feet.

'My!' Veronica wrinkled her pert nose. 'What a ghastly smell!'

Tallien coughed. He had noticed the aroma once before when he had come to look over the house for Stotenburg, prior to offering it for sale. He presumed that some rodents had become trapped beneath the flooring and had slowly decomposed. They should have rotted away by now. That had been almost six weeks ago.

'The place needs airing,' somehow he managed not to heave. 'These old buildings get very stale when they're shut up for months, sometimes years, on end.'

'Stale!' Veronica Pennant had a tissue pressed to her nose. 'It's like the sewers are blocked up, only worse.'

'Let's open some windows.' The agent crossed to the one nearest to the door and tugged at the sash. Nothing happened. He pulled again, narder this time. Suddenly the yellowed dusty cord snapped and he staggered back, almost sprawling full length.

'Never mind,' Pennant was hastily lighting another Rossli and blowing out clouds of smoke. 'Let's take a look around.'

As he dropped the cigar case back into his pocket he felt small fingers closing over his, squeezing tightly. He glanced down. Tod was clutching at him, looking up with wide eyes, a mute plea. *Oh, Dad, this place scares me!*

Pennant smiled reassuringly. For the moment his son had shelved the task of growing up. Then Tallien was pushing past them, angrily determined to overcome the obstacles which seemed to be barring a quick sale.

'A nice lounge.' He threw open an adjoining door, gesturing into a room which was laden with dust, the diamond-shaped window panes so caked that the sunlight had difficulty penetrating the glass.

'Spacious. Note the large stone fireplace, the exposed

beams, and the furniture and fittings which are all included in the asking price.'

'What's that?' Veronica was pointing at the far wall, her hand shaking.

They all stared. Tod shrank back. Tallien pursed his lips, then licked them slowly, nervously. He had forgotten the display of torture-instruments which adorned the wall. He remembered seeing them on his last visit. It was tactless of him just to walk in here with a party of prospective buyers without warning them, especially as one of them was a female. It would do the boy good, though. Shake him up a bit.

'Er . . . I'm sorry.' He turned apologetically as though trying to screen the items from Veronica's view. 'I should have warned you. Some museum pieces . . . very old . . . probably never used except for show even . . . '

'I mean that!' Veronica pushed him to one side and pointed again. There was a thick brown stain on the dusty off-white wall, a dozen or more dried trickles running down until they met the floor, where they had soaked into the floorboards leaving a dark unmistakable patch. *'It's blood, isn't it?'*

'Well . . . no, I doubt it,' Tallien sought a feasible explanation like a schoolboy caught raiding an orchard, his pockets crammed with apples, trying to convince his captor that they were merely horsechestnuts. 'I don't think so . . . '

'Of course it's blood,' Veronica Pennant was frightened and angry, insulted by the other's denial of the obvious. 'Something's happened in here at some time. Look, those manacles are bloodstained, too. And . . . and . . . that's a whip lying on the floor over there. Ugh! What a ghastly instrument. See the metal tip. There's blood on that, too. *Somebody's been fastened to the wall and flogged!'*

'Let's take a look in another room,' Al could feel Tod shaking with fear and thought he detected a whimper from him. 'You go ahead, Tallien, and make sure there aren't any more horrors in store for us.'

Tallien crossed the hall and made for a doorway on the opposite side. He was searching his memory, wondering if there had been anything else in here on his last visit which he had overlooked. He ought to have done something about that collection adorning the lounge wall, but it was even more careless of him not to have noticed the blood. Now the kid was going to start crying and that redheaded, loud-mouthed bitch might even get hysterical. In that case Pennant wouldn't buy. He'd blab it around that the Reichenbach residence was full of torture weapons, that there were bloodstains on the wall, and that the place stank like a latrine in the height of summer which hadn't been cleaned out.

'From here there is a magnificent view of the top of the falls,' Tallien shouted back, relief and hope surging through him. The windows here were not so dusty as the others and the lashing spring rains had washed the glass on the outside.

The contrast was electrifying. In a matter of seconds the horrors around them seemed to evaporate. Al Pennant, Tod, still holding his hand, and Veronica at his shoulder, clustered in the large bow window. They watched in fascination as the foaming spray from the Falls scintillated in the bright sunlight. Beyond, a group of tourists stood, totally oblivious of the house nearby, laughing and chattering.

'It's beautiful,' Veronica murmured. 'Just out of this world.'

'And that's only part of it.' Tallien was quick to press home the advantage, motivated by the apparent turn of events. 'Let me show you the upstairs rooms, the panoramic views, possibly the finest in Switzerland.'

They followed him up the wide oak staircase to the first floor, Tod coughing as dust rose beneath their feet. He still held Al's hand tightly, and his uneasiness did not appear to have lessened. *Dad, I don't like this place.*

'As I said,' Tallien smiled, and stood to one side so that they could see the view from the bedroom window. They pressed close. The panes were grimed and it was difficult to look outside. 'And, as I said before, all the furniture is included,' he nodded towards a large fourposter bed.

The tour of inspection continued up to the third floor and then on to the fourth. Decay everywhere, but nothing that could not be rectified.

'A firm of contractors would clean the whole house up in

a few days' – the property agent's hopes were rising fast – 'and the garden, too. You won't recognise it then.'

'That smell seems to have gone,' Veronica commented as they arrived back in the hallway on the ground floor. 'Peculiar, the way it's just disappeared.'

'The house has been shut up for a long time,' Tallien replied. 'It's amazing what wonders a little fresh air will work.'

'You never told me' – Pennant released Tod's hand and tossed the butt of his cigar out through the open front door – 'where this place came from, why it rests on stilts.'

'I haven't the slightest idea.' Tallien shrugged his shoulders. 'Nobody has. What does it matter?'

'I'm just interested, naturally. I like to know the history of places I buy.'

'You'll be shipping it back to the States?'

'Maybe. In due course. We'll probably live in Switzerland for a while.'

Tallien smiled. Another tax fiddle. He knew that Pennant had an account with the Bank of Switzerland in Geneva. A million dollars on deposit. The manager, Naniescu, had told him. Or rather he had told Stotenburg. Naniescu had a vested interest in the latter's property deals. It was Naniescu who advised the sale of *La Maison des Fleurs* to an American. They paid good money in the States for houses like that.

'I take it you're going to buy then, Mr Pennant?'

'It depends.' The American looked at Veronica. Not that her opinion would sway his decision; his mind was already made up. But he had to go through the formality of asking for it.

'It's nice.' She looked beyond the wooden steps across to the shrubbery. 'It's also horrible.'

'That's nonsense.'

'You know what I mean.'

'But you wouldn't object to living here for a while.' It was a statement, not a question.

'I don't suppose so.' There was no point in arguing. Al was the boss. He'd do what he wanted, anyway.

'Tod?'

The boy looked up, his face white and drawn. His voice trembled when he spoke. 'Dad, I don't . . . like it here. It's . . . I'm scared.'

'Don't you worry, son.' Al Pennant ruffled Tod's blond hair. 'When I've had this place cleaned up you won't recognise it.'

'You . . . you won't be able to get rid of . . . of . . .'

'Of what, Tod?'

'I don't know, Dad, but . . .'

'There, you see, you don't know what it is you're frightened of. It's dirty and smelly. Nothing else. You're imagining bogeymen. Like you did when we stayed at that motel in Nevada last fall.'

'There *was* something there.' Tod was insistent to the point of defiance. 'An old woman. She was groaning in the grounds . . .'

'The boy has a vivid imagination,' Pennant told Tallien. 'Too many of these horror comics at school. We don't allow him to have them at home.'

'I don't read horror comics,' Tod mumbled, 'because they don't frighten me. I'm only scared of real spooks.'

'There aren't such things as spooks,' Al snapped, becoming angry.

'They . . .' The boy fell silent. He was trembling violently, his hand now seeking Veronica's.

Veronica pulled him to her. It was two against two; herself and Tod versus Al Pennant and Tallien. But they had no chance against the other two. None whatsoever. If Al said they were going to live here, then that was exactly what they would do.

'They'll get to like it.' Al walked down the steps, Tallien following him.

'You're going to purchase?' Hope. Tension.

'Maybe. It depends.'

'On what?'

'The price.'

'It's a bargain at half a million dollars.'

'It would be, if it were situated somewhere in Boston or Philadelphia. It'll cost a fortune to get it back to the States.'

'You'll still make your profit.'

'A reduced one. Tell you what, I'll take it at four hundred thousand, and you'll still be doing well on ten per cent.'

'I don't know.' Tallien walked away, careful not to let the other see his expression. Stotenburg had said they could afford to come down to three hundred and fifty thousand. He'd be delighted with four. But Pennant musn't know that. The haggling had to stop. 'I'll have to discuss it with Stotenburg. I'll ring you tomorrow.'

'Make it this evening. Before nine. We're booked in at the Bernerhof. We'll be at the casino by nine.'

'I'll ring.' Tallien permitted himself a faint smile. 'But don't bank your hopes. I can't promise anything. And there's somebody else coming to look at this place tomorrow.'

Pennant grinned. There was always a mythical third party in any property deal. It would have seemed phoney without one.

It was 8.30 when Tallien's call came through. Even as he walked towards the reception desk where the receiver lay off the hook, Pennant knew the deal had gone through.

It was August when the Pennants returned to Interlaken. A long vacation lay ahead of them. A week at the Bernerhof, whilst they attended to the final details, to ensure that the contractors from Geneva had restored *La Maison des Fleurs* and made it habitable. Then they would move in, maybe not returning to New York until the spring, by which time Al would have arranged for the house to be taken down in sections and shipped back home.

Al was jubilant as he and Veronica sipped iced bourbons in the residents' lounge of the hotel. Tod was upstairs in bed.

'I'm worried about the boy,' Veronica wrinkled her narrow forehead into a frown.

'He's just moody,' Al had more important things on his mind than Tod.

'No. It goes deeper than that. He's withdrawn. He's gotten more and more so ever since that day we first saw the house. Just as though . . . something has happened to him. Changed him.'

'He doesn't like being away from New York, that's the

trouble with him. If we'd let him, he'd vegetate, spend all day in his room reading, and that's no way to bring up a boy. He needs the open air. Look how pale he is. These mountains will soon put some colour back into him.'

'He's scared, Al.' Veronica looked at her husband closely. 'And so am I if it comes to that.'

'Jeez! I get one of the best deals in years and you and the boy are doing your best to screw it up.'

'We don't have to live in the place. You could comply with the terms of the sale simply by leaving the house empty where it is and shipping it back sometime next year. In the meantime we could have lived normally on 72nd Street.'

'I got news for you,' Al Pennant swilled his drink around the glass, clinking the cubes of ice like a child's xylophone. 'I sold our place just before we left!'

'You what?'

'I sold up. Bought a vacant plot on Long Island. Magnificent coastal view. This Reichenbach house will be worth a mint when we put it up for sale over there.'

Veronica Pennant choked back her retort. What was the use? This was the second time during their marriage that Al had decided on a move and gone ahead without her consent. It was no partnership. She was the 'little woman', trailing along behind, doing as she was told. It was a waste of time complaining. If it hadn't been for Tod she might have gone back home to her folks in Washington.

'Tod doesn't like the house,' she said. 'He'll like it even less when he knows.'

'It'll grow on him.'

'And what d'you think it's going to do to him in the meantime, Al?'

'Look, we both know the boy's unusually sensitive.'

'Psychic.'

'Rubbish. He's over-imaginative.'

She sighed. You couldn't talk to Al. Except about cash-flow and profits.

'We'd better get an early night.' He drained his glass. 'The house has got to be gotten spick-and-span this week. We want it looking its best for the big party.'

Parties! She was sick of parties. Al's parties weren't like

ordinary parties. Showpieces. Every new property he bought had to be shown off. It was part of his make-up. Flamboyant. Arrogant.

'I've invited Parlane,' he grinned.

'Just to make him jealous?'

'He's not a bad guy. Knows his stuff where property like this is concerned. He'll go green at the gills to begin with but then he'll start to give me advice. A lot of it is bullshit, but you can learn from him.'

'I don't like his wife.'

'She's OK. You're just being bitchy.'

'It isn't what she says. She hardly says anything at all, but she's thinking it.'

'How d'you know what she's thinking.'

'I just do.'

'*You're* psychic,' he laughed, 'but I'll tell you what she'll be thinking this time. She'll be thinking that her darling Bruce isn't so clever after all, because if he was he'd've been out here and struck a deal with Stotenburg and Tallien before I'd had a chance to jet out from New York.'

God, how I wish he had, she thought.

Tod had spent most of the afternoon in the garden. The mountain breezes kept the temperature down, and it was just pleasantly warm in spite of the blazing sun. For an hour or so he'd tried to read a juvenile adventure story which he had picked up in Interlaken. He couldn't concentrate, and after a while he dropped the book on to the closely-cut grass and lay staring up at the house.

He didn't like the house even in broad daylight. It was unfriendly. Grim. Certainly it was more homelike than it had been on that day when they had first visited it. The windows were clean, the woodwork had been washed down, and it looked as though those rows of carved flowers had been polished. He tried to figure out why the snowdrops were so out of place. They should not have been. They were as much a wild mountain-flower as any of the other varieties. It was some time before he hit upon the reason. They were bigger, not carved to scale; not much, but enough to upset the symmetry. They made you want to look at them. You tried to focus your attention on something else but always your eyes were drawn back to the snowdrops.

He shivered and stood up. His parents were inside the house. Stotenburg was here today, a heavily-jowled man to whom the boy had taken an instant dislike. The property dealer had called to see Al Pennant, just a social visit now that the deal was concluded. They were drinking in the lounge. Veronica would be busying herself in the kitchen, making preparations for the big party on Friday night. She was always in the kitchen, as though it was her rightful place. Tod had heard her and his father arguing about it many times. Al Pennant said that she should be socialising, chatting with his guests instead of doing a skivvy's job. But Tod knew that she preferred to keep out of the way. She was shy, like himself.

He got to thinking about his father. They had never been close. Dad was either away on business or too busy to devote any time to him. In a way they were like strangers. Mom said that it would be different here in Switzerland. Get the party over and it would be a six-month holiday with no business pressures. There were lots of exciting places to visit. The Jungfraujoch with its Ice Palace over 11,000 feet up in the mountains, a frozen world even in the midst of summer. You could also have a ride on a sleigh pulled by huskies. Trips on Lakes Thun and Brienz. Geneva (Dad had to make a trip there to see the bank manager), Lucerne.

Yet they always had to return to this place. *La Maison des Fleurs.* It wasn't officially called that, Tod knew. Either Stotenburg or Tallien had given it that name. It sounded nice . . . until you saw it! He shivered. The house was a brooding monster, squatting on its stilts, as though it resented having been transported here from some distant place. He could imagine it in its former setting, desolate marshland, thick mist rolling across the mire, veiling it from human eyes.

He walked on down to a sunken garden below the top tier of lawns and flowerbeds. The shrubberies seemed to hem him in here, almost as though they were living creatures that would suddenly form a complete circle and cut off his retreat. He kept glancing behind him, but nothing moved.

In the centre of this small garden an ornamental fishpond had been installed. There was a fountain, the water gushing up out of a statue of a naked girl with a large basket on her head. Tod had heard his mother telling his father that it was obscene and Al Pennant had laughed harshly. Mother was like that; prudish to the extreme. There were no sexual details on the stone girl – Tod had already looked – her legs were pressed tightly together and her breasts were merely two raised lumps, not even a trace of a nipple.

He resented his mother's prudishness. She had never even explained to him how babies were born. She probably thought he didn't know even now, three months after his tenth birthday. He had had to rely on the other boys at school to fill him in on the details. They had been cruel about it, and he hadn't forgotten. Neither had they. He hated school. That was one reason he didn't mind being away from New York. But worse than any school was this house. He didn't know why, but it frightened him. There was *something* there, not just in the building itself but in the grounds. Everywhere. As though whatever it was was following him around . . . He glanced over his shoulder again.

He stepped forward and looked down into the pool. It was octagonal, about three yards in diameter, the statue in the centre. The water was pure and clear, and his eyes searched for the ornamental fish which his father had put in.

Then he saw them. All ten of them, floating on their sides, gently bobbing against the opposite bank in the swell caused by the fountain. *Dead.*

He was running feverishly, scrambling and falling up the flight of stone steps that led to the upper garden. Branches brushed his face and hands as though they had suddenly come to life and were trying to pull him down, dragging him back into the tiny enclosed garden below, *their* domain.

He screamed and tore at them frantically. A twig whipped him viciously across the face. A creeper tangled with his ankle and brought him down heavily. Somehow he made it on to the lawn, gasping and sobbing, closing his eyes in an attempt to shut everything out. It was then that he smelled the odour, faint yet recognisable, that same smell of putrefaction which had been in *La Maison des Fleurs* on their first visit.

'Tod!'

He turned, looking towards the house, peering through the fingers of the hands which were clasped over his eyes. They were all there, his father, the two property agents, and his mother. Veronica Pennant was running frantically towards him.

'Tod! What is it? What's the matter?'

'I . . . I.' He had difficulty in speaking amidst the gasps, and the fear which was knotting his stomach muscles into a tight ball. 'Down there . . . in the garden . . . '

'What's down there in the garden?' Al Pennant demanded, anger in his tone. Tod's fears were becoming an embarrassment to him.

'The fish,' Tod gulped. 'They're all dead.'

'Oh.' The lives of a few colourful fish were of little importance to Al Pennant, particularly at this moment.

'And the smell, Dad' – the boy's voice was on the verge of hysteria – 'that awful smell, the rotting one we smelled when we first came here. I smelled it again!'

'Of course you did,' Pennant snapped. 'Dead fish floating on a pool in midsummer are bound to smell nasty. Now pull yourself together.' He turned half-apologetically to Stotenburg. 'I'm afraid my son is frightened of his own shadow.'

Stotenburg looked at his watch and then at Tallien. 'It's time we were going,' he muttered, and the other nodded.

'I'm sure Tod's fears will subside once he has been here for a few days.' Stotenburg spoke gutturally, his jowls seeming to quiver. 'And I'm so glad that you and Mrs Pennant are happy with the place. Maybe after a few weeks you will decide that Switzerland is preferable to the hustle and bustle of America.'

Al Pennant walked across the lawn with them. Tod was sobbing in Veronica's arms, and Al made a mental note to take a stern line with his son. Fantasy had to be replaced with reality if the boy was to succeed in life.

Tod's bedroom was on the third floor, immediately above the one in which his parents slept. Veronica would rather their son was in closer proximity but Al pointed out that all the second floor bedrooms were large ones and would be used for guests. The boy would be much better in one of the smaller ones. In the end she had agreed. It was no good hoping that her husband might have a change of mind.

'Now, you'll be all right, won't you?' She smiled down at Tod as she turned back from drawing the curtains. His features were pallid against the pinkness of the pillowcover and this worried her.

He nodded. 'I guess so, Mom,' and added, 'when are we going back to New York?'

'Oh, in the spring some time.' She hadn't told him about Long Island yet. Let him settle here first.

'I wish we could go home now, Mom.'

He echoed her own thoughts. She experienced a sudden feeling of homesickness and longed for the constant rumble of traffic, flashing neon lights and nights that never really darkened.

Sleep eluded Tod. Through a chink in the curtains he watched dusk blending into darkness, heard the soughing of the wind in the trees outside and the distant thunder of the Reichenbach Falls.

His thoughts went back to the sunken garden, and no way could he push the events of the afternoon from his mind. He shuddered. He had not been alone down there. He knew it. The whole place, the trees, the vegetation, seemed to take on a life of their own, controlled by powerful evil forces. *They* had killed the fish. There was no doubt in Tod's mind about that. *They* had destroyed them because the fish were alien to these surroundings. The mysterious powers were determined to preserve their own domain; not just in the case of animal life, but humans also. It was a terrifying thought. And that stench – it had not come from the decomposing fish. It was the smell of whatever lurked in this house and its gardens.

Tod's fear was mounting with the advent of darkness. He wanted to get out of bed, to run to his parents' room, to yell at them to get out of here before some terrible disaster happened. Then he thought of his father, the anger, the ridicule, and he slid down the bed and pulled the sheets right up over his head. He determined to remain there until morning, even to the point of suffocation.

Some time later he heard his parents coming to bed, the closing of doors, running water in the bathroom below, the flushing of the w.c. Normal everyday sounds that seemed to temper his fears, and in due course he dozed. The night was sultry, and instinctively he pushed the sheets back from his face.

Suddenly he was wide awake. It took him some seconds to remember exactly where he was, and as reality flooded back the fear began to mount inside him again. He wondered what had awoken him. The creaking of old timber? Something falling?

Oh, God, no, it was the stench of putrefaction!

The choking, awful smell scorched his lungs with its vileness. Terror prompted his first action, a frenzied grope for the light-pull which hung a foot or so above his head. His fingers found the knob, closed over it, tugged. A click, but no welcoming electric light flooding the room. *Click. Click.* Nothing. He pulled with all his force and the cord snapped, snaking uselessly across the bedcover.

He cowered back. *Oh, please, no.* He wanted to scream. He couldn't. His vocal chords refused to function. His back was pressing into the wooden headboard, carvings gouging his flesh. Sobbing. Whimpering.

Everywhere was total blackness. Not a single sliver of grey light filtered in from outside. A blackness that was complete and alive like the atmosphere during a thunderstorm as powerful forces converged. He felt their presence, the cold clammy sweat pouring from him.

Then he heard the screams. Not of one person, but of a dozen. More. Anguished yells that came from souls in torment and in the background low laughter. Cruel. Sadistic. On and on, screams for mercy that was not granted.

Tod was down the bed again, pulling the sheets over him, burying his face so that he should not see, clasping his ears in an attempt to shut out the noise. It was impossible.

The stench became worse. Overpowering. His senses reeled and he felt himself hovering over a black abyss. Falling . . . falling . . . floating.

Unconsciousness spared him further torment, and when he finally came to, beams of early morning sunlight were streaming into the room through the gaps in the curtains, bringing with them the sweet fresh scent of early morning. The foul atmosphere of the night had gone.

Tod sat up in bed. It might just have been an awful nightmare, vividly realistic in the darkest hours of the night. But it wasn't. On the floor, coiled like a viper basking in the warmth of a summer's day, lay the broken pull-cord. He climbed out of bed and crossed the room to the light-switch by the door. He flicked it downwards and the bulb inside the shade over the bed blazed into life. It was in perfect working order.

Such was his terror then that Tod ran hard for the stairs and down to the storey below, where his parents' bedroom was situated.

2

THE FIRST DEATH

Friday.

The guests had been arriving at *La Maison des Fleurs* since early afternoon, a steady stream of baggage-laden people, the weariness of a long journey stamped on them. Tod watched from his bedroom window. He had counted over fifty people so far, a few of whom he recognised vaguely from parties which his father had held in their big house back in New York.

He recognised Bruce Parlane but he had not seen his wife before. In some ways the Englishman reminded him of his father. In others he was a total contrast. Tall, with a mass of jet black hair that fell to his collar, and not a grey hair to be seen although he was surely around forty. Confident, but not arrogant. Tod had once seen him wearing glasses, so his eyesight could not be all that good. Another thing, he didn't treat his wife like Dad treated Mom. It was much more of a partnership. Even as they crossed the big lawn on to the drive they were holding hands and they must have been married a few years because their son, Rusty, was Tod's age.

Anthea was tall and slim with short dark hair, her most striking feature her clear blue eyes. Bruce claimed that that was because she was Welsh. Welsh brunettes were noted for their blue eyes, he said. Her thighs were shapely. On a shorter female they might have been considered bulky. She always wore either Wranglers or a trouser-suit because, she said laughingly, her legs were too thin to go on show. And she was shy, more so than Veronica. But there the similarity ended.

Tod wondered where Rusty was. His parents always called him Richard, but to everyone else he was Rusty. Most likely he was back in England being looked after by his grandparents. Tod envied him wistfully. Anywhere would be preferable to *La Maison des Fleurs* and its sinister, frightening environment.

He watched Parlane and his wife go inside. In the distance he heard the cable-car beginning its journey back down the mountainside, a noise that sent prickles up and down his spine like the time he'd run his fingernails along the side of a coach. That was another thing that made him feel uneasy. The funicular. You took it for granted; a speedy trip down to Meiringen and back, but if anything went wrong with it you were marooned as surely as if you were on a desert island. Trapped. Up here with . . . with what? He shivered.

So peaceful. Magnificent. But fall was only a few weeks away. Then winter, and the snows. They'd be shut in. His father didn't seem bothered about it, but he sensed his mother's uneasiness, a tension that was building up inside her. Her nerves were tautening. One day they might snap. A powder keg with the fuse spluttering.

Tod had been keeping out of his father's way these last few days. Ever since the morning when he had burst into his parents' bedroom sobbing incoherently, shaking with fear. His mother had tried to comfort him but all that Al Pennant had to offer was scorn.

'There's something wrong with you,' Al Pennant's lower lip had curled in a sneer. 'You're nuts. Come on, let's go and look in your bedroom.'

Naturally, there was nothing there. Whatever it was had vanished hours ago, retired to its hiding place, waiting for night to come again. Lurking unseen, a psychic force that had them all at its mercy, was playing with them. And, of course, the light worked perfectly. Only the broken pull-cord was evidence of Tod's nocturnal terrors, and that might have snapped anyway.

'You're just being ridiculous.' Pennant glanced at his watch and saw that it was not yet 6 a.m. 'Frightened of your own shadow. What you need is a damned good larruping to shake you up.'

Al Pennant's sarcasm continued at the breakfast table, and Tod couldn't wait to get away. He went outside, but the grounds held their own restrictions for him. He dared not go back down to the sunken garden. It stank of evil, an evil that was so powerful that it commanded even the trees and shrubs.

Beyond the gates at the end of the driveway was a patch of scrubland. It was warm sitting there in the morning sunlight, sheltered from the wind. Much more than that, it had a feeling of freedom about it and Tod knew that whatever lurked in the house did not come this far. He felt safe.

His thoughts ran in a circle and ended back in his bedroom. Now, watching the guests arriving from his window, he experienced the yearnings of a prisoner serving a long sentence. Freedom taunted him, the gigantic falls in the distance, the water rushing on its way to the valley below; a raven, gliding, scarcely a flap of the huge outstretched black wings; a group of tourists making a pilgrimage to the shrine of their fictional hero. They were free to leave. Tod was not.

The mounting tension within the house was temporarily destroyed. Voices; laughter. The brooding silence of decades was broken. Tod listened, trying to identify various accents, catching snatches of conversation. '. . . like a palace. Trust Al to find himself a place like this . . . talk about Treetops . . .'

The boy sighed. These folks were all like his father.

Insensitive. Atmosphere was lost on them. They couldn't *feel* the brooding evil, its hate for those who trespassed in its domain. *He* felt it, even now, in broad daylight. It was there, an invisible smouldering malevolence. Waiting, determined to wreak its vengeance on them for some unknown reason.

Tod feared the coming of nightfall. Dusk had an uncertainty about it, lingering, as though daylight was determined not to surrender to darkness until the last possible moment.

Veronica Pennant came into his room whilst he was still at the window, her long flowing dress a kaleidoscope of bright colours, flamboyant to the extreme. Al had paid five hundred dollars for it. The style and pattern were his choice, not hers. As always.

'C'mon now, Tod.' She smacked him playfully on the bottom. 'Bedtime.'

'Aw, Mom.' He sought her hand. 'You know how I hate going to bed.'

'I know.' She stooped and kissed him. 'But you'll be all right. There's loads of people in the house. And you were all right last night. And the night before, weren't you?'

'Yes,' he nodded reluctantly, 'but only because *it* let me alone. It's still here. All the time.'

'You're overwrought,' she murmured. 'It's the atmosphere of all these old places. Spooky. It's in your own mind really. There's nothing to hurt you.'

'But there *is* something here' – he clutched at her – 'I know. It was in the sunken garden, too. It killed all the fish in the pond. And it made me frightened so that we'd all go away and leave it in peace.'

'No.' She sounded unconvincing, even to herself. 'There's nothing to be frightened of, Tod. If . . . if anything . . . well, if you should get scared run down to our room.'

'Dad'll larrup me if I do.'

'No, he won't. I won't let him.'

Tod began to unbutton his shirt. There was no point in arguing. He was trapped in this environment along with everyone else; his mother, these guests. And it was all his father's doing.

The party was in full swing by ten o'clock. The long dining-room and the lounge had tables laden with food and drink, and the spacious hall had been cleared for dancing. The stereo was playing a smoochy number and a dozen or so couples moved slowly in time with the music.

Bruce Parlane held Veronica Pennant close, feeling the tightness of her dress. He knew the garment was Al's choice. A showpiece. Sexy. The American wanted every guy in the place to be mentally screwing Veronica. But if anybody so much as propositioned her . . . Jesus! That was how Al got his kicks in life, making everybody else covet his own acquisitions, including his wife. And Parlane knew that he himself was one of the victims. There were two things he wanted right now – this house, and Veronica naked on that four-poster upstairs. But he knew that he wasn't likely to get either.

'Al's in his element.' Parlane laughed softly and nodded towards the far corner of the room, where Pennant was being fawned upon by three cigar-smoking, well-known international antique dealers, their diamond rings and tiepins scintillating like a myraid of stars on a frosty night.

'I just wish someone would make him a big enough offer so that he'd sell,' Veronica replied wistfully.

'I offered him half a million,' Bruce Parlane grinned, and added, '*pounds*.'

'At the moment, I'm afraid, money just wouldn't buy this house. Al's a king in his palace. The sooner it wears off, the better.'

'You don't like it?'

'I *hate* it. God, I loathe the place!'

'I think it's rather cosy.'

'It's awful. Like a monster. There's something about it that terrifies me. Tod's nearly out of his mind with fear. That's what worries me most. I'm afraid that if we stop here this winter he might crack. It could do irreparable damage to his mind. Worse, I have to keep on pretending everything's all right. I'm lying . . . to all of us.'

'Ghosts and bogeymen and things that go bump in the night?'

'Don't joke about it, Bruce, please. I'm deadly serious. I can't tell you what it is. Sometimes there's a ghastly smell. That's when whatever it is is close.'

'You've not seen anything yourself?'

She shook her head, and found herself wishing that he didn't have to go back to England in a couple of days' time. Surprisingly, she felt herself relaxing. A kind of easing of the tension, but then when everybody left it would come surging back again.

Elizabeth Quilmer did not like *La Maison des Fleurs.* Neither did she like Al Pennant. His wife was a bitch. And any affection which she might have had for her husband, Wallace K. Quilmer, had long since faded.

It was the same at all these parties when one of the menfolk bought a new property to try and outdo their colleagues. Lavishness to the extreme, the dealers congregating in a corner where dollars dominated the conversation, the women left either to sit it out or to indulge in a mild flirtation. And, to be perfectly candid with herself, Elizabeth knew that none of the males wanted to flirt with her.

Once she had had a passable figure that in some ways compensated for her coarse features. Wallace, of course, had married her for her money. Her old man's money, and at eighty-five her father was still alive and Wallace was still waiting. Then something had gone wrong with her glands. Her weight had soared from 154 pounds to 190 pounds in two years. She had spent thousands of dollars on consultants but in the end they had told her that there was nothing they could do. She put on another 20 pounds and then her heart began to object. A strict diet meant that she had to abstain from the food and drink at these functions. Men no longer found her attractive, and with her husband likely to be engaged in conversation with Al Pennant for the next hour or two, it was going to be a long night.

Elizabeth's head ached. It usually did after an exhausting journey, particularly by air. The palpitations would start soon. She recognised the signs, a slight quickening of her pulses that would develop into a rapid pumping of blood through the arteries. The altitude was responsible for that.

She was forty-four next birthday. She didn't think she would make it to fifty.

Bed was a comforting thought. A man between the sheets would have been a bonus, but that wasn't likely to happen for some hours until Wallace retired for the night, not that *he* made much difference. Sex only took place on infrequent occasions. Her gaze flicked over Bruce Parlane. Now he *was* her type . . . oh, hell, it was a waste of time conjuring up fantasies!

She slipped out of the crowded room and made her way up the stairs to their bedroom on the fourth floor. By the time she gained the top landing she was panting heavily and the backs of her legs quivered and ached. The palpitations were already starting.

She went into the bedroom and closed the door. Her nostrils wrinkled. There was a musty smell, one that she had not noticed on their arrival. But what else could you expect in these old places? It was crazy; an apartment on Park Avenue and Wallace had to drag her out to a restored shack on stilts in the wilds of the Swiss mountains.

She undressed slowly, wheezing all the time. There was a full-length mirror on the wardrobe door and she tried not to look in it. The less Elizabeth Quilmer saw of Elizabeth Quilmer, the better.

Phew! She flung herself on to the bed, and with an effort reached up and tugged the light-pull. Darkness. A cooling relief, easing the ache behind her eyeballs, slowing the pounding in her pulses. She closed her eyes and hoped that she might fall asleep fairly quickly.

Oblivion, but not for long. Elizabeth Quilmer stubbed her toe at the top of a long flight of stone steps and felt herself falling. The ground below rushed up to meet her and the impact shot her from the depths of slumber into wakefulness.

She lay there, trembling. Every vein in her body seemed to be being strummed like a guitar. Her head felt as though it was coming apart down the centre like a child's Easter egg. *And the smell!*

She coughed and tried not to breathe, but she couldn't hold her breath for more than a few seconds. A foul, rancid odour. God, there had to be a leaking cesspit somewhere close at hand. It was cold, too. Freezing.

She tried to struggle up and then she saw the figure standing there in the blackness of the room. Her scream of terror died away to a gurgle. Whether it was man or woman, human or inhuman, there was no way of telling. A face, the mouth a long bloody slit that stretched from cheek to cheek, the skull hairless, bleeding. Eyes filled with pain and hate, accusing. The mouth opened; torn crimson toothless gums.

Elizabeth Quilmer recoiled. Her heart was pounding like a ram struggling to pump a water supply on an uphill course. No! No! *No!* She forced her head away, afraid to look into those eyes. The blackness was total, cold and clammy, an invisible mountain fog swirling around her.

The stench was worse, suffocating. She gasped for breath, phlegm rattling in her throat. Unseen hands were clawing at her, dragging her eyes back so that she was compelled to gaze upon . . . *that!*

This time the shock was even greater. The face was still there but it had changed. The mouth had miraculously healed into a small, compressed, bloodless line. The top of the head was whole, no longer a scarlet morass, with short cropped hair. The features were fuller, yet a thousand times more repulsive. The flesh was in a state of decomposition, the cheekbones showing white where it had rotted away, the eyes glowing in sunken sockets, the nostrils two black holes.

The mouth opened, a cavity that spilled out soundless words, a mirthless grin. Hate, yet dominant, cruelly in command.

Voices. Distant to begin with, coming closer, a meaningless jumble of sound. Screams that were cut off only to be replaced by others.

Elizabeth felt the pain, like a screwdriver being scraped across her breasts, gouging deeply. Her vision was blurred, the face shimmering, the mouth contorted, shouting its venom. She could neither hear nor understand, yet the message blazing from those eyes was only too clear. *Death.*

She writhed, limbs flailing feebly. The face was closer, the thing leaning over her, its fetid breath an icy wind on her forehead. Her eyes were drawn upwards as though some force was ripping them from their sockets, bulging. And then she fell backwards and lay still.

It was after 3 a.m. when Wallace K. Quilmer came up to bed. His step was unsteady and he belched loudly as he entered the room. He closed the door and expelled more wind. He had been forcibly holding it in for far too long.

He reached for the light-switch, then changed his mind. Silhouetted against the whiteness of the crumpled sheets was the form of Elizabeth, thighs wide, arms splayed. He grinned in the darkness and belched again.

God, that Parlane wench had turned him on. He'd been watching her on the dance floor, noting the way her body moved lithely, feeling his own reacting as though the two of them had been indulging in love-play. Fantasy. And why not?

He tugged off his clothes, nearly overbalancing as a foot became caught in his trousers, and steadying himself. The fantasy would go on from where it left off. Elizabeth would never know that his thoughts were centred on another woman. It was dark and he wouldn't be able to see the way her bulbous frame quivered like a jelly when she orgasmed.

Awkwardly he knelt in between those spread legs, supporting himself with his hands on her shoulders. Her flesh felt unusually cold, and there was no response from her as he fumbled clumsily with the lower regions of her body.

It was not until he was struggling to achieve a penetration that he realised that something was wrong. Shaken, he drew back and groped with podgy fingers for the lightswitch.

As the room flooded with light and he gazed down on the contorted features of his wife, Wallace K. Quilmer knew without a doubt that she was dead. Her eyes, inflated in their sockets, stared sightlessly up towards the decorative ceiling, and her lips were frozen in a scream of anguish that was still trapped in her throat.

He scrambled away, heedless of his nakedness, and rushed out on to the landing. Even before he began to yell for help he was aware of the pungent, putrid odour which cloyed his nostrils.

Much as she disliked her husband's flamboyant parties, Veronica Pennant experienced a sense of helplessness as she watched the Parlanes walking down towards the funicular. Nobody had planned on leaving before Monday, but by Sunday afternoon *La Maison des Fleurs* was empty except for Al, Tod and herself. Elizabeth Quilmer's unexpected death (a local doctor thought it was a coronary thrombosis but the post-mortem on Tuesday would either confirm or deny this) had brought the festivities to an abrupt end. Death, even from natural causes, had a habit of instilling terror into the average person.

And Veronica was frightened. Terrified because now the three of them had to face whatever it was in this dreadful house on their own. She pulled herself together with a supreme effort and walked down the driveway to where Tod was sitting on the rough grass outside the gates. Lately it seemed to be his favourite daytime refuge, as though even the garden held terrors for him.

As she approached him she could see that he was lying facing away from her, an open book propped up in front of him. But he was not reading. He was staring fixedly in the direction of the Reichenbach Falls, his features pale and drawn. Veronica recognised fear when she saw it. He did not appear to be aware of her approach even when she was standing only a yard or so behind him.

'Tod,' she said softly, kindly.

He turned. 'Hi, Mommy.' It was as though he was having to make a supreme effort to drag himself away from his distant thoughts.

'Are you all right, Tod?'

'Yes, Mommy.' He had stopped calling her 'Mommy' two or three years ago. Suddenly his rapid process of growing-up seemed to have been halted.

'What were you thinking about, Tod?'

'About . . . ' he hesitated and dropped his gaze to the ground, 'about . . . Mrs Quilmer . . . *they* killed her.'

'She had a heart attack. The doctor thinks so, anyway, but they'll know for sure on Tuesday.'

'Even if she did have a heart attack they killed her. Just like they killed the fish in the sunken garden. *And they're getting more angry now*. I heard them the night she died.'

'It was probably the noise from the party downstairs.'

'No. It was *them*. They were in my room to start with. I know. Then they went away. Mommy, when are we going to leave here?'

'Your daddy says we're stopping until the spring.'

'*No!*' He struggled up and flung himself at her. 'We can't. We've got to go before they kill us, too. They don't like us being here.' He was on the verge of hysteria.

'Calm yourself.' She stroked his head, sharing his own fears but trying to hide them. 'I don't for one moment believe that there's anything there. It's just a spooky old house that creaks and groans in the dead of night and . . . '

'And smells. When you can smell that horrible stink it means they're around.'

'There's probably something wrong with the sewerage,' she said. 'We'll have to get some plumbers out to come and look at it. In the meantime I'll talk to your daddy and see if there's any chance of us going away for a few days. Maybe a trip to Austria would do us all good and when we come back we'd feel a lot better. We're all depressed because Mrs Quilmer died. She had a bad heart. It would probably have happened, anyway.'

Tod followed her back towards the house. He knew that going away for a while wasn't going to change anything. Nothing at all.

Veronica Pennant was uneasy. Sleep eluded her and she lay listening, wondering if Tod was all right in the bedroom directly above. He was frightened. Terrified. But Al would not hear of having him sleep in their room.

'Hell, the boy's ten,' Al had snapped. 'Time he stopped imagining bogeymen and all that kind of crap. If we start letting him sleep in with us it won't help him any. He's just gotta grow out of it.'

Al was sleeping heavily by her side, snoring. That meant he was lying on his back.

Somewhere a board creaked and there was a rustling. Rats. She hated rats, but most of the old properties Al bought had a few and it was a job to get rid of them. A scurrying, as though the rodents were playing some game. Then silence. That was worse. Total silence like the whole house was waiting for something to happen.

She dozed and then woke again. She was uncomfortable and knew that a trip across the landing to the w.c. was inevitable. Oh, sod it! She told herself that she didn't want to go because it was a nuisance and she might wake Al, or disturb Tod and scare him. A little voice somewhere inside her said, *You don't want to go because you're frightened.*

She slid out of bed, found her slippers and housecoat, and tiptoed towards the door. It groaned its protest as she edged it open. She thought about switching on the light but decided against it. She'd only be a couple of minutes.

It was pitch black out on the landing. It made her uneasy but she tried to shrug off the feeling. The w.c. was ahead of her, slightly to the left. She moved forward, groping, arms outstretched, and heaved a sigh of relief when her fingers located the door she sought. She turned the handle, stepped inside, and the light-pull brushed against her like some gigantic spider's thread.

She pulled. It clicked, but nothing happened. Damn! She tried it again and cursed more strongly, making a mental note to tell Al that the bulb must have blown. Maybe there was a fault in the wiring. That was the trouble with these old places. It could be dangerous.

She finished, and was just about to step out on to the landing again when she heard a faint noise, a swishing sound like thin material wafting in the wind. It might even have been the noise of the Reichenbach Falls in the distance.

Veronica paused, and heard it again. No, it wasn't the falls. It seemed to come from the landing directly above. Tod's bedroom. Maybe he was having another nightmare, even sleepwalking.

'Tod,' she called softly, anxiously.

There was no answer. Just a sudden silence, an awful stillness that had the muscles in her stomach constricting. Panic hit her like a missile out of the stygian blackness, forcing her limbs into sudden movement. She was running, tripping and almost falling as the hem of her nightdress became entangled with her feet. Sobbing. Forcing herself not to scream.

Her fingers searched frantically along the panelled wall until they came to a door, found the brass knob, turned it. Inside. Slamming the door behind her, leaning her full weight back against it as though to shut out whatever was lurking on the landing.

'Al,' she croaked, 'oh, Al. There's . . .'

Her voice tailed off as the awful realisation dawned on her. *She was in the wrong room.* The boards beneath her feet were rough and unpolished. There was no furniture, just a square enclosure of dust and emptiness, a stale musty odour. Oh, God in heaven, this was the trunk-room adjoining their bedroom, the room they had not yet got around to cleaning or furnishing.

Veronica Pennant cowered there, afraid to move. There was a light-switch by her hand, but she knew it was useless. There was no bulb in the socket.

She whimpered and opened her mouth to scream, but no sound came. The muscles in her throat seemed paralysed. She beat upon the wall, but her puny fist made no more noise than a mouse trapped behind the skirting-board.

And at that moment she knew that she was not alone in the room.

It didn't occur to her that she was able to see the boy crouching in the far corner although there was no light, not even from the uncurtained square of window. He saw her, turned his face, and the sight of his emaciated features had her heart leaping and pounding, her throat tight as though a noose encircled it. She tried to jerk her eyes away, but it was impossible.

He was no more than twelve years of age, and at first she thought that he was naked. Then she saw the remnants of clothing hanging from his frame, a jacket that had no arms, just a collar and lapels, the rest ribbons of torn cloth. Short trousers; no, they had rotted just above the knees, jagged and unsightly like the cut-off jeans the kids back home wore. No shoes. The feet were blistering and bleeding, one with part of a sock adhering to it. And the face, oh Jesus! Eyes stared out of black sockets, the nose appeared to be inverted, a hole from which mucus and blood bubbled as he laboured for breath, and the mouth was like a cartoon caricature, a slit that stretched high up into the cheeks, a toothless gap from which trickled scarlet spittle.

Unrecognisable. It could have been Tod. There was no way of telling. Veronica pressed herself back into the corner by the door.

Help me.

The words were plain enough, yet there appeared to be no sound coming from those slitted, mutilated lips. Such was their grotesqueness that it would have been equally impossible to lip-read them. But she understood.

Help me.

Pathetic. And terrifying. She wanted to speak, to say words which her brain was having difficulty in transmitting to her vocal organs. Nothing came out, but the other seemed to understand whatever was being asked in the unfathomable recesses of her mind.

He's killed everybody else. There's only me left. And he's coming for me now!

Who? For God's sake, who?

Him. Can't you hear him?

No, I can't . . .

Then she heard whoever the poor wretch was referring to. Heard him, and smelled his vile, nauseating stench. Slow, dragging footsteps on the other side of the door. A pause. A rattling of phlegm. Wheezing.

The smell was overpowering. It was like recently exhumed corpses from a mass grave; the odour of death and decomposition, of the slow rotting of human flesh.

Veronica felt the door behind her starting to open, pushing her forward. Trapped. The boy before her had no right to be alive with such ghastly wounds inflicted upon him. Whatever was behind her had no right to exist in any corner of the universe. Her tortured brain could accept neither.

She fell to the floor and lay there, her face drawn towards the opening door, gasping for breath in the putrid atmosphere.

The man, if indeed he was human, was inside the room now, seeming not to be aware of her presence as he shuffled his way towards the cringing thing in the corner. His face was terrible to behold, a skull with strips of flesh still adhering to it like sticking-plaster over innumerable wounds. A uniform of some kind, colourless; a peaked cap that was tilted forward as though the wearer was self-conscious of his ghoulish features; thin cruel lips that moved and spoke soundlessly; a whip of some kind dangling from the skeletal fingers of the right hand.

You cannot escape me, boy.

A stifled whimper, hands covering the bloody face. Kneeling. Surrendering.

They're all dead except you. Dead and in the grave. Lying there . . . waiting for you!

Veronica saw the whip raised, stared transfixed as it found its mark unerringly between the splayed, futile defence of those juvenile fingers, gouging an eye in its sunken hole and dragging it out like a stoat seizing a rabbit from its burrow. A scream. The other eye hung by a thread, dangling above the gashed mouth.

Blinded, the boy fell back, lying there as the lash continued its merciless flogging, destroying his bloody, mutilated face, whipping it into a scarlet mulch, spraying blood across the room. A drop flecked Veronica's lips. She tasted it, sour and vile like rancid urine, and retched.

The frail body twitched but there was no respite as the whip continued to flay it, biting deep into the brittle bones, and only when the faint whimpering ceased did the tormentor stop.

He turned slowly, and for the first time seemed to notice Veronica lying by the door. She stared upwards, unable to avoid those penetrating orbs that reflected the ultimate in malevolence and cruelty, felt their power burning deep into her brain. And fainted.

3

THE PUTRID MAN

'I tell you, Al, Tod and I are leaving this house, no matter what you say.'

Al Pennant's annoyance was evident in the way he paced the bedroom, paused to look out of the window in the direction of the Reichenbach Falls and turned back towards Veronica, who lay in bed, propped up by a pile of pillows. Her face was distraught, panic flickering in her eyes. A doctor would have diagnosed her state as being on the verge of a nervous breakdown; the early stages of a mental illness. But Al Pennant had no time for the medical profession, preferring to rely upon his own findings. Veronica was scared to hell. The silly bitch was taking after their son. Hysteria was infectious. And the only way to stop it was to take a firm line. Sympathise, and he would find himself believing that Count Dracula and Frankenstein's monster lurked in this very building. When that happened they were all destined for the mad-house.

'Look,' Al was tight-lipped, two scarlet spots showing on his cheek, 'you went sleepwalking and had a nightmare, blundered into the trunk-room and gave yourself a scare. Nothing more.'

'There *was* something there. A boy who had been starved and tortured until there was nothing left of him, and a . . . a . . . creature who . . . '

'I once had a dream about a werewolf when I was a kid.' Pennant's lips curled in a sneer. 'I had to go to school the next day just the same.'

'We're leaving and that's final.'

Al Pennant sighed and selected a Rossli from his case. Maybe he ought to get rid of his wife and son back to the States. Life would certainly be more peaceful without them. The only snag was that there would be nobody to cook and clean, and he didn't fancy doing the chores himself. Doubtless somebody could be hired from Meiringen or Interlaken, but that was a risk. You didn't know who you were getting and there was a lot of valuable stuff in *La Maison des Fleurs*. Try and talk her round, Al. Use your gift of the gab.

'Anyway, you wouldn't be fit to travel right now,' he said.

'We'd manage. Just get us down to Meiringen and we'll make our own way to Geneva. We'll be back in New York . . . '

'Long Island,' he corrected her. 'We don't own any place in New York any more.'

'I could go back to my folks.'

'No,' he smiled with an effort. 'Your mother has a weak heart and she has all her time cut out looking after your father . . . '

'So I'm trapped here. Tod and I have got to winter it out with . . . with *these things*.'

'If there had been any murdering or flogging during the night hours I should most certainly have heard it in the next room.'

'But it's not like that, I keep telling you. Tod hears and sees things which I don't and vice versa. They don't manifest themselves to all and sundry.'

'Which proves it's all in the mind.'

'You're impossible,' she grimaced.

'And another thing. If, as you say, a boy was flogged to death, blood splattering the room, then there would be *some* evidence of what happened. I've examined the trunk-room myself. The only signs of anyone having been in there last night are your footmarks in the dust.'

'But they're spirits, Al. Evil spirits. They don't leave tangible evidence of their presence. Jeez, they've left their mark on me; I can still feel my ticker going like a crazy pendulum.'

'All you need to do is to rest up for a day or two.'

'Al,' her voice was low and trembling, 'when we get this place back to Long Island, you are going to sell it, aren't you?'

He took a long drag on his cigar and blew a cloud of brown smoke up to the ceiling. 'Maybe,' he said, 'and maybe not. It all depends.'

'On what?'

'Well, on whether anybody's prepared to pay the price I want.'

'Parlane would.'

'I'm not sure that I want to sell to him.'

'Professional jealousy. Cutting off your nose to spite your face. And what if you can't get the extortionate price you're going to ask.'

'Then we'll have a home that will be the envy of the President himself.'

'Oh, God,' Veronica groaned. 'I couldn't live forever in this place. I'd . . . ' She was about to say 'I'd leave you' but she checked herself. Walking out on a millionaire several times over took an awful lot of courage. Maybe Al would see reason in the end.

'Tell you what,' he grinned and fogged another cloud of smoke up at the ceiling. 'We'll let Tod sleep in here with us. How's that? And if there's anybody prowling round after dark then Big Al himself is gonna be asking them a few hard questions.'

She nodded and thought *you stupid conceited sod.* That guy with the putrefied face wasn't going to back down for Al Pennant or anybody else. Whatever the thing was, it had power. *Real power.*

She tried another angle. 'Once the snows come, we won't have any way of getting down. The foot-tracks will be covered over and the funicular will be frozen up. And we don't have a phone.'

'I'd get us ferried out by chopper in an emergency.'

'Suppose one of us was ill. Tod, say. An appendicitis. How'd you let anybody know.'

'My radio,' he replied smugly. She had forgotten all about her husband's radio. He had it all worked out, planned to perfection . . . to suit himself. Only you couldn't make plans in a house like *La Maison des Fleurs.*

Fall was moving fast towards winter. Al Pennant turned up the collar of his sheepskin-lined carcoat as he walked through the grounds. Earlier in the day there had been a few snowflakes in the wind and there was every chance that by morning there would be a light covering on the ground. That was OK, he grinned to himself. Folks paid a fortune to come to Switzerland for the snow. What was Switzerland without snow?

He was trying to work out what to do with this hectare of land once the house had gone. The obvious answer was to build another in its place. It was virtually the only place around the Reichenbach Falls where there was any flat land. A hotel; put a manager in, someone reliable who wouldn't fiddle more than ten per cent of the takings. Name it '221 B'. Say, that was a stroke of genius! The bookings would be heavy all the year round, nutty guys who wore deerstalker caps and Norfolk jackets, smoked bent Peterson pipes and kept their shag tobacco in a smelly Persian slipper. *Al, my boy, you're on to a winner. You've hit the jackpot this time.*

He was whistling tunelessly to himself as he negotiated the rocky steps down to the sunken garden. Overhanging branches sprang back at him as he forced a passage through them. One whipped him across the face and he cursed aloud. Hell, somebody had to do some pruning here.

Another thought struck him. Once the hotel was built, put the rumour around that this was the site of the original building in which the 'tec and his sidekick stayed overnight before that historic plunge over the falls. A double bonus. The followers wouldn't be entirely satisfied just by visiting 221 B. They'd make a pilgrimage out to Long Island, dip into their savings coffers just to walk the hallowed wooden floors of the house itself. He'd really do the place out, everything they expected to see and a lot more besides.

Already he could hear the dollar bills rustling. He stood there looking down into the empty ornamental pond. He'd let the water out a week ago otherwise the frost might have damaged the structure. Pity about those fish. Hell, what did they call 'em? It didn't matter. The guy at the aquarium store in Interlaken would fix him up with some more next spring. They would probably have died in the winter, anyway.

Night was coming fast, dusk turning to darkness with hardly a respectable pause. He looked up at the sky and noted the banks of heavy cloud moving in from the west, leaden grey, loaded with snow. He shivered.

And then Al Pennant saw the man standing in the shadow of a rhododendron bush on the opposite side of the pond, some twenty feet away, just an outline, silently watching him.

Al started. Hell, that stupid bugger had made him jump and what the fuck did he think he was doing here, anyway?

'Hi, you. What the hell d'you think you're doing in my garden?' Pennant's tone was harsh but he could not disguise the slight tremor in it.

No answer. Not so much as a movement. The stranger did not appear even to have heard him.

'Are you bloody well deaf?'

Al took a step forward and then, for some inexplicable reason, checked. He didn't know why, except that a tingling feeling ran down his spine as though somebody had tipped a glass of iced water down his collar.

He licked his lips. His mouth had suddenly gone dry. Fuck it, this bum had no business here. He had to be a hobo living rough in the mountains who had found himself a nice snug patch of shelter from the elements. Well, he wasn't staying here. Al Pennant didn't provide buckshee lodgings for dropouts, not even in his garden.

'You can fuck off. D'you hear me?' Talk rough to him, frighten him, even if he doesn't understand English. '*Tête de chien!*' The biggest insult he could think of right off. Most of the Swiss spoke either French or German.

The intruder gave no sign that he had heard. No movement. Al Pennant was puzzled. He backed away a step and was instantly ashamed of his cowardice. Hell, he wasn't afraid of any punk, and certainly not on his own land.

'Now, see here...'

His voice tailed off and his whole body became rigid, as though he had been rendered paralytic, mouth wide, staring in total disbelief... *for he had caught his first glimpse of the other's face!*

It just had to be a figment of some warped, delirious dream. That face, with its peeling flesh hanging down in strips like rotting carcases on a gamekeeper's gibbet. Eyes that were not eyes, sockets that glowed their hate. A dark-coloured uniform with polished jackboots. A hand was raised, a fleshless finger pointing at Al Pennant, stabbing the air accusingly. The lips were almost invisible, the mouth a cancerous slot that oozed yellow pus, which ran down the chin in tiny rivulets.

For the first time in his life Pennant experienced real *fear* . . . the ultimate in dread. His mouth formed words that were never uttered, mute gibberish, a mixture of pleas, apologies. Apologies for being here, for his very existence.

Leave my house alone. Be gone!

The message came on the icy breeze, the smell of putrefaction wafting with it.

If you remain in my house you will die. All of you.

Al found himself nodding, and muttering something about 'we'll go'. A chill wind, a strengthening of the breeze, bringing the clouds closer, suffocating the remaining dusk. Night.

The stranger was gone. Al Pennant sensed it. He could no longer see across the sunken garden but suddenly the evil had lifted, leaving in its wake the remnants of that foul stench as a reminder.

He turned, somehow found the steps and rushed heedlessly up them. A trailing briar caught at his ankle, ripping the flesh through his sock. He ignored it. Branches parted at his progress, slashing back at him. He cursed. He was running the gauntlet of evil, and terror stabbed at his heart. He had to make it to the upper lawn. Like Tod had done. The boy had told the truth. So had Veronica. There was . . . *something* here.

At last he was on higher ground, wheezing and gasping for breath. Thirty yards or so in front of him the lights of the house winked their welcome. He knew how lost seafarers felt when they glimpsed a lighthouse. Safety. Not really. A temporary lull. He had been warned; it was up to him. Not just his own life was at stake but those of his wife and son.

Unless . . . another thought occurred to him and with it came light relief. It had to be a trick of some kind. Nothing like that thing he had seen down there could possibly exist. That was it! He gave a hollow laugh which he scarcely recognised as his own before the wind whipped it away.

Now who the hell stood to gain anything by scaring seven sorts of shit out of the Pennant family? One of the Reichenbachs who had just heard that the family home had been sold and was determined to evict the new owners? Hell, no, he'd start a law suit. A rival dealer, somebody who had been at the party? A more likely solution but, according to Veronica and Tod, all this business had started long before these other dealers saw the place. A nutcase, some local who had an obsession about Swiss property being bought by foreigners? Maybe. But it had to be somebody, a human being. It could *not* be anything else. Bogeymen were handy reasons for getting your kids down the bed at night and stopping them from larking about. Spooks had their uses; film producers and writers made a fortune out of them all because folks actually *liked* to be frightened. But not Big Al. No, sir!

He winced when he recalled those few moments. The odour still lingered in his nostrils; it would take some getting out of his system. Before he realised it he was placing a Rossli between his lips and feeling for his cigar lighter. There was a remedy for everything.

Al Pennant drew the smoke down into his lungs and exhaled it slowly. Snowflakes were starting to fall, but he wasn't going inside for a few minutes. Shit, he'd been startled, not really scared. Nevertheless, the business couldn't be ignored completely. If it was some crank then it could be dangerous. They'd got Kennedy in spite of all the tight security precautions. Others, too. It would have to be handled carefully.

The snow thickened, almost to blizzard proportions, and he headed for the flight of wooden steps. They were already slippery beneath his feet, and he had to hold on to the rail. He shook his coat in the porch and went inside.

'Al, I . . . ' Veronica came out of the kitchen doorway and stopped, staring at him in amazement. 'Al, whatever's the matter?'

'Nothing.' He took a deep drag on his cigar and removed it from his lips, aware that his hand was shaking. 'Why?'

'You look ill. You're trembling like you've got the ague.'

'It's the cold,' he laughed, a harsh, unnatural sound. 'Freezing out there. Snowing hard, too.'

'You've had a fright of some kind, haven't you?'

Damn this so-called woman's intuition! He hung his coat up on the hallstand, taking his time, keeping his back to her. Jeez, that guy had really shaken him.

'Where's Tod?' he asked.

'Upstairs. Reading. Supper will be about ten minutes. Longer if you don't come clean.'

'Some joker's making a nuisance of himself. Trying to drive us out. Who the hell he is I haven't a clue, but I don't want Tod to know.'

'Oh.' She paled but could not hold back a faint grin. 'I wondered how long it would be before you saw it.'

'It was human,' he snapped. 'Dressed up for the part.'

'What did he look like?'

'Some kind of uniform. Had stuff stuck all over his face to make it look as though the flesh was peeling off.'

'That's him! The one I saw. The one Tod's seen.'

'Sure. He ain't gonna invest in a wardrobe of different disguises. He's out to scare us away.'

'And the smell?'

'Yeah. A handful of kid's stinkbombs crushed under his boot would see to that.'

'You're impossible, Al!' She half turned back towards the kitchen door.

'However,' – he had almost convinced himself that his explanation for the presence of the stranger was the correct one. Convince them now, but don't take any chances at the same time – 'however, we can't have a maniac running riot for the rest of the winter. Tomorrow we'll go down to Meiringen and see the gendarme. We'll get some police protection.'

'So you *are* scared, underneath your usual façade.' Biting sarcasm. But the truth.

'Concerned is the word. I can't take chances with you and Tod around.'

'We should go back to the States. Stay in an hotel for the winter if need be.'

'Just because of one nutter?'

'It's not human, Al. You know that yourself although you won't admit it. The police won't be able to do anything. *Please*, if not for my sake, then for Tod's, let's get out whilst we still can.'

'Tell you what.' He walked across to the table and crushed the butt of his cigar into an ashtray. 'If we can't get police protection then I'll take you both to a place of safety.'

'Promise?' Relief showed on her strained features.

'Promise.'

Strangely, Al Pennant felt relieved at the prospect of going away. For once he wasn't going to insist too hard on protection by the law. He could not get the sight of that grotesque figure down by the fishpond out of his mind.

Armand Heron had been chief gendarme in Meiringen for the past five years. It was a good post, much more relaxed than his previous one in Zürich. A sleepy little place for eight months of the year. Then from May until the end of August the Sauvage, Hirschen and Weisses Kreuz were fully booked. All because of one fictional detective. The main township of the Hasli Valley, a home weaving centre, overflowed with sightseers, all making for the one goal: the Reichenbach Falls. They thronged the Aareschlucht, many of them camping out. All nationalities.

'Où est le poste de police? . . . Wo ist die Polizei? . . . Dov'è la polizia?' From his office in the summertime Armand could hear their interrogation of local tradesmen. They asked for the police first, came trooping in. Such importance was placed on their pilgrimage to the falls that they didn't want to waste time wandering along the Aareschlucht just hoping to come upon the place they sought.

But a foreigner in winter was so unusual that Armand ushered the cigar-smoking American to his private office and closed the door.

'Now, monsieur, how can I be of assistance to you?' The gendarme seated himself behind the flimsy wooden desk, stroked his short-clipped moustache and toyed with a pencil in anticipation of taking notes.

'Pennant's the name.' Al paused, searching for some sign

of recognition on the other's face at the mention of his name, slightly annoyed when he saw none. 'Al Pennant, owner of *La Maison des Fleurs*.'

'Ah!' the policeman's eyes widened, his brow furrowed. 'Oui, oui . . . of course. The American.'

'Yeah.'

'You . . . like living up there?' a narrowing of the eyes.

'Sure. But we gotta problem.'

'Yes?'

'Some crack's japing us.'

'Pardon?'

'There's a guy trying to scare hell out of us. My wife and kid are on the verge of a breakdown.'

'Please explain.'

Al Pennant recounted the experiences of both Veronica and Tod, then told him about the man with the putrid face in the sunken garden.

'I see.' Armand tried to keep an impassive expression. He licked his lips slowly and stroked his moustache. 'I take it you know the story of the Reichenbachs.'

'I've heard bits and pieces.'

'The man you describe, the one you yourself saw, he was wearing a uniform?'

'Yeah, kinda dark-coloured, peaked cap, knee-boots. It was too dark to make out much detail.'

'None the less, it is evident to me that it was a Gestapo uniform.'

'So what?'

'The last Reichenbach, the one that disappeared, was a notorious Gestapo torturer. Several thousand people died at his hands.'

'Look,' – Al Pennant felt his anger rising – 'I know what you're driving at. But if somebody wanted to scare the crap out of me, make out they were Reichenbach, ain't that just the costume they'd use?'

'Perhaps.' Heron sucked the end of his pencil. 'If that is what is happening, although I very much doubt that the answer is so simple.'

'What's your theory, then?'

'I speak only from hearsay, monsieur. Reichenbach had

disappeared five years before I came to Meiringen. *La Maison des Fleurs* is a house with a history which it has revealed to none. Nobody knows whence it came, although there are locals who say that it appeared during the war years, springing up like a Black Forest mushroom, transported here secretly in sections under the directions of the Führer himself, a hiding place for him when the Allied forces overran Germany. Instead, with Hitler dead, Reichenbach fled here.

'Others say that the house was there decades before, owned by a succession of Reichenbachs, and that it was hidden by the trees which have since been felled. Do not forget, monsieur, it is only since the advent of travel on the scale that we know it today that crowds have flocked here. One hectare of ground containing a house that was hidden by trees could pass unnoticed in a remote part of Switzerland.'

'Sure,' Pennant snapped. 'But you haven't told me your theory about this guy with the peeling face.'

'My theory, monsieur,' – Armand removed the pencil from his mouth and began doodling on the pad in front of him – 'is that the man you saw was Reichenbach himself . . . or, to be more precise, his spirit.'

'Shit,' Pennant said. 'I don't believe in ghosts.'

'I have an open mind, monsieur,' the gendarme replied. 'There have been rumours of screams coming from that place, heard by climbers who have lost their way and wandered close to the house. Rumours also that towards the end of the war, when Reichenbach was already in hiding in *La Maison des Fleurs*, the Gestapo brought prisoners to him secretly . . . for him to torture to death! The house cannot have failed to absorb that atmosphere of pain and death, if that was, indeed, the case.'

'Shit,' Al Pennant said again.

'I am sorry that I cannot be of any more help to you, monsieur.'

'You haven't heard my request yet.'

'Oh?' Armand scrutinised the other carefully.

'I still say it's some crazy punk who wants us out of the house for some reason of his own,' Al Pennant said. 'But he's still a threat. I need police protection for my family.'

Armand Heron shook his head slowly, pursing his lips. 'I am afraid not, monsieur,' he murmured. 'I do not have the men available, and even if I did, my superiors would never permit it. In another week or two the funicular will probably be frozen up, anyway. I am sorry, monsieur, I would like to help but . . . but allow me to offer you some personal advice. *I* would not spend a single night in *La Maison des Fleurs*, not for a million francs. Get out now, whilst you *still can*!

Al Pennant joined Veronica and Tod in the lounge of the Weisses Kreuz. His expression was grim, yet there was a faint flicker of relief in his eyes.

'We're movin' out,' he told them, when he'd ordered two bourbons and a coke for Tod. 'I'll book seats on a flight from Geneva right away. We'd best get moving before the snows come. Can't take chances with a maniac at large, and only country cops to rely on who wouldn't even be able to get to you. We'll go back to New York. Winter in an hotel. Then I'll come back in the spring.'

'And . . . and what then?' Veronica asked apprehensively.

'We'll start shipping the old place back to the States.'

'But . . . but what about . . . whatever it is that's in the house?'

Pennant laughed, hearty now in the crowded atmosphere of a modern hotel lounge. 'Well, if you persist in believing in bogeymen I guess this particular one's going to find it a bit uncomfortable without a roof over its head.'

The other two did not share his mirth. They were already thinking ahead to the following year, envisaging an old mansion on stilts within sight of the rolling breakers on the shores of Long Island. The nocturnal hours there would not be any different. And if perchance the spirits of the torturer and his victims should make the voyage along with their home, those forces of darkness might be enraged to unbelievable ferocity out of their own environment.

4

THE COMMUNAL GRAVE

April 10th. Al Pennant stepped off the plane at Geneva Airport and buttoned up his sheepskin carcoat. Winter had lingered on and there was still snow on the mountains, but a transatlantic telephone call to Armand Heron at Meiringen had confirmed that the funicular up to the Reichenbach Falls was working normally. Morc phone calls. The contractors from Zürich were ready to start. The site had already been inspected, and there would be the additional cost of cranes and cable trucks to transport the sections of the house down to low-level. An estimate of $150,000 in all. That was OK, but get cracking, build a second funicular if need be, only don't hang about. The shipping date was May 30th from Trieste. It all had to be taken down, packed, railed across country, then loaded on to the ship. Time was at a premium. It was money, not just for Al Pennant but for the merchant shippers. They were on a bonus. Al knew how to dangle his carrots.

He arrived in Meiringen late in the afternoon and booked in at the Sauvage. He was uneasy. Hell, it was just because he was tired; nothing that a good dinner, a few whiskies and a night's rest wouldn't put right. He'd be staying at the Sauvage until *La Maison des Fleurs* was on its way to Long Island. Not that he was bothered about spending nights up there alone. But you couldn't live in a place that was in the process of being dismantled.

The contractors were already on site when Al arrived the following morning. It had snowed during the night, just a shower or two, enough to give the ground a slight covering, but it would melt before mid-day.

It was as Al came back out of the house, down the flight of steps, that something caught his eye. Red icing on white, carelessness by the baker, yet adding to the effect rather than spoiling it.

He stared at the lone snowdrop and a chill ran over him

that was in no way due to the crisp mountain air. The flower stood there, proud and erect, out of a quarter of an inch of snow, yet around its base there was a spreading crimson stain approximately the size of a dinner plate.

'Jeez!' He approached nervously and tried to find reasons for what he saw. It was blood, there was no doubt about that. Fresh, too. An animal of the wild that had squatted there, some anal infection causing it to bleed. But there were neither droppings nor urine stains. Just blood.

He licked his lips and called to a workman who was in the act of removing one of the lower windowsills.

'Hey, what d'you make of this?'

The man came across slowly, unwillingly, his Tyrolean-style hat perched on the back of his head. He looked at Pennant. '*Je ne comprends pas.*'

'*Parlez-vous anglais?*'

The man shook his head.

'*Qu'est-ce que c'est?*'

'*Je ne sais pas.*' Sullenly the other turned and went back to his work.

Pennant stared down at the snowdrop again. The stained snow appeared to have lost some of its brightness. *It was more of a pinkish hue, as though the blood was draining back into the earth.* But that was impossible. The snow would melt in that case. Crazy.

He moved away, still turning the matter over in his mind. The foreman wanted to speak to him, a whole list of queries. They were all easily answered, but it was evident to Pennant that he would have to remain in Switzerland until the job was completed. There seemed to be a distinct lack of decision-making ability amongst these contractors. They worked to a finger-and-thumb rule; had to have it all written down, preferably not in English. They weren't interested in the job, just the money.

By mid-afternoon the atmosphere was milder, the crispness of an extended winter seeming ready to make way for the warmth of spring. Al took off his carcoat and hung it up in the hall. A mild spell would help to keep the work on schedule, perhaps even get ahead.

He went back outside again. A group of men were busily

working on the front of the house taking out the lower windows. One was climbing a ladder, on his way to begin the removal of the wooden floral decorations. Pennant's gaze passed him, irresistibly drawn up to those snowdrops, fascinated by them.

Almost apprehensively he glanced down at the one on the ground again. He started. The snow around it had melted completely, revealing the rocky soil, tufts of grass already beginning to take on the lush green of spring. Even so it was odd. Uncanny. This side of the house was shaded from the sun, and would be for another half hour. The snow was still lying . . . *except around the snowdrop*!

Pennant shivered. Jeez, this place was really starting to give him the creeps now. Then he heard the scream above him . . .

His head went up like a string puppet that had been jerked hard. Aghast, he saw the man on the ladder swaying outside one of the first floor windows.

'*Mon Dieu!*'

The workman's back was arched, his hands flung up, not to grip the ladder but to protect his face from some unseen danger. His feet were stuck between the rungs as he fell back, taking the ladder with him. For some seconds everything seemed to come to a standstill, the ladder upright, hovering on its point of balance as though undecided whether to crash back to safety against the side of the house or to pitch outwards. It tottered, fell outwards. Slow motion, the man slipping, held upside down by one trapped foot. Screaming.

Pennant wanted to wrench his gaze away and clasp his hands over his eyes so that he should not witness the finale, the sickening crunch, the splintering of wood and bone, the smashed and mangled body writhing in its death throes, moaning for help. He saw it all before it happened, then watched the re-run, almost identical but more horrific.

The heavy ladder had pinned its victim to the ground, bent double, legs splayed at an unnatural angle. The back was broken, it couldn't be anything else. The head was turned towards the watchers, blood streaming from mouth, nose and ears. *And he still lived!*

Men rushed forward, then hung back, knowing it was hopeless. There was nothing anybody could do. Death was the only outcome and the sooner it came the better for everybody.

Al Pennant stood where he was, eyes riveted on the bloody mangled heap. *Die, you poor bastard; hurry up and die!*

The mouth was moving, spitting blood and broken teeth as the lips tried to form words, the vocal chords struggling to produce sound. Garbled at first, a brief coherent spell, then back to gibberish, only the wide pain and terror-filled eyes able to move freely. Pupils dilated, they stared past the group of men, up towards that first floor window. Words and blood spilled out, jumbled French and German which Pennant was unable to understand so fast was it spoken, as though the injured man knew that he was going to die and had to get some message over first.

The speech died away to a gurgle. The head slumped to one side. It was all over.

A dozen faces turned, staring upwards at that window, every one wearing an expression of shock, horror. Lips moving, mumbling; a few praying, crossing themselves. Now they were looking towards Al Pennant with hate and accusation, tight-lipped, only their eyes speaking.

Murderer! You knew. You knew all the time what was in that room!

Al Pennant had always boasted of an ability to make split-second decisions, to act quickly. But for once he just stood there, white-faced, open-mouthed, wilting beneath the mute barrage of hate, unable to present his own case.

'We'd best get a doctor up here.' He pulled himself together with a conscious effort, singling out the foreman.

'A doctor will be no good. Pieter has only need of an undertaker.'

'Why . . . why did he fall?'

Another volley of malevolent expressions. Al Pennant glared back defiantly.

'What is in this house, monsieur, which you did not tell us about?'

'Nothing. Nothing at all.'

'It is a lie. Pieter saw something . . . something which mortals have no right to gaze upon, one who has returned from the grave to walk with the living!'

'Rubbish. Utter crap.' Pennant was visibly shaken and reached for his cigars. It was like a dream, everything going crazy. That snowdrop. Something in . . . it just occurred to him which room it was . . . *the trunk-room*! 'There's nothing here, I can assure you. Just an old house.'

The men were not listening. Even their dead colleague was ignored as they clustered into a group, jabbering in low, fearful voices. Pennant stood there watching them, making no effort to translate the chatter. He knew only too well what they were saying, and it spelled trouble in a big way.

The black-bearded foreman turned and came towards him, arrogant in spite of his obvious fear, spitting contemptuously on the ground.

'The men will not work here any longer,' he growled.

'You've got to.' Al Pennant had to restrain himself from shouting, 'You're under contract.'

'We are leaving. All of us. Now. We will report what has happened.'

The American stood there with clenched fists as the workers hastened through the gates, almost breaking into a run, heading towards the funicular, and he cursed them until he ran out of obscenities. Finally he turned and went back inside for his coat. He thought about going up to the first storey and checking on the trunk-room, but decided against it. Just a waste of time and effort. There would be nothing there. There had not been before, only Veronica's footmarks in the dust.

As he turned to leave, he thought he detected a faint rancid odour in the musty atmosphere of the hall but he could not be sure. Nevertheless, it was with some relief that he stepped out into the sunlight and closed the door behind him. He breathed deeply, relishing the clear mountain air.

He averted his gaze in order not to see the pulped heap beneath the fallen ladder which had once been a human being. Everyday, somewhere, people died in accidents. Building workers and steeplejacks fell from scaffolding, motorists were killed on the road, terminal diseases took a slow toll. Death was part of life. You lived with it and hoped that it would be somebody else and not yourself.

By the time he reached the funicular platform he had almost got Pieter out of his system. Don't think of him again until the inquest. There had been nothing in that room. That snowdrop . . . it hadn't been blood on the snow. Reddish clay. Even a trick of the light. He had to wait half an hour for the cable-car to come back up. By then the workmen would be well on the road to Zürich. Al Pennant was going to make some very angry phone calls once he got back to his hotel.

He used the telephone in the manager's office at the Sauvage. First to Chandu in Zürich. *Sorry, Mr Pennant, we'd like to finish the job but if we try to force the men we'll have a full-scale labour stoppage. Yes, we appreciate there's a contract but there's nothing we can do about it. Why don't you try Dupins? A small firm. They might be glad of the work.*

Al Pennant went round to Dupins on foot, ten minutes' walk from the hotel. The yard was small, backing on to Lake Brienz, and stacked with piles of softwood that had not yet been peeled. Monsieur Dupin was out, he was informed by a dwarf-like man in yellow overalls who conversed whilst operating a chain-saw, but he would be back shortly. At least that was what Al Pennant thought the midget said. Lip-reading in a foreign language had its complications.

He waited. It was almost dark when Dupin drove into the yard in a crimson Volvo, parking it by the side of a precariously stacked pile of sawn trunks. The man was short and thick set, heavy lips giving him a sullen expression.

'You'd better come into the office,' he grunted when Al Pennant had introduced himself, leading the way without looking back to see if the other was following. He did not offer his visitor a seat so Al took one. Otherwise, psychologically he was at a disadvantage, an office-boy summoned before the boss for a bawling out.

'Chandu recommended you to try us?' Dupin's eyebrows lifted in surprise. 'That is strange, indeed. Usually he poaches jobs, big ones anyway, not gives them away.'

'One of the men got killed this morning. Fell off a ladder. The others got chicken and there was a walk-out.'

'Chicken? *Je ne comprends pas.*'

'Frightened.'

'Why? Workers know the risks. A percentage have to die every year from falls, by the law of averages.'

'They'd been listening to too many rumours about *La Maison des Fleurs.*'

'*La Maison des Fleurs.* Now that is different, Mr Pennant.'

'It shouldn't be. All I want is the place taken down, packed up and put on the rail to Trieste.'

'Any other place would be no problem. But the Reichenbach house . . . '

'It's no different from thousands of other ancient properties throughout the world.'

'I'm afraid it is, Mr Pennant. Not that I'm superstitious myself' – Dupin smiled weakly – 'but you know what local workmen are. They hear stories, they believe them.'

'I'm willing to pay over the odds.'

Dupin regarded him steadily. 'Of course, with the men, money goes a long way. They are not prepared to . . . to take risks for an average day's pay.'

'Chandu quoted me $150,000,' Pennant spoke slowly, hearing the rustle of dollar bills again, this time being wafted away on a Swiss mountain breeze. 'I'm prepared to offer $200,000. That'll give you a good profit margin, even after you've given your men a fair bonus.'

'Hmm.' Dupin pursed his lips, trying to hide his satisfaction, but no way could he disguise the glint of greed in his round dark eyes. He drummed his fingers on the desk. 'I don't know . . . it's hard to say . . . if only it wasn't *La Maison des Fleurs.*'

'If it wasn't, you wouldn't be getting that kind of money,' Al Pennant snapped. 'Look, I'm not prepared to hang about. I'll fly contractors in from the States if necessary.'

'No, no,' Dupin raised a hand. 'Don't be hasty about this, Mr Pennant.'

'I've gotta be. Time's money, and . . . '

'I'll phone you this evening.' The other's mind was

already made up, but he wasn't committing himself on the spur of the moment. 'I'll have to contact my site manager. We've got a demolition job at Brienz but we're well ahead of schedule. We could pull some men off there for a few weeks. However, I can't promise right now, but I'll give you a definite answer before ten o'clock tonight.'

Al Pennant was in high spirits as he strolled back to the hotel, pausing to stare into the windows of closed shops. His own reflection, that determined look on his features, gave him the added confidence he needed at the end of a disastrous day. The deal would go through all right.

Dupin telephoned his acceptance at 9.40. Fifteen men were being drafted to the Reichenbach Falls first thing next morning. He had also fixed with Chandu to hire the heavy plant already up there. *La Maison des Fleurs* would be at Trieste by May 30th. He, personally, guaranteed it.

There was a different atmosphere around the house on the Reichenbach Falls. Efficient, workmanlike. The men worked tirelessly, cutting their breaks down to a minimum. Pennant didn't know the wages, but he guessed Dupin had made some sort of a productivity deal. There was obviously no union involved, hence the absence of chaos.

Every item of furniture was crated and on its way by April 13th. The outer facings, the carvings and some of the top floor were cleared by the 15th. The roof came off easily and the slates were carefully stacked in wooden boxes, then the rafters, and from thereon it was merely a question of dismantling a storey at a time.

'That's how I like to see men work,' Al Pennant complimented Dupin, on one of the latter's infrequent visits to the site. 'Everything will be in Trieste well before the sailing date. Oh, and another thing, Dupin. I want to export some of the garden. Just a few of each flower and shrub, enough to help me create the original picture back home.'

'Of course, of course,' Dupin smiled. 'No trouble there. Just make a note of what you want. My men will see to it.'

Only then did Pennant remember the snowdrop by the steps. After Dupin had left, he found a trowel and went in search of the plant in question. The flower had died down after its brief spring showing. The bulb would provide years of future growth. He scraped away at the rocky surface, dug down with some difficulty and unearthed several ounces of fine powdery soil. Scraping it to one side, he found the bulb. Just an ordinary small tuber, no different from those which you bought by the packet in any departmental store.

He scooped it up and dropped it into a small polythene bag, together with some of the rocky soil. Even as he was fastening the neck, the smell hit him, a stench that might have come from the foulest New York sewer. He recoiled, and shuddered as he recognised the odour. It was identical to that in the sunken garden the night that spectre of evil had given its warning; the same as they had smelled the first time they entered *La Maison des Fleurs. A breath of foul air from the depths of Hades.*

He threw the bag into a crate containing other small items that were due for shipment, and swayed uncertainly on his feet. Now where the hell had that stink come from? It was logical to conclude that it had come up from the ground. In which case there *was* something wrong with the sewage system after all. A blocked pipe, maybe even a burst, overflowing its contents instead of carrying them on down to the cess-pit at the far end of the grounds.

Al Pennant grinned. He'd solved where that foul stink was coming from. And it was a logical explanation. Already his lingering fears of the man with the putrid face were diminishing.

Just a nagging thought, though. That *had* looked like blood around the snowdrop the other week. But it was impossible, so why worry about it?

May 4th. Only the ground floor and the foundations, including the supporting stilts, remained. A week's work at the most. The floor was on its way to Trieste within three days. Al Pennant checked. Everything was arriving OK at the other end. Things were going smoothly.

The stilts were buried deep in the ground. They had to be to support four storeys.

The JCB was working overtime, throwing up a huge mound of soil and rocks on to the upper lawn, burying its greenery. Pennant reminded the driver that everything had to be put back and levelled when the job was finished.

May 6th. The JCB was working in a deep pit below where the wooden entrance steps had stood. The blade pushed up several more tons of rock and soil and sent its load cascading down the slope on top of the last one.

Two of the men attaching chains to the last of the stilts turned and stared. Whiteness glinted amidst the greyish-brown of the earth. Bones. *Skeletons.*

'Che cosa è questo?' The first man, an Italian, knew what they were even as he asked the question. He closed his eyes and began to cross himself fervently.

The second man shouted. Others came running. Al Pennant, who had been on his way down to the funicular, retraced his steps hurriedly. There was a knotted feeling in his stomach. Things had gone far too smoothly for his liking so far. No hitches. It was uncanny.

'Mon Dieu!' The foreman had scrambled down into the pit, treading warily, staring at a number of other half-exposed skeletal limbs which had not yet been dug out. 'A graveyard. Beneath the house of evil. The hell-house. So the stories were right.'

'They're old,' Al Pennant shouted, foreseeing another walk-out by the workmen. 'Years old. Mouldering bones of centuries ago. There must be scores of forgotten cemeteries scattered around the countryside.'

'This is no cemetery,' the foreman muttered. *'It is a communal grave in unconsecrated ground. The burial place of the Reichenbach torture victims.'*

'We'll have to get the gendarme up here.' Al Pennant's fingers were shaking as he struck a match to light his cigar. 'In the meantime we'd better call a halt to excavations.'

Armand Heron grimaced as he stood watching the mechanical digger throw out a dozen or more skeletons. The JCB went back, then came forward again, pushing another two feet of soil before it. This time only odd limbs were being churned out.

Two gendarmes were dragging the skeletons out of the excavated soil and laying them in a row, like corpses after a military skirmish awaiting identification for a ceremonial burial.

'Seventeen, Armand.'

'This is what I was telling you, Mr Pennant.' The policeman turned to the man at his side. 'The Reichenbach rumours were not just rumours. They were true. Look at these. Every one of these people has been tortured. Some have had limbs amputated. Look at that one, a mere boy!'

Pennant remembered what Veronica had told him and tasted bile in his mouth. He thought of Tod.

'And that one; look, the body has been crushed into a ball by some devilish instrument of torture. Note those limbs which have been pulled from their sockets by the rack. See, some still wear their shackles.'

'He must've been a madman.' Al had to say something. He couldn't put his own feelings into words.

'Probably. Certainly obsessional. A man who might have been the devil's henchman. He never accepted defeat, hiding out here and wreaking a terrible vengeance on the last of his country's enemies as they were brought to him. Possibly a few of his Gestapo colleagues are still alive in various parts of the world. Anyway, the commissioner will have to see these remains and determine whether or not an inquest will be held. It all depends on their age.'

'Well, there's just that one support and a few shrubs from the garden to be loaded,' Pennant said, 'and then you'll be rid of the Reichenbach house for good.'

'Yes,' the gendarme smiled mirthlessly, 'but we shall not miss it. Mr Pennant, I have said it before and I make no apology for saying it again. Not for a million francs would I spend a night in *La Maison des Fleurs*, let alone live in it. With such evil perpetrated within its four walls, the very woodwork with which it is constructed cannot have failed to absorb the souls of tormentor and tormented, the screams and groans of the dying, the curses of the monster who afflicted these atrocities upon them. And beneath all this, the dead were buried in a vile pit, their disfigured bodies rotting slowly. A house of death, Mr Pennant, which will never be rid of its atmosphere. You are more than welcome to it!'

Al Pennant was ill at ease when he returned to the

Sauvage that evening. Moving the house would be a good thing. On Long Island it would look exactly as it had done in Switzerland and its atmosphere would take on a new serenity; the horrors of Reichenbach, the beast of torture, would remain in the place where they had originated. If spirits lurked there then in future they must haunt a barren site. It had been a long hard fight to wrest *La Maison des Fleurs* from their clutches.

5

HORROR AT SEA

May 31st.

Dave Giovanni was not impressed with merchant seafaring. He had come to this decision the second day after they had left New York harbour. At eighteen years of age he had not fully made up his mind on a career, but in the meantime he needed money. His old man had just progressed to a 1979 Mustang and that seemed to be the ultimate in ambitions. Dave would have a 1972 VW Beetle upon his return. His wages for the trip would just about run to it, and he was hopeful of a loan from his mother to enable him to get it on the road. Further than that, he had no plans. But one thing was certain. He wasn't going to sea again. Not even for a Mustang.

The night was sultry as he sat on a packing case in the stern of the boat. The chugging of the engine was getting on his nerves. It was like a dicky heart, missing every so often, giving you a funny sort of feeling if you were listening hard. The VW had sounded like that the afternoon he went on a test-run. The mechanic had said it was because it was only firing on three cylinders. The replacement of the fourth lead had done the trick. Maybe that was what was the matter with this old tub. They wouldn't thank him for his opinion, though. No, sir! Furthermore, they weren't going to get the benefit of his astute observations. Sod 'em all, right down from Captain Stacey to Chips, the stoker.

He lit the last of his Camel cigarettes, then crumpled up the empty packet and committed it solemnly to the Adriatic. He made another decision. He wasn't going down below to his bunk tonight or any other night. This wasn't the navy, you could sleep where you bloody well liked.

He'd had enough after last night. Going ashore had been more of an experience than an enjoyment. Sallinger and two or three of the others had taken him along with them to this brothel in Trieste. If only he'd tried it with the girls back home first, Dave decided, then maybe it wouldn't have been such a disaster. The young Italian whore had gone berserk when he'd shot all over her whilst they were still playing about. It wasn't his fault. He couldn't hold back any longer. Neither could he help not being able to get a second erection. After his orgasm the whole thing had seemed so sordid, a sheer waste of money. One consolation, he wasn't likely to catch a dose.

He'd never have guessed, though, that Sallinger and the others were queers into the bargain. That trip to the brothel had been a kind of seduction, a softening up process. They'd all screwed hussies but when they got back on board it was obvious that they'd only been whetting their appetites. They were lusting for a nice eighteen-year-old boy, queuing up at at his bunk. He'd had to let them have their way otherwise they would have beaten him up and then had it anyway. He was disgusted with himself for getting a hard-on in the midst of it all, ashamed that he had come. That meant he found it exciting and in that case he was as bad as them. No, never. It was the thought of the way that harlot had kissed his penis that had made him ejaculate. Nothing at all to do with being homosexual. If he was gay then he'd be down below right now, giving himself freely to the crew of the *Zinal*. And there was no chance of that happening. The filthy bilge rats!

Dave decided that he would keep out of their way until they docked back in the States. It might not be easy. Right now they were probably eagerly anticipating his arrival down below. They'd be disappointed. He grinned, thinking of how they might satisfy their warped lust.

Another thought struck him, a rather frightening one. Suppose they came looking for him. Hell, if they'd got the urge they might search the whole boat, and when they found him they'd teach him a lesson. Rape would be a pleasure after what they'd do to him first. He cupped the palms of his hands around his cigarette as he drew on it, masking the glow of the tobacco so that it would not give away his position.

The engine slowed, then picked up again. He noted its faster rhythm. He liked it when they speeded up; it made New York seem nearer.

He settled down and tried to make himself comfortable. It wasn't easy. He wouldn't sleep, anyway, not for a long while yet. There was too much to think about. Italy, for instance. That was one of the reasons he'd come along. His father was Italian, his mother American. Well, Italy meant nothing to Dave. A couple of hours ashore had convinced him of that. Give him li'l ol' New York any day. Even if Americans were as crazy as coots. They had to be. If they weren't they wouldn't buy houses in distant countries and bring 'em all the way back to the States. It didn't make sense. There were millions of houses and apartments for sale in America, so why go to the expense of importing an old junky one? That's what it was, a load of crap. Dave knew because he'd examined some of the timber sections down in the hold. Woodworm. And it hadn't even been treated.

Christ, the feller had even brought some of the garden along! You had to be nuts to want a garden. He'd seen enough of his old man's efforts in their back yard. He spent hours fiddling about with a few puny vegetables that usually withered and died in the end when you could buy 'em pre-packed, washed too, or even canned.

He shook his head in bewilderment, took a last drag at the remains of the Camel, and ruefully tossed it overboard. No more smokes till they hit NY. Unless he traded his body for them down below. No chance. He'd sweat it out.

There was a movement somewhere amidst the piles of crates behind him. He felt the vibrations, like somebody walking overhead. You didn't exactly hear it. You were aware of it.

Dave Giovanni stiffened and ducked lower. His mouth was dry, bitter from the taste of tobacco. His heart was pounding in time with the old engine down in the hold. He licked his lips. There weren't many places to hide; there was too much fucking rubbish stashed in packing crates that took up all the room. Fuck that loony guy and his rotton old shack.

Another movement. He tensed. Sallinger with a hard-on was his greatest fear, seething with lust and vengeance. He stared into the darkness towards the bows. And then he saw the boy, crouching, running, coming towards him.

Help me. Hide me. He is after me.

The plea for help was like a distant echo in Dave Giovanni's brain. *He is after me . . . after me . . . me . . .*

'Over here,' Dave whispered hoarsely.

The fugitive turned, stopped, came closer, a curious shambling gait. And then Dave saw his face.

'*Mother of God!*' he whimpered, unable to believe what he saw. The features were a matt of clotted blood, indiscernible. Tufts of hair adhered to the scalp, as though the boy was either suffering from some form of mange or else whole handfuls had been torn from his head. Ragged clothing. The ribs standing out through the emaciated shrunken torso.

'What . . . who . . . ?' Dave Giovanni could not get the words out. A fleeting sensation of pity turned to horror.

Hide me. Please.

Dave backed away. The other was not looking at him. The unnaturally bright eyes were searching desperately around, coming to rest upon a niche between two crates. The Italian youth had examined the hole earlier, but it had been too narrow to offer any concealment.

Don't let him find me.

Who? What? Who are you? Questions hammered at Giovanni's brain but when he tried to ask them there was only a choking sound. Dumbstruck, he watched the stranger forcing his way into the gap, panicking, ignoring protruding nails.

Dave whirled round. He had sensed the approach of somebody else, heard constricted breathing somewhere in the darkness behind him. A man stood there, the blackness around him seeming to melt to the greyness of a winter dawn until every detail was visible. Sheer revulsion, enough to destroy the sanity of any mortal being. Peeling flesh, from which maggots fell like a leaking tap, cascading down the dark uniform; eyes that stared from sunken holes; living decay that smelled of ancient death and evil.

'Cap'n . . . Cap'n Stacey . . . ?' It was a vain hope on Dave's part, praying that this was some terrible hoax played by the captain and his crew in their desperate search for homosexual pleasure.

Giovanni's voice failed miserably. *I'll do what you want, cap'n . . . anything . . . I enjoy it . . . I wasn't trying to hide from you . . . just resting . . . I promise I'll let you . . .*

Where is the boy?

Oh, God, it's him they want, not me. They don't need me. They don't want me. They won't harm me!

It was impossible to tear his eyes away from the thing which confronted him. Dave's left arm moved, a tremendous effort, pointing vaguely in the direction where the juvenile fugitive had sought refuge amongst the crates. *He's there. Take him. Don't harm me. There!*

You lie. There is nobody there!

Honest, he's hiding there. I promise.

The man was closer now, distorted nostrils flaring in anger, giving off vile fumes. A white, fleshless hand was raised, gripping the handle of a whip.

Where is the boy?

He's over there. I promise.

Liar. Then you must take his punishment!

Dave's brain was refusing to cope with the situation. His body was numb. Naked, too. He had no recollection of the clothes being removed from his body, nor of his hands being lashed to an overhanging beam so that his feet barely touched the boards beneath him.

You are the one I seek. You cannot fool me.

No. I promise. The boy you seek was here. Let me go. I've done nothing. You're mistaken. It's him you want.

You must pay for the crimes of your parents.

Crazy. His mind was fogged. He couldn't think of any crime his mother and father had committed. He wanted to close his eyes, shut it all out, and when he opened them again find that he was alone on deck, fully clad. This wasn't happening. It was some kind of nightmare. But his eyes would not close. It was as if the lids had been glued so that he was forced to watch what was happening.

He screamed as the lash bit deep into his lower regions, the pain shooting up through his stomach and spreading out over the rest of his body. Again. And again. He was even denied the freedom to writhe, he discovered. His ankles had been tied to some immovable object on the ground, legs splayed apart. He tried to faint but his senses always came back to base after a brief orbit. The pain reached a peak and then dulled. Every nerve in his body was destroyed; anything else wouldn't hurt.

His tormentor had dispensed with the whip. Something else was gripped firmly in the long skeleton fingers. Steel that flashed dully amidst the dark stains on it. Dave Giovanni had only once seen an open razor, one his father kept on top of the shaving cabinet in the bathroom. It had belonged to his grandfather.

The thin lips of the uniformed man parted in a sadistic grin.

Still you remain silent. Your mouth must be enlarged.

Oh, Holy Mary, save me! Dave clamped his mouth shut but it made no difference. He felt the blade slitting upwards from the corners of his lips and grinding on the cheekbone, warm blood gushing down his chin and on to his neck. Within seconds, a lifetime's disfiguration was completed. He was screaming. Surely somebody down below must hear him. But nobody came.

His scalp was grasped firmly, lifting it away from the skull, the razor blade nicking with the expertise of a taxidermist. Blood ran into his eyes and blinded him. He could no longer see. The smell was worse, a foul gas that had him coughing, retching, vomiting.

He felt his scalp leave his head, one swift tug that tore it free.

He gibbered through a mouthful of blood. 'Kill me!'

You will die . . . eventually!

Dave Giovanni was aware of being untied, lowered to the floor and dragged along. Beneath the warm, bitter blood which enveloped him, he was crying. Rough planks tore at his naked body, splinters embedding themselves in his flesh.

Suddenly he was falling, floating. His overheated skin was being cooled. So beautifully serene, the pain fading altogether. He opened his mouth to draw breath, and started to panic when his lungs filled with liquid. Water everywhere, above and below him. Threshing, his arms and legs beating, then failing as fatigue overcame him. He could close his eyes now, but it didn't shut out the sight of that thing on the deck, the mouth wide in sadistic, triumphant laughter.

The boy was there, too. Cringing in a corner, weeping, awaiting his turn. Then everything was fading in a scarlet mist. Dave Giovanni made one last effort to fight off the blackness hovering around him but it was to no avail.

Captain Stacey radioed the mainland to the effect that one of his crew was missing, presumed lost overboard. A brief helicopter search was made, but there was no sign of Dave Giovanni.

Stacey made out his report and the *Zinal* continued on its way, the engines on full power. A schedule had to be maintained. The crew could not afford to lose a bonus just because an eighteen-year-old youth was presumed drowned.

'I figured you'd be turning up sometime before the year was out.' Al Pennant poured two large whiskies from the decanter on the cocktail cabinet and fixed an iced vodka for Veronica. Bruce Parlane's visit to *La Maison des Fleurs* on its new site on Long Island was his crowning triumph. *Crow a mite, Al. Rub it in. You don't often get the chance.*

'I didn't make the journey specially.' Parlane took the glass offered to him and tasted it. Johnny Walker, Black Label. There were still things which these brash Americans relied upon Britain for. 'I was in Brooklyn to conclude a deal. I read in the papers that you'd already got the house up. You didn't waste any time.'

'A record, I guess.' Pennant saw his visitor's eyes flick over Veronica approvingly, maybe longingly. 'I told you we'd be spending Christmas in it. Why don't you fly Anthea out and we'll make a party of it?'

'I don't think Anthea's too keen on house-warming parties in the Reichenbach place,' Bruce Parlane said. Not after last time, anyway.'

'Wallace K. Quilmer's married again, by the way,' Pennant laughed. 'He didn't waste any time, either.'

'I don't think that's funny,' Veronica snapped, and then her gaze went back to Parlane. She would have liked him to stay for the festival so long as Anthea didn't fly out to join him. That would sure spoil it.

'You've had a few mishaps since I last saw you,' the Englishman went on. 'The British newspapers picked up the story about a communal grave under the place.'

'Could've been there for decades.' Al had to play it down in front of Veronica. 'Probably even nothing to do with the house. It might've been there a century before the place was erected on the Reichenbach Falls. Who knows? Who *cares*? A lot of unrelated incidents got blown up out of all proportion. A workman fell off a ladder and his mates tried to make out some spook had given him a push. Then some stupid kid fell overboard on the boat coming across.'

'Just fated then, Al.'

'I don't believe in rubbish like that. Anyway, the place is here, with one of the best views on Long Island from its windows, and if there *was* something going on in Switzerland then that's all been left behind.'

I just hope so, Veronica thought. At least nothing untoward had happened during the week since they had moved in. Tod seemed more settled, too. She prayed that everything was going to be all right. For all their sakes.

'Tell you what,' Parlane had moved across to the bow window, watching the breakers foaming across a wide expanse of golden sand. From where he stood it could have been taken for summer, the sun shining out of a deep blue sky overhead. Outside, the wind was cold and there was no mistaking the season.

'What are you gonna tell me, Bruce?' Pennant came to join him, revelling in the view.

'That offer I made you in Switzerland, Al. I'll up it another hundred thousand. Dollars, of course. You could build yourself a big modern house, all mod cons for Veronica and . . .'

'Money wouldn't buy. Not even the IMF could raise enough to tempt me to sell.'

'No, I guess not,' Parlane smiled. 'But if ever you do decide to part with it . . .'

'No chance. Try Jimmy. You've more chance of buying the White House than *La Maison des Fleurs*. By the way, are you going to stay overnight? We have a kitchen staff now, nothing so primitive as camping out in the Swiss mountains.'

'Thanks. I'll have to leave early tomorrow, though. I've another call to make before I fly home.'

'We rise at seven. It's good for the constitution.'

The room looked no different from the last time Bruce Parlane had stayed at *La Maison des Fleurs*. With the curtains drawn, the constant pounding of the Atlantic might have been mistaken for the roar of the Reichenbach Falls. Louder perhaps, but not much in it.

He undressed slowly. The builders had made a good job of the erection: not a single flaw to destroy its antiquity. Much the same could be said for whoever had moved it in the first place. It would have been much more difficult then, without modern machinery.

He got into bed and put out the light. No matter what Veronica might say, the atmosphere hadn't changed. Unless, of course, Big Al had a ready source of canned or aerosol flavourings that gave the necessary musty smell. There was more to it than that, though. A damp eeriness that you couldn't conjure up. Parlane wondered if removing the house to England would change it any. It was cold and inhospitable, in spite of the central heating radiators which had been fitted behind the oak panelling.

Al wouldn't sell. Not at present. In a year or two perhaps, but by then Pennant's own rate of inflation would have put it way out of Parlane's price range. He wondered how

Anthea would feel about living in the place . . . in England, of course. There was no country like England. The splendours of the world couldn't compare when it came to a final totting up of points. Too many people were intent on spoiling it. What it needed was more attention paid to the past and a bit less to the future. Pennant wasn't helping any. If the American had his way the whole of Great Britain would end up in the States and be replaced by modern housing estates. That had happened after he'd shipped that Elizabethan cottage out of Stratford-on-Avon, less than a mile from Parlane's own home. It had really rankled. Some gazumping had gone on. A backhander for the agent, a few hundred more on the asking price, and just when Parlane thought he'd got it all sewn up, Al was signing the contract and making shipping arrangements. Dirty. But they all did it at some time or other. Even Bruce Parlane.

He lay there, dozing comfortably, the sound of the Atlantic a distant lullaby. That was one thing man could not transport. Something that was really unchanging, timeless.

Somebody was crying. Gradually the sound filtered through to him via the crashing breakers. He listened, trying to work out where it was coming from. Strange, there was nobody on the floor above. Tod was down on the same landing as his parents.

Parlane sat up, thought about switching on the light, but decided against it.

Words were just audible. *Help me . . . hide me . . . he is after me.* Incoherent babbling. Sobbing.

Parlane got out of bed. It was cold, several degrees colder than it had been when he had retired for the night. He found his dressing-gown, shrugged it over his shoulders and crossed to the door.

Outside on the landing he fumbled around until he found a light-switch. He pressed it. Nothing happened. Just like Al: spend a million and overlook a blown bulb.

Silence. The weeping had died away. Even the Atlantic breakers seemed to have relented in their attempts to conquer dry land.

Bruce Parlane stood there for some minutes. Maybe he

had been mistaken, a dream that had extended from slumber into semi-wakefulness. He didn't think so. So it had to be Tod. The boy was starting to have those awful nightmares again. In which case Al *might* just be persuaded to sell up. Don't be so bloody selfish.

For some reason, he didn't know why, Bruce Parlane tried the light-switch again. A soft red glow illuminated the wide oak landing.

'Well, I'll be . . . ' He shook his head in bewilderment and went back into his room.

Breakfast was served at 7.30 a.m. Bruce was surprised, on entering the dining-room, to find Veronica and Tod already started on their grapefruits.

'Hi.' He glanced at Tod, trying to make it seem no more than an early morning appraisal. 'Nice to see some young boys get up bright and early. I must tell Richard. I trust you slept well.'

'Yes, thank you, Mr Parlane.' Tod spooned up a mouthful of segments. 'You sleep well?'

'Excellent, thank you.' Parlane sensed a faint prickling of his scalp and tried to convince himself that last night had just been in his imagination after all.

6

PURSUED

Tod knew that nothing had changed. *They* had come to Long Island with *La Maison des Fleurs*. He had heard them infrequently during the winter nights. Mostly cries for help. Twice he had identified the harsh, cruel voice of the man with the rotting face. But it was not so bad. It scared him, but so far they had left him alone. Mostly they confined their activities to the top storeys, almost as though they were intent on keeping as far away as possible from the human inhabitants of the house.

Sometimes he heard a boy calling for help. Always it ended in sobbing and weeping. There was the man who cursed also, not the putrid, sadistic beast, but one who was subjected to his tortures. The curses died away to incoherent babblings.

Tod thought it all out, tried to find a reason. Two factions existed. The torturer who held sway and inflicted pain and terror, and his victims. None were able to rest, their souls were trapped within this place, unable to escape. They could have no quarrel with the living, although their tormentor obviously resented human intrusion and relished carrying on his evil deeds. Was there no solution to the problem? No way in which they could all have been freed from their terrible psychic bonds?

Tod was grateful when his schooling began again. His father had talked about a private tutor and had even gone as far as interviewing one for the job. The man had turned it down and said outright that the house gave him the creeps. The boy understood. Al Pennant didn't. Anyway, Tod appreciated the opportunity to be away from the atmosphere of *La Maison des Fleurs* for a few hours.

Spring came early and the shrubs and plants which had been transported from Switzerland came into bud. For them, the climate must have seemed almost tropical.

Tod had breakfasted early with his parents, as was his custom, and had time to spare before setting out on the short walk to school. He went out on to the verandah above the flight of wooden steps. He had noticed the snowdrop several days before, the way it had flowered in a lush creamy colour as though appreciative of its change of soil. Al Pennant himself had planted it. Tod remembered because it was unusual to see his father performing any small task himself about the place. Al had embedded the bulb with care a short distance from the driveway, where it was sheltered by an overhanging laurel.

Now the boy stared, holding on to the balustrade with trembling fingers. *The plant was starkly outlined by an uneven circle of crimson, like a blob of redcurrant sauce poured on to a bowl of cream.*

He saw, but did not believe. It was impossible. The snow

flakes, now red crystals, had not even melted.

'Dad!' he yelled. 'Dad!'

Al Pennant knew that something was amiss. 'Dad' had become a warning cry, a shout of terror which had been absent since their return from Switzerland. He came on the run down the first flight of stairs, dishevelled, shaving foam a fluffy white beard on his heavy chin.

'What is it?' He burst out through the front door and then stopped as his gaze followed Tod's. *Christ alive!*

'Pa . . . *it's blood*!'

'No, it ain't.' He pushed past the boy and went down the steps, feeling them slippery with snow beneath his feet. He crossed the driveway and dropped into a crouch, staring fixedly at the scarlet-based flower. Gingerly he stabbed a forefinger into the snow and drew it out; on the end was a red blob. Hesitantly he extended his tongue, closed his eyes in revulsion and licked his finger.

He spat instinctively, and heaved at the vile taste on his palate.

Oh, God! It *was* blood! There was no mistaking the rancid flavour.

'Dad.' Tod was scrambling down the steps, running across to join him. 'It . . . it is blood . . . isn't it?'

'No.' He looked away so that his son should not see that he lied. 'It wasn't. It's . . . it's some kind of sediment in the soil.'

He didn't know whether or not Tod believed him. 'Now don't get letting that wild imagination of yours scare the pants off you every few minutes. You get ready for school, boy.'

'I am ready, Dad.'

There was no answer to that. Al Pennant went back upstairs to finish his shaving. He cursed softly when he nicked his upper lip with the safety razor. The sight of the thin trickle of blood in the mirror made him feel sick. He ought to change to an electric or a battery-operated razor. Old habits died hard. It wouldn't stop his hand from shaking, though, whatever he used.

A quarter of an hour later Tod went back outside. He opened the door stealthily, fearfully. Wide-eyed, he peeped out, afraid to emerge in case . . . A long sigh of relief escaped his lips. The snowdrop protruded out of a bed of dark soil. All the snow had melted, even in the shade.

Tod was trembling as he walked down the driveway. He was scared, not just because of what had happened, but because his father was scared. Like that night when he came in from the sunken garden . . .

They were becoming more angry; angrier and noisier than they had been in Switzerland. Tod heard them every night now, almost as though the incident of the snowdrop in the garden had summoned them from a winter of inactivity. His fear began from the moment his mother kissed him goodnight and left him, until the first rays of daylight came creeping softly in through the windows.

His terror was one from which there was no escape. He dreaded the night when one of those awful beings would confront him. But, so far, they seemed content to confine their activities to the upper regions of *La Maison des Fleurs.*

'Mom.' He clung to Veronica's hand as she leaned over his bed. 'Do . . . do you hear them nights?'

'Yes.' She closed her eyes. A question which she had been dreading but she could not lie. 'I heard them last night. And the night before.'

'When is Dad going to sell the place so we can go away?'

'I don't know, Tod.'

'Has he heard them?'

'No. I told him about it, but he refuses to believe me. He says it's just imagination, and if there was anything in Switzerland then it couldn't have followed us here. Every time I mention it he gets angry.'

'Couldn't . . . couldn't you and I . . . go away, Mom?'

Oh, God, he seemed to read her thoughts. He was psychic. She had always said he was.

'Please, Mom.'

'I'll have to think about it.'

'We could go to Nan's.'

Yes, he was psychic, all right. She had been dwelling on that idea these last few days. They'd be safe there, and perhaps it would force Al into selling this dreadful house.

'Now don't you worry, Tod.' She extricated her hand from his and moved quickly towards the door. 'If they don't stop, then we'll go to Nan's, whether your father likes it or not.'

It was only when she stepped out on to the landing that she realised that her body was bathed in cold sweat. Things were getting really bad. She couldn't delay a decision much longer. Very soon she would have to make a stand against Al.

Tod lay there thinking for a long time after his mother had gone. He wondered about the significance of the snowdrop. Somehow there was a link. He was beginning to get afraid of the garden again now that everything was coming to life. Branches of trees and shrubs moved in the wind, beckoning. *Come closer Tod. Let us touch you. Hold you. Kill you! You have no right here. You were warned.*

He pulled the sheets up over his head. Any night now one of them was going to appear in his bedroom. He prayed that it would not be the one with the putrid face. He was the most dangerous, the most evil of all of them.

It was a week before it happened. The night was filled with weeping and groaning, screams and pleadings, and the boy knew that one of them would come. He hadn't expected his visitor to be a young girl, though. She was standing at the foot of his bed, a torn white sheet clasped around her puny body. Her face had once been pretty; now it was scarred, disfigured, part of her lower lip missing, as if it had been ripped forcibly away. Her eyes were puffed and swollen, her fair hair matted with dried blood.

In some way she was more terrifying than any of the others. So pathetic, yet whatever they had done to her had scarred her soul, embittered her.

You have exiled us. As though it wasn't bad enough before. It is a thousand times worse now.

Tod tried to tell her. Jumbled words which he hoped she'd understand. He and his mother were going to leave his father. Dad would sell up then.

That will not help us. Someone else will buy the house. If we are fated not to be at peace then at least return us to our native land.

It was her eyes which frightened him most. They were old, as though they had been prised from some evil old hag and transplanted into her tender sockets. They stared balefully, with smouldering malevolence that might burst into flames at any second.

You must order your father to return this house whence he brought it.

I will. I will. I promise.

Then she was gone, and he lay there trembling in the cold blackness. He had stalled her. It was no good trying to say anything to his father. Al would cut him short with scorn and sarcasm. If he persisted, then Al Pennant's wrath would fall on him. It was up to his mother. If she couldn't do anything, then . . . oh, God, he'd run away! Thousands of kids ran away from home every week, a lot with less reason to leave than he had. He tried to think where he would go. Nan's was no good. She would send him straight back home. And the police would be looking for him. They found a high percentage of the kids who went missing. Some of them were dead, their bodies mutilated, sexually assaulted, buried or stuffed down drain covers.

Tod licked his dry lips. He wasn't as frightened of death as he was of these . . . these *living dead*. He'd watched a late-night movie on TV once when his parents were out and the baby-sitter had let him stop up. Zombies, creatures that came out of their graves when darkness fell and prowled the countryside, growling like wild animals. *Those* were laughable. But these things in *La Maison des Fleurs* were enough to send you out of your mind.

Some time towards dawn he fell into an exhausted sleep.

When Tod arrived home from school the next afternoon his parents were out. His mother had left a note on the table in the hall, in big red capital letters so he couldn't miss it. They'd gone into town. They'd be back by six. There was a cheeseburger in the warm oven under the cooker and a can of coke in the fridge.

He sighed. Dad had gone to buy Mom some new clothes,

he guessed from the hurried decision to go to town. Somebody was coming to stay shortly or else they were going to a party somewhere. Either way it was important and his mother had to have the latest fashions. His father would choose them in the store, then write out the cheque with a flourish, cigar ash cascading all over the pay desk, flamboyant to the extreme.

Tod hoped it was somebody coming to stay. It would help to ease the tension. Particularly if it was Mr Parlane. As he munched his cheeseburger and swigged coke out of the can he thought about the young girl. His greatest fear was her return after darkness fell. He hadn't said anything to his father. He hadn't had a chance yet, and he doubted whether he had the courage, anyway. It would just be a waste of time. But he *had* promised. He sighed. Maybe, when his parents returned, he would try and say something in a roundabout way. Just enough to fulfil his promise.

He went up to his room and changed out of his school clothes into a T-shirt and jeans. Outside, the sun was shining and it was a warm evening. He didn't fancy staying indoors on his own. Neither did he like the idea of playing in the garden. Those plants and trees watched his every move as though they understood . . . as though they were biding their time, awaiting their chance to lure him into the depths of the shrubberies and close in on him with suffocating, strangling vegetation.

He decided on the beach. It was only a few minutes' walk and his parents didn't mind him going there so long as he promised not to go in the sea. The currents were strong and, worse, there was always the danger of sharks lying inshore.

He'd take his space-hopper, the one Mr Parlane had given him at Christmas. Just for half an hour. An escape.

He tried to remember where the space-hopper was. It had lain in a corner of his bedroom for some weeks and then it was missing. Doubtless Mom had put it away somewhere on one of her infrequent tidying-up sessions. He attempted to reason where she might have put it. It had to be in either the garden shed or the trunk-room. He'd look in the trunk-room first, and if it wasn't there then he'd check the shed on his way-out.

He went back upstairs to the first floor. The trunk-room next to his parent's bedroom was now in use and full of lumber. Mom just tossed everything in there. One day, she said, she'd have a good sort-out.

He opened the door and looked inside. Boxes and items of infrequent household use were piled and strewn haphazardly over the floor as though Veronica Pennant had thrown them in from the doorway because she was afraid to go inside.

Afraid . . . afraid.

Tod hesitated and almost drew back on to the landing. He licked his lips, nervously glancing about him. He was uneasy. He didn't like this room. He liked it less than all the rooms in the house except perhaps the attic, which was gloomy and dirty, the rafters dust-covered and spilling cobwebs down so that they brushed your face like the artificial ones on the spook trains at carnivals.

But the early evening sunlight streamed in through the window at the far end, its golden rays warm and friendly. *Come inside, Tod. Don't be afraid.*

He stepped over the threshold. Dust rose beneath his feet and he could see it billowing up through the beams of sunlight. He coughed and stepped over a pile of broken curtain rods. He could see the space-hopper wedged between two tea-chests over by the window. In order to reach it, he would have to clamber across some stacked chairs and a sideboard.

Tod began his climb. It wasn't easy. Unstable items shifted beneath his feet and he gripped the sides of the sideboard to support himself, then hauled himself up on to it and perched there. He was breathing heavily and trembling. Previously he had been nervous, unwilling to enter this room. Suddenly he realised that he was afraid, more afraid than he'd been in his life before.

He swallowed and glanced apprehensively around. He started. For one moment he thought there was somebody standing in the corner by the door. There was nobody. He licked his lips. Maybe he wouldn't bother about the space-hopper after all. He didn't really need it. He could take a ball down on to the beach.

You're nearly there. That oversized horned ball is less than a yard away. You've done the hardest bit, why give up now?

He turned back towards the object of his quest: a huge horned rubber devil, mouth wide and leering, two black eyes that seemed to move and then fix on him with a stare, holding his gaze. *Come and get me . . . if you can.*

He'd never really studied its face before. Just a few meaningless black daubs, millions like it, mass-produced. Now it was an individual. It saw him. It *understood.*

A dull thud. He jumped and turned his head. *The door had closed.* Panic. He almost fell from his precarious perch.

Don't be frightened. A draught has blown it shut. Nothing to worry about.

There could be somebody outside on the landing . . . or in here!

He glanced around jerkily, furtively. Nobody. Only that . . . toy. A heavy-duty rubber balloon. A bag of air. Harmless. But those eyes . . .

He saw the window again. He was level with it and could see right outside, to the garden, the shrubs and flowers. A laurel bush, its protective evergreen foliage shielding a plant that grew close to its base. A snowdrop. Something was odd, wrong. That white flower, alive and full. It had no right to be. It was too late in the season. It should have wilted, its narrow leaves should be brown and decaying.

Tod couldn't take his eyes off it. A phenomenon. Sinister. A freak of nature.

The sun was no longer shining. It didn't suddenly happen, it must have been setting for some time, only he hadn't noticed it. Now it was gone, a pinkish hue in the western sky marking its departure. He glanced down at his wristwatch and saw that it was nearly eight o'clock. That couldn't be right. He'd only been here a few minutes. Yet the sun said it was. It was chilly now, much colder. It'd be dark soon.

He wrenched his eyes away from the flower down in the garden below and felt them being drawn back to the rubber monster in the corner, a grotesque spider, sadistically delighting in the fly caught in its web. Grinning.

It can't hurt you. It can. It's only a toy. It's alive, breath-

ing. It can't move. It's turned round so that it can watch you. Get out. Now!

Tod dragged his trembling limbs into action and slid from the sideboard. His feet landed on the pile of curtain rods. They shifted beneath his weight, rolled and cascaded down like a miniature landslide. He felt himself falling and made a despairing grab for a table which stood on its side close by, but missed.

He hit the floor, landing on his face. Choking dust rose in a cloud and clogged his nostrils. He coughed. Struggled up. It was nearly dark; he could barely discern the objects around him.

The door was only a few feet away, ominously closed, barring his escape, trapping him there . . . with what? A noise behind him, a hollow sound like a big beach ball being bounced. Oh, God, it could move after all. It *was* alive!

He caught his foot on a rolled-up mat and stumbled. He would have fallen again had it not been for the door. He felt his shoulder against it, solid oak, centuries old, unyielding. His hands groped frantically in search of the knob.

It's no use. It's going to be locked. It has to be.

But it wasn't. The knob turned as smoothly as though it had recently been oiled. The door creaked open.

The boy stood there, heart pounding, pulses racing like a pneumatic drill on full throttle. Blackness everywhere. Night had fallen.

That hollow bouncing noise again inside the room . . . the space-hopper . . . it was coming after him, a beast of prey, rolling, jumping. He let out a low cry of fear and somehow managed to move his legs. Something hard barred his progress. Stout wooden railings. The bannister. *Follow its course, keep to the stairs.*

He fell, but picked himself up again. Wooden steps. The stairs. *Hold on to the rail. That noise again. Keep going, don't stop, don't look back . . . run.*

A sudden awful thought, and it was too late to do anything about it. *He was travelling upstairs instead of down. And that egg-shaped fiend was following him!*

A landing. *Run into one of the rooms, close the door and*

keep it out. No, don't. Something else could be in there, something worse. Keep going.

More stairs. Up . . . up. Falling, crying, dragging himself along on the rails. His left ankle hurt him, he could hardly stand on it. That had been when he'd slid with the pile of rails. Listening. Noises everywhere. Woodwork creaking, groaning as though the entire house was coming to life with the advent of darkness. A door banged somewhere; a window frame rattled . . . *bounce* . . . *bounce* . . .

He dared not look back as he continued his flight. That painted face would no longer be grinning, the black lines had straightened into an expression of fury. *Come here, boy. I want you . . . want you . . . want you.*

The fourth floor. The air was stagnant and musty. His lungs heaved their rebellion as he took a deep breath. He clasped his hands over his ears. He dared not listen. He closed his eyes in case they might behold something terrible in the blackness. Blood pounded in his head. *Flee. Flee.* But where to? The attic.

His hands brushed against the vertical ladder and he gripped the rungs, hauling his feet clear of the ground. Somewhere in the ceiling above him a small square hole yawned. That was whence the stale air came, from the attic, an area of blackness, a void in which there was nothing but rafters and dust.

His pursuer would not be able to negotiate the ladder. A small sigh of relief at the thought. *Get up there and close the hatch. Stop there until Mom and Dad get back. Where were they? Oh, please God, send them back.*

The square awning. The trap-door was closed. He held on to the ladder with one hand, and pushed upwards with the other. The wooden frame gave a little way, then checked. Something was holding it. Shaking fingers traversed its perimeter. A bolt. It shot back with unexpected ease, gouging his thumb. He scarcely noticed the wound.

He pushed his head and shoulders up through the opening. *And then he heard them.*

They were somewhere over on the far side of the attic area, sobbing, weeping, groaning, too weak to scream. A man was cursing in a foreign language.

Come in, Tod. There's no escape for any of us. We're locked in here until we die. He wants you, too. And your folks.

Tod was rigid with fear. He'd known all along that they were up in the attic, wanting him, calling him. He'd kept away so they'd sent their terrible servant to shepherd him here.

He managed to step back a rung and looked down past his feet. It was squatting there at the foot of the ladder like a great crab, eyes elevated so that they met his. There was no escape.

'Let me go, oh, God, let me go.'

You have not kept your promise to return us to our native land.

A chorus of jeers. Insults. He could see them now, huddled in a corner, a dozen or more, women trying to protect children, the men furious, defiant, especially the tall stooping one with the slit mouth.

You'll join us, boy, and find out about the death where you do not die, the eternal suffering of mind and body.

No! Tod backed down a rung and saw the two dilated orbs of the space-hopper below, waiting for him.

I want you, boy. I want you dead!

He clung to the ladder. Death above, death below. There wasn't anything to choose. No escape, unless . . . He saw the black square beyond the bannister, the stairwell yawning, an abyss, offering a remote chance. Life or death. At least the latter would be swift . . . and final!

Tod aged in the time that it took him to make up his mind. He did not understand, but he knew what he had to do. There was no way of reasoning, no means of knowing why the dead did not die and a rubber toy became a fearful creature. Perhaps it was better that way.

He leaped out into space. Diving, as if he had been practising in a swimming pool, swallow-like, then hurtling clumsily, sideways, somersaulting. A sickening thud that hammered every bone in his body, a foot caught between narrowly spaced rails, slipping free, falling again, head-first, plummeting. Seconds that seemed hours. He started to scream, then laughed. He'd cheated them, all of them. They were leaning over watching him: the people in the attic, the space-hopper.

Come back . . . come back . . . back . . . back . . . back.

The final sickening crunch, not even time to feel the pain from a hundred fractures. Instant oblivion. And then the silence came surging softly backwards.

Lieutenant Kiernan had come fast the moment he'd received the call on his radio. Not that he thought there was any urgency. The kid was dead. It was more a case of an instant desire to break the monotony of routine patrol work. Most of the time there was nothing doing on Long Island. Even shark scares at the height of the season had become boring. Mostly they were put about by scaremongers, sensation-seekers. They oughta be charged with wasting police time, he reflected, but you'd never get a shark to give evidence. Particularly if it wasn't there in the first place. A stupid line of thought. Some sick firm somewhere were plugging a useful line in artificial shark fins. Plastic, but life-like at a distance. You strapped 'em on like water-wings and swam below water with the triangles just protruding above the surface. Mass hysteria every time. Folks fled the beach like sheep that had caught the scent of a prowling puma. That was the Shark Patrol's pigeon. Except that they put through a call before they got their choppers airborne. *Clear the beaches, lieutenant.* Sounded easy with most of the crowds spilling up beyond the tide-line. It was the sensation-seekers that caused the trouble, guys grabbing their cameras and thinking there was a few thousand bucks in it for them if they got the right picture.

But now there weren't any sharks, real or plastic. Just one dead kid in that new place that had been shipped all the way out from somewhere or other. Al Pennant was as bad as the shark jokes. He interfered with the environment and now it had backfired on him.

It was 11.04 when Kiernan arrived at *La Maison des Fleurs* and braked to a halt with gravel flying. He gunned the engine a couple of times before cutting it, just to let them know he'd arrived. He hated ringing bells or knocking on doors. It reminded him of the time he'd been a sales-pusher in Brooklyn.

He noted the two parked cars. Pennant's Chevrolet, Dr Savage's Pontiac. Good, the doc was here. That made it easier, just left him with the police work. Road accidents were the worst, particularly if you got there before the ambulance crews. It wasn't so bad if all the victims were dead. It was when the road and mashed vehicles were crammed with living mutilated bodies that you puked. There was nothing you could do, like that time after a head-on when some guy was staggering around with the severed head of his wife in his arms, kissing and crooning to it. *Don't you dare touch my baby, you bastard. Don't worry pal, I ain't gonna touch your baby. No, sir!* The baby had gone through the windscreen and into the grill of an oncoming car. Sliced into French fries. *No, pal, I ain't gonna touch your baby.*

Kiernan remembered the time they'd seized some underground comics on a porn raid. He'd taken one home to read, just out of curiosity. One of the characters had been a ghoul who'd lurked near accident zones, polythene bag at the ready, nicking dismembered parts of the human body, pickling them in jars in his cellar. It was laughable. The guy who wrote that had obviously never seen a *real* crash. He'd puke and shit himself if ever he did.

Yeah, Kiernan reflected as he heaved his huge bulk out of the car and looked towards the lighted windows of the house, the dead were no problem. They hurt nobody.

Dr Savage appeared in the lighted doorway, tall and grey-haired, staring owlishly from behind heavy rimmed spectacles, his expression inscrutable.

'Good evening, lieutenant.' He pressed back to make room for the other to step inside. 'I haven't moved anything. The boy fell from the fourth floor, right the way down to the hallway. Accidental. He was on his own in the house. Mrs Pennant's under sedation in the bedroom.'

Kiernan nodded. He could see the boy from where he stood, a sprawled form, legs bent in an unnatural posture, neck twisted, eyes staring sightlessly, the expression of terror trapped and frozen on impact. Christ, anybody would be terrified if they realised they were falling the whole length of the stairwell and were going to hit the bottom deck any second.

'Multiple fractures,' the doctor said.

Kiernan nodded. Like a rabbit that had got under a tractor wheel. The coroner would fill in the details. The policeman's report would be short, a generalisation.

'I'll have to talk to the parents.' He didn't relish the task but it had to be done. Not that he was sentimental or anything like that; simply that it took a long time to get a statement out of folks who were weeping and wailing.

'The woman's cut up,' Savage replied. 'Bad.'

'Uh-huh.' The lieutenant wiped the back of his hand across his mouth. 'But I still gotta talk to her.'

'First floor. Second door on the left.'

Kiernan mounted the stairs slowly, glancing around him as he did so. Shit-awful place this. Stank. Like somebody had used the john and not flushed it. Probably it was the kid's bowels shot when he landed. He wrinkled his nose but by the time he reached the landing the smell had disappeared.

He pushed open the door and went inside, nodding sombrely to the occupants. He knew them by sight, the woman lying in the bed, deathly white, the guy in the chair by the window, grim, silent.

'I'm sorry,' Kiernan said. He wasn't really but you always started like that, got them on your side and they co-operated more freely.

'It was bound to happen.' Veronica stared at him blankly through puffed eyes. 'Couldn't end any other way. Not with them around. I told Al, warned him' – her voice began to rise to a crescendo – 'but he wouldn't listen. He won't now. Says it was just an accident. But it was *them*. *They* pushed my Tod down the stairwell.'

'And who're *they*, ma'am?'

'The . . . the spirits that live in this place.'

'I see, ma'am.' She was really up the horned road, this one, Kiernan thought. 'OK we'll deal with them later but first we'll have to have a few facts.'

'Deal with them!' Veronica hoisted herself up on to an elbow, her expression one of scorn. 'And how do you think you're going to deal with them, lieutenant? Arrest them, lock them up?'

The policeman looked at Al Pennant for help and received an understanding nod, no more.

'You're as bad as him,' Veronica shrieked, pointing at her husband. 'He's seen one of 'em and still he won't believe that there's anything here. And we're all goin' to die.'

That's right, ma'am. Every one of us when our time comes. Shitfire, let's get down to facts.

'Where were you when it happened?' He addressed Al.

'In town. We'd gone shopping. Something went wrong with the car and held us up.'

'Like what?'

'Never found out. The mechanics went all over it. Couldn't find anything amiss. Then suddenly it started as though there'd never been a fault.'

'You usually leave the kid in the house on his own?'

'No' – defiance in Pennant's expression – 'never. We shoulda been back by six. As it was, we were assing around for hours. Thought he'd be OK.'

'Did he usually climb the stair-rails? A lotta kids like to slide right from the top to the bottom. Dozens get killed in big hotels and departmental stores.'

'No, he wasn't that kind of a kid. Studious. Spent too much time reading. Sorta withdrawn.'

'Withdrawn!' Veronica screeched. 'He was studious. Intelligent. He would've made a . . . ' Choking sobs drowned her words. Tod might've made it to the top, but now it was all over.

'OK, OK, he was the quiet type,' Kiernan cut in. 'So you left him in the house, had some kind of an automobile breakdown that kept you in town, and when you got back . . . it had all happened.'

Silence. The lieutenant knew he'd got it right. No bother. Half a page of report. All the same, he had to give the place a lookover.

'If you need me, just give me a call.' *And I hope to God you don't. With a bit of luck this can all be tied up, barring the autopsy, by tomorrow morning.*

He went out, closing the door without looking back. He

was glad Sal hadn't wanted children. A thing like this could have happened to anybody. Just another accident.

The remaining floors were much of a muchness, to Burt Kiernan anyway. He wondered briefly why anybody wanted to live in a place like this. It was OK if you hadn't got anywhere else, but as for paying a fortune to import a heap of ageing timber. Well, it took all sorts.

He was glad to pause on the fourth storey. He was breathing heavily. He needed to lose some weight. About thirty pounds. Sal had put him on a diet, salads and fruit with no bread, but it hadn't worked. She didn't know about his daily quota of hamburgers. She'd . . .

His practised eye noticed something, a piece of bright orange material in the corner of the landing, torn and all scuffed up. He picked it up, straightened it out and saw the face painted on the thick rubber beneath the protruding horns.

'One o' them space-hopper things that were all the craze.' He turned it over, examined it, then tossed it back where he'd found it. 'Bust, just like a carnival balloon. Never thought them things would puncture.'

Then he detected that mysterious odour again, just a faint wafting, enough to make him twitch his nose in disgust. *Jeez, the john's sure stopped up somewhere,* he decided, and started back down the stairs.

7

THE FUNERAL

Veronica Pennant had the feeling that the funeral had all happened before. It should have been over and finished, only the grief remaining to scar her for life. But there was something so horribly familiar about it all as though the bearers had fetched the coffin back from the grave in the fir-lined churchyard and now they had to go through the proceedings all over again.

Father O'Rourke mumbled inaudibly, holding a prayer book between his large pink fingers. What was he doing here? He should have been in New York. Maybe Al had had him flown out specially. Or were they all in New York? She'd expressed a desire to have Tod buried there. She couldn't remember whether Al had agreed or not. And Al always had the final word.

They were back at the graveside again, all grouping round, the mourners pressing forward, ghoulishly watching the ropes being fastened around the coffin containing . . . oh, God, get it over and let my baby rest!

A sea of blurred faces. She did not recognise a single one. Only Father O'Rourke and she couldn't be sure now that it was him.

The grave was stark, the damp smell of fresh earth making her feel heady. She thought she was going to faint but she didn't. Somebody was holding her by the arms from behind, tightly gripping her. Al? It didn't matter. Throw me in, too. Let me lie there on the coffin, shovel the soil back in and finish this nightmare for good. Let me be with my boy.

The coffin was being lowered. She watched it fixedly, disbelievingly. Tod wasn't in there. He couldn't be. It was all a sick joke. He was back home, reading. Maybe playing . . . with his space-hopper. Oh, God, that loathsome thing. The police had decided he'd been fooling with it on the bannisters when he'd . . . but he hadn't fallen. He was still alive. *He's dead, Mrs Pennant. We killed him.* Liars. He's alive. I know it.

That awful artificial grass. Why try to pretend that the soil isn't all mounded up beneath it? Just another way of lying. But you can't hide that flower beyond the grave, growing by Father O'Rourke's feet. He'll step on it if he moves any further forward. Blossoming in the fullness of life. A snowdrop. Like the one that Tod saw last spring, growing out of rich red soil.

The coffin was down. Everybody was bending forward, peering. Gloating. Unrecognisable faces. Was there nobody here she knew? Where was Al? Why all these strangers?

Father O'Rourke raised his head and looked directly at her. *And then she knew.* It was not him. Instead, the flesh peeled and hung from his cheekbones, bluebottles swarmed and buzzed all over his forehead, crawling around the eyes, feeding. The pink flesh on the hands was gone, now they were just bones. Something dropped from those fingers into the oblong hole and thudded on to the coffin. The prayer book. Contempt.

The stench was overpowering, as though they were engaged in the exhumation of a partially decomposed corpse. She stared. It was no good trying to scream.

Something was attempting to climb out of the grave, small hands failing to secure a grip on the loose earth, soil showering back.

Tod! Oh, my poor boy. He's not dead. Let him climb out.

She struggled but she was powerless in the grip that held her. She beat with her fists at the grinning distorted faces crowding in on her and felt the pain as her knuckles smashed against skulls uncushioned by flesh. They pulled her down to the ground but she could still see the grave, the boy almost out now, dragging himself up.

It wasn't Tod. No way did her son resemble that pathetic emaciated creature in tattered rags, the wasted flesh revealing every bone. Weeping, pleading.

Help me. Somebody help me.

The man who was not Father O'Rourke was wielding a whip, lashing venomously, slashing at the face of the screaming boy who somehow managed to maintain his puny grip on clods of soil. Each cut was like a .22 pistol explosion, reverberating and echoing in the enclosed graveyard.

Finally, blinded and bleeding, the victim slid back and was lost from sight. Veronica could hear him groaning in the depths of that hell-hole. Others stepped forward as though to help him but fell back. The beast who blasphemed in priest's clothing held terror for every one of them. Except Veronica.

Suddenly, her fear was gone and in its place came anger, a fury that gripped her and drove all else from her mind. Her strength returned, greater than ever before, fired by her rage.

She shook off her captors, slipping from their skeletal grasp, running forward, fists flailing like windmills. Whether she lived or died was of no importance to her. Nothing mattered, except to wreak her vengeance on this unspeakable fiend.

Her fist took him straight in his stinking face, squelching on rotting flesh and bluebottles, sinking into the mulch. Momentarily he swayed and then he had her by the wrists, gripping her with unbelievable force, bearing her to the ground, lowering his full weight on to her, pinning her down helplessly, his foul breath pumping into her mouth and nostrils.

Even now she could not faint. The ultimate in degradation was about to take place . . . the mating between human and inhuman! She closed her eyes and prayed for death.

'Veronica!'

Struggling, fighting this terrible adversary with every weapon she had, ripping fingernails gouging at the awful face, pummelling fists, kicking, biting, drawing blood. *You'll have to kill me if you want me.*

'Veronica!'

Her name was called again in a familiar voice, penetrating her haze of anger, seeping into her numbed brain. She checked, tensing. Blinding light dazzling her.

'Al!'

It was crazy. She was mad. Everything and everybody was mad. She should have been sprawled on the damp earth of Tern Hill cemetery beneath the man she believed was the terrible Reichenbach himself, returned in some ghastly inexplicable form.

She wasn't in the cemetery at all. She was in bed, lying amidst rumpled sheets that were damp with her sweat, Al Pennant kneeling over her, his features scratched and bruised.

'Al,' she muttered, struggling to understand. 'Whatever . . . why . . . the funeral . . .'

'The funeral was over a week ago.' He spoke softly, almost sympathetically, wiping away a trickle of blood from a gash on his cheek. 'You've been in bed ever since. You've had another nightmare, only they're getting worse.'

'It . . . it was real,' she muttered. 'They were all there . . . these people . . . that man . . . Reichenbach.'

'They don't exist.' He spoke sharply. 'It's all in your mind.'

'No!' She struggled up to a sitting position and caught a glimpse of herself in a mirror on the opposite side of the room. Her hair was matted with sweat, her face sunken, cheekbones white and prominent, eyes black ringed and staring wildly, her whole body shaking. 'Don't keep giving me that, Al, please. They killed Tod, and they'll kill us until they get their house back so that they can continue their vile sadism . . . or rather *he* can. They're under his power. They want to be free to die in peace but he won't let them. They're forced to unite against us. Oh, Al, please let's go away. Sell the house.'

'Dr Savage will be here first thing in the morning.' He leaned across and took a brown bottle down from the bedside table, unscrewed it and shook three white tablets out into the palm of his hand. 'Here, take these. They'll help you to sleep.'

Her eyes were riveted on the bottle. Her brow furrowed. Oh, why hadn't she thought of it before? It was the only way out. More than that. She could be with Tod again, beyond the reach of these fiends.

She took the tablets which he gave her, dropped them into her mouth, and swallowed them with the help of some water from the plastic mug by her side. Then she lay back.

'Put the light out, please, Al.'

'Aren't you sure you'd rather it was left on for a while?' He regarded her steadily. She had calmed too quickly this time, before the sedatives had had a chance to penetrate her system. He didn't like it one little bit. He didn't trust her, especially when he was asleep and defenceless.

'All right.' He pulled the cord and plunged the room back into darkness. 'If you want anything, just wake me.'

'All right.'

Silence. Except for Al Pennant's heavy regular breathing. Veronica was listening to him, trying to fight off the drowsiness which threatened to engulf her. She mustn't sleep . . . mustn't sleep . . . *keep awake . . . it's your only chance.*

It was an effort to move. Her right arm stretched out, groping, fumbling, her fingers brushing the mug of water and nearly overturning it. Something hard. A glass bottle. It rattled as she picked it up.

She rested, cradling the small drug container against her cheek, kissing it with pouted lips. Oh why, oh why, hadn't she thought of the tablets when Dr Savage prescribed them the day after the funeral when she really started to go to pieces? She could see the label plainly in her mind. Three tablets to be taken four times a day. *Warning: an overdose could prove fatal.* It would. She'd see to that.

The cap was screwed on tightly. Too tightly. Sweat poured down her face as her weakened grip struggled to unscrew it. Typical Al; he never did anything by halves. She tried again, exerting every ounce of physical and mental strength. *Oh, please God, let me go to Tod. Take me away from these things.*

The cap gave suddenly. She was panting with the exertion, and even as she began to pour the contents into the cupped palm of her left hand she knew that she might be too late. She felt the presence of Reichenbach in the room although she could not see him. Her overheated body was cooling in the sudden drop in the temperature. Shivering, trembling. That stench was beginning . . .

You're too late! She was laughing, jeering, some of the pills filtering between her fingers on to the bedclothes, rolling and bouncing across the floor. *I'll cheat you yet. I'll have something you never managed. Death. I'll be really dead, beyond your reach . . . with Tod.*

Tod isn't dead. He's one of us. Suffering.

Oh, merciful God! They've done that *to my boy!*

Tod doesn't love you as his mother. He hates you. Both of you.

She hesitated. Death no longer beckoned a welcoming finger. A void, without Tod, unable to be with him, to comfort him, the boy tortured beyond human understanding by this fiend.

She began to pray, and then he was upon her just as he had been in the cemetery, grabbing her by the wrists, knocking the bottle from her fingers together with a shower of tiny white capsules. She heard them spilling across the floorboards and then she started to scream.

'Veronica! For Christ's sake, you stupid bitch!'

Al's voice, but it wasn't Al. It couldn't be, not with that stinking fetid breath and fleshless fingers that bit into her skin where they gripped her.

'Let my boy go. You've no right to him. Release his soul and take mine in exchange.' In desperation her crazed mind hit upon the idea of a pact. It didn't matter what happened to her. She didn't care.

'Shut up!' The blow across the face exploded a blaze of brilliant colours before her eyes. Light. It was light. Blinding light. She couldn't see.

'Take me, and let Tod go.'

It was Al. At least she thought so. She couldn't see because her face was pressed into the pillow, a solid weight crushing her body, knees digging into her sides. She was a prisoner.

A familiar sound, the whirring and clicking of a telephone dial. The phone by the bedside. She could hear it ringing at the other end, and Al's heavy breathing whilst he waited. It was him. She tried to shout to him to let go of her but her voice was muffled in the pillow.

'Doc,' Al Pennant's voice was urgent, strained. Somebody was saying something on the other end of the line but Veronica couldn't catch the words. The line crackled badly like a needle-scarred record. 'Doc, you gotta come . . . yeah, right now . . . bad, very bad . . . tried to . . . yeah, the tablets . . . daren't leave her . . . OK make it fast, though.'

After that Veronica couldn't collate her thoughts. She was held there, imprisoned beneath her husband, his grip hard and vicious as though he wanted to squeeze the breath from her. He hated her all right, and he was up to something. Sly cunning. He'd conned the doc, all part of his plan. Al was in with *them* after all. She ought to have seen through him but it was too late now. Reichenbach had got him on *their* side. *Get rid of the boy and your wife, then we'll all have the house to ourselves.* So simple.

Her brain couldn't cope. She was aware of logical reasoning slipping away from her. She grasped at it, threads left in her fingers. *Al, please, for Tod's sake.* But Al wasn't listening.

Being carried downstairs, a kind of portable invalid chair. Now a stretcher. Inside a small enclosure, dimmed lights, people moving about, watching her, conversing in low tones. A vehicle of some kind, moving smoothly, stopping, starting. No conception of time. Carried on the stretcher down long corridors with white-washed walls, the sharp pungent odour of disinfectants.

A room. Small, very small. Lying on a bed. Alone. She reached out a hand, touched the wall behind her head. Soft, kind of spongy like foam rubber. Just one bulb giving a faint blue glow. Nothing else.

She wanted to get up, hammer on the door, scream, make them let her out. She tried, but her limbs refused to co-operate. Somebody was coming. A rattle of keys, the lock clicking back.

Veronica couldn't turn her head. It hurt her eyes trying to see from this angle so she closed them. It would be the man known as Reichenbach for sure, but she wasn't scared any more. He'd taken everything she'd got so the rest didn't matter. Maybe he'd even let her be with Tod for a while, allow them to suffer together.

Al Pennant sat alone in the bedroom after they had taken Veronica away. Dr Savage had given him some pills and a ticket to get some more from the drugstore in the morning. He hadn't taken them and he wouldn't be buying any more. They wouldn't help, not now.

Funny guy, Savage. A thought suddenly occurred to Al and he gave a hollow laugh, listening to it echo off the walls in the empty room. There'd been a film years ago about a Doc Savage. He hadn't seen it, just the bills posted on subway walls and quarter page ads in the papers. Any connection? Hell, no, the doc was stereotyped, did his job efficiently and that was it. Nothing more. Characterless. We'll take your wife away for a while, Mr Pennant. Shit, he hadn't the courage to say we'll take your wife away for keeps, Mr Pennant. She wouldn't be coming back, that much was clear; not in her state.

It was daylight long before Al Pennant was aware of it. He rose to his feet jerkily and went downstairs. He felt weak and ill, drained of every vestige of vitality and clear thinking. It was as though he had been ill during the nocturnal hours and a fever had gripped him, infuriated him, made him hate Veronica for everything. He had wanted to kill her, brutally throttle or beat her to death. He had known all along about her plan to take an overdose. He had lain there listening to her, willing her to swallow a handful of those sedatives. Then suddenly he had seemed himself again. Just in time. He had saved her life, but nobody could save her sanity. Not even Dr Savage.

He walked almost drunkenly towards the telephone, picked up the receiver and in hoarse tones asked the operator for a transatlantic call.

'Parlane? P-A-R-L-A-N-E.'

'Yeah, that's right. A personal call.'

'We'll call you back.'

He replaced the receiver and sank into a nearby chair. He'd always hated Bruce deep down. Never realised it until now. Slick, a real shit when it came to a deal. Parlane had blocked a couple of those Stratford deals, using his influence with the authorities to get protection orders, probably backdated. A real shit. But he could have *La Maison des Fleurs.* Oh, sure he could have it. And that snowdrop could go with it. He'd even transfer it to the tub on the verandah to make sure it went. Funny that, but he wasn't even going to try to fathom it out. That was Bruce Parlane's problem. Yeah, a real shit that bastard.

The telephone buzzed sharply, startling him. He drew his hand across his forehead. Sweating like a pig. Maybe he had a fever last night and it had left its mark. It would pass, though.

He reached out, fumbled the phone, croaked, 'Yeah?'

'Your call to Stratford-upon-Avon, England' – a girl's voice this time – 'A Mr Parlane for you, sir.'

PART TWO:

RUSTY

8

THE GARDEN OF SILENCE

'D'you think it's wise?' Anthea Parlane's eyes narrowed thoughtfully as she watched furniture being unloaded from the removal van and carried, with difficulty, up the long flight of wooden steps to the front door.

'You've been a long time expressing your reservations.' Bruce glanced at her, the sunlight slanting down through the branches of the tall pines which fringed the lawn. He hadn't really looked at her lately, not properly, anyhow. The low-cut blouse showed her small breasts off to perfection, the cut of those Wranglers did the same for her hips. The Welsh combination of blue eyes and dark hair completed the picture. He'd missed out on a lot these last twelve months whilst he'd been over in the States negotiating the sale and export of *La Maison des Fleurs.*

'It's just that' – her brow puckered into a frown – 'that . . . I never gave a thought to the whole business until . . . until I heard Veronica had died.'

'It was a stroke.' He turned away so that she could not read the expression in his eyes. 'She lasted ten months in Tern Hill. A gradual process of deterioration. She never looked up since Tod was killed.'

Anthea understood. It would be the same if anything happened to Rusty. She wouldn't want to live. But there was no doubt about it, the house had a history of tragedy, the legends growing right up into the 1980s. It was worse when you knew the people.

'Well, we're lumbered now,' Bruce said. 'I gave Al his price and we've got to give it a go. We can always sell if' – (if anything happens) – 'if we don't like it.'

He fell silent, watching the workmen carry the last of the furniture inside, remembering that night just before Christmas two years ago. That weeping. It had been Tod, of course. That business of the landing light – a temporary electrical fault or maybe he hadn't flicked the switch properly. One thing that would always be on his conscience, that space-hopper. They reckoned the boy had been fooling with it, maybe trying stunt rodeo tricks on the stair-rail. It could have been different, a bicycle carelessly ridden across the road into the path of an oncoming car, a dinghy that had been caught in a swift current and swept out to sea. He threw these sops to his conscience. It flung them back. Hard.

A football came bouncing into view across the lawn, followed by a red-haired boy in a blue tracksuit. He pulled up, saw his parents watching him and grinned. A mass of freckles, just like Anthea's. Blue eyes, too. At twelve years of age there was more of his mother than his father in him.

'Hi, Dad.' Rusty came towards them, still dribbling the ball. 'Can we go inside yet?'

'Won't be long,' Parlane grinned and found himself comparing his own son with Tod Pennant. It hurt. He had to shake this depression off. Of course, it was a natural reaction after what had happened. The house made it worse. Maybe he would sell soon and get everything off his back.

La Maison des Fleurs was just the same as it had always been, Bruce Parlane reflected smugly. Two recent moves hadn't made it look any different. That was because these firms knew their job. They were experts, disguising tiny flaws so that every board of wood retained its character.

Rusty was busy conducting his own exploration. So many rooms, exciting corners and passageways; his own bedroom. He paused, staring from the window down at the lush Warwickshire greenery below. A feeling of sadness came over him. He didn't know why.

He went back out on to the landing. His mother was standing at the foot of the stairs looking up. She had a worried expression on her face which she tried to hide with a smile. She was too late to fool him, though.

'What's up, Mum?' he asked.

'Nothing . . . nothing really.' She dropped her eyes to the floor.

'You don't like the house, do you?' He came down a few steps.

'I . . . I don't know, Richard.' She had never liked the 'Rusty' tag, although she used it frequently herself. 'I guess it's . . . just different. Not what we've been used to.'

'Which was Tod's bedroom, Mum?'

'I . . . I don't really know. I've never thought about it.'

'He slept in my bedroom.'

'Why d'you say that, Richard?'

'I just know. I went in there now and I . . . I could feel that it was his.'

'You're imagining things.'

'No, I'm not. I know. I liked Tod. You remember that time the Pennants came to stay and we all went on a boat down the river.'

'Yes,' she nodded, and stared down at the floorboards again. These were the same stairs where Tod had fallen and killed himself, right from top to bottom. There was only one place he could have landed. She had scrutinised it. There were no marks, thankfully. No bloodstains. Probably they'd been cleaned up. It was a terrible thought and she knew that she would never be able to get it off her mind as long as they lived there.

'Well, everything seems satisfactory.' Bruce came out of one of the rooms and stared down over the stair-rail at his wife and son, 'all ready to be lived in.'

They both nodded. Outside, the sun had gone down and dusk was creeping in from the Cotswolds. Suddenly everything had taken on a gloomy atmosphere; not frightening, just drab and dull and very old. The house smelled damp and musty.

Summer faded into autumn, the chill east winds bringing winter a month in advance. An early November snowfall cast its white mantle over the Heart of England. Anthea's anxiety had eased. So far nothing untoward had occurred and the house seemed if not more friendly then at least less hostile. No longer did she stretch an arm inside a room to press the light-switch before entering. She slept easier, too.

The snow melted and then came again a fortnight later.

This time it was deeper, drifting in the narrow lanes between Newbold-on-Stour and Armscote. On the first Monday morning there was no way Rusty could get to school. The snow-ploughs probably wouldn't be on the scene until later in the day, so having rushed through the 'homework' which his father had set, he went outside.

It was bitterly cold. In some ways he regretted not being able to go to school. It had been all right when they had lived virtually on the edge of Stratford, and there were always some of his mates to be found mooching the streets or playing down by the river behind the theatre. Not so now. Isolation. A few farms but no children his own age. Anyway, he consoled himself, he was having a bike for Christmas and then he'd be able to go into town whenever he wanted. The holidays wouldn't seem nearly so bad then.

He pulled on a pair of wellington boots and made his way round to the back of the house, walking beneath the big stilts. He liked that. Not many boys were able to boast that they walked under their home.

The garden comprised about an acre, long and narrow, gently sloping downhill until it reached the narrow stream at the bottom. Bruce Parlane had purchased this rough strip of field from the neighbouring farmer, and after much difficulty with the planning authorities had managed to obtain permission to erect *La Maison des Fleurs* on it. There had been some objections from the scattered residents in the beginning but now that they saw the house they were satisfied. It blended into the historic countryside, gave it prestige.

Rusty paused and looked back at the house. Fresh snow capped the carved floral decorations, giving them added beauty. Especially the snowdrops. He had never bothered much about flowers up until now. Suddenly he found them fascinating.

The lower part of the rear garden was still uncultivated, masses of dead bracken and brambles crushed beneath the weight of the snow. Rusty walked on top of them, sinking down in places above his rubber boots. The air was crisp and invigorating. Maybe he'd follow the course of the stream as it meandered through the white countryside.

A rabbit scuttled into the thick hawthorn hedge at his

approach, and a resting woodpigeon clattered out of a holly bush. It was a pity, he thought, that the landscape gardeners would be devastating nature's own garden in the spring. It was much more natural as it was. So beautiful. So quiet. Silent.

He was nearly at the length of sheep-netting which the farmer had erected to segregate the grounds of *La Maison des Fleurs* from the pastureland when he noticed the boy standing there. As Rusty approached he saw that the boy was on the nearside of the fence, watching him.

'Hi,' Rusty shouted, tried to hurry forward and sank up to his thighs in a snowdrift.

The boy did not reply, his gaze fixed unwaveringly on Rusty. As Rusty extricated himself and clambered up a short bank he suddenly felt uneasy. He didn't know why. It wasn't as though he was alone.

'Hi,' he said again, and stopped within three feet of the stranger. The latter was dressed in denim trousers and a thick hand-knitted sweater. The mop of blond hair, together with the reflected whiteness of the snow, gave his features a deathly hue. Probably he was anaemic, Rusty thought. He didn't look well. He was glancing about him as though he wanted to flee the place but didn't know how to get out. Maybe he was too weak to climb the wire-netting.

The boy looked away without speaking. Rusty felt uncomfortable, embarrassed.

'Would you like to come for a walk with me along the stream?' Rusty asked, aware that his mouth had suddenly gone dry. 'I've only come to live here recently and I don't know the countryside.'

The other did not answer. Instead, he turned and began to walk along the inside of the fence, heading towards a thick clump of rhododendrons in the corner. Rusty watched him. Icy prickles began to form on the back of his neck, running up into his scalp. He was annoyed, too. Rude devil, at least he might have had the good manners to reply.

The sky was clouding over again, bringing with it a few light flurries of snow. Rusty glanced up, and when he looked back again the strange boy had disappeared. He was hiding in the bushes, of course. Perhaps it was some kind of a game, or else strangers were resented in the locality. Anyway, the other was trespassing. He had no right to be there.

Rusty was angry. He'd find the boy and tell him to clear off, if that was his attitude. He headed towards the rhododendrons. They were dense from two or three decades of growth, and about seven or eight feet high. A kind of miniature forest, just the place to play in during the summer, cool and shaded, mysterious . . . eerie.

Rusty stopped. He was frightened and he did not know why. Just because the stranger was rude it was no reason to . . . Where on earth had he gone? Branches formed an impenetrable wall, weighed down heavily with snow. And nowhere had they been disturbed.

Rusty looked to the right and left. He had expected to find a track of some sort leading into the bushes, a regular path or even a well-worn run made by rabbits or hares. There was nothing at all.

'Hey, come on out,' he shouted, surprised and ashamed at the way his voice quavered.

Silence.

Rusty licked his lips. He thought about forcing his way inside, then changed his mind. If the other had not knocked the snow from the branches then he couldn't be in there. That was logical. In which case, where was he? There was nowhere else he could have gone or hidden without Rusty seeing him.

A sudden idea. There had to be footmarks, tracks in the snow. They only had to be followed and Rusty would find him. Simple. He began to look around for them.

He saw his own footprints, the criss-cross patterns of his wellington boots, places where he had scuffed the snow. It was ridiculous. His scalp was prickling again and he glanced behind him. The feeling of being watched returned. *There were no other tracks except his own!*

There had to be but there weren't. It was impossible. The boy had been standing over there by the fence, between the second and third posts. He went and looked, sucked in his breath and backed away. *There was nothing but unmarked, virgin snow!*

Rusty was scared, too scared to stay down there on his

own. He backed away. A fir branch brushed his cheek and he let out a cry. He was sure he hadn't touched it to make it spring.

Run! He panicked, stumbling through the snow. It was up to his thighs in places where it had drifted. His foot caught against something, wrenching his ankle, pulling him down. He screamed. It was as though steely fingers had reached out to stop his escape.

He scrambled up. His ankle pained him and he could scarcely put his full weight on it. Hobbling, not daring now to look behind. Pursued. A roaring in his ears, heart pumping madly. Any second now he would be pulled back, dragged down to the rhododendrons. *Keep going, you might make it.* A briar clutched at his sleeve with its sharp thorns and he felt them tearing into his forearm. He ignored the pain and wrenched himself free.

He made it to the garden, the part that had already been levelled. He could see the house from there. *But keep going ... keep going ...*

Rusty was breathless by the time he reached the steps. He started to climb them, having to use his arms on the rail to drag himself up. The pain in his ankle was excruciating. His forearm was bleeding and his lungs felt as though they might collapse at any second. And no way could he stop his skin from goosepimpling.

'Rusty, whatever's the matter? Are you hurt?'

Anthea opened the front door, staring wide-eyed. She saw her son's dishevelled state, the way he limped, the blood on his hand.

'I . . . I . . . I don't know.' He couldn't halt the sudden flood of tears, the way his knees sagged and collapsed him into his mother's arms.

'What a state you're in.' She flung an arm around him as a support. 'Let's get you into the kitchen and have a look at you.'

His brain seemed numbed now that he was safe. He lay back on the old settee, eyes closed, as Anthea began bathing the six-inch briar wound with TCP. It stung and he clamped his teeth together. His ankle was even more painful as she bandaged it tightly.

'You'll live.' She tried to make light of it, but there was no getting away from the fact that her son had had a very nasty shock. 'Now, suppose you tell me what it was all about. Been climbing trees again?'

He looked up at her and almost said 'Yes, that's right, the big oak down by the stream!' Now, back in the safety of the kitchen it all seemed so silly. He felt foolish. But the fact remained that it had all happened.

'There was this boy down at the bottom of the garden,' he began, licking his lips, still trembling. 'He didn't speak. Just walked away into the bushes and when I tried to follow he wasn't there anymore. And . . . there weren't any footmarks in the snow.'

'He was probably hiding.'

'There'd still have been footprints.'

'Perhaps you obliterated them with your own or else this blizzard that's raging now covered them up.'

No, that was just trying to find silly reasons to put his mind at rest. He was too old to be taken in. A couple of years ago, maybe . . .

'I got scared and ran, Mum. It was as if the trees and bushes were trying to grab me.'

'That was just your panic.'

Well, she was probably right there, he decided. Bushes didn't do things like that except in science fiction stories.

'Look, let's have a cup of tea and forget all about it.' She stood up and walked across to the Tiba stove on the other side of the room where the kettle was already boiling. 'You'll have to take it easy for the rest of the day. Don't go outside again. You can play with your Meccano set.' She filled the teapot, a thoughtful expression on her freckled face. 'Oh, and another thing, Rusty. I shouldn't play down at the bottom of the garden again. Not just yet, anyway.'

'Why not, Mum?' He looked at her sharply, tensing. 'D'you . . . think there's something . . . *wrong* down there?'

'No, of course not.' She turned away so that he could not see her expression. 'It's just that . . . well, it's a bit dangerous. Thick briars hiding rabbit holes that could break your leg. But it won't be long until we've got it all landscaped. Another few months, as soon as winter's over.'

Rusty wasn't listening. He was staring fixedly at the wall, not seeing it but visualising in his mind that strange boy again. The white face, it was vaguely familiar, that unruly blond hair, the wild eyes. The body was too thin, scraggy. It jogged his memory.

It couldn't be. Similar, but like . . . like . . .

Tod Pennant!

'Oh, God!'

Anthea whirled round, spilling some tea, flooding the saucer.

'What's the matter?'

'The boy, the one in the garden. He was like . . . like Tod.'

'Don't be silly. Tod's . . . not here any more.'

'He's dead. Why don't you say it, Mum? Why gloss over it, make it sound as if he's just disappeared? We know what happened to him. He was fooling with that space-hopper Dad gave him for Christmas and . . . '

'Rusty. Don't say that!'

'Why not? It's true.'

She sighed heavily as she set his tea down on the table.

'Anyway, it couldn't be Tod you saw so stop thinking such silly thoughts. There's a logical explanation for everything if you only look for it.'

Nevertheless, Anthea Parlane was uneasy. She was glad when Rusty hobbled away to go and play with his Meccano set in his room. The likeness between the mysterious boy and Tod Pennant *had* to be just a coincidence. It couldn't be anything else. Tod's death had started to play on Rusty's nerves. They ought not to have put him in that bedroom. More than that, they should never have bought the house in the first place. A whim of Bruce's. Hers, too, if it came to that. The temptation to live in a centuries-old Swiss mansion had been too much for her.

She tried to pull herself together. Things like ghosts didn't really exist, not to ordinary people. You had to be psychic, on the same wavelength, absorb an atmosphere.

Rusty wasn't like that either. He was a perfectly normal boy, not even studious like Tod Pennant. Tod had been a quiet boy, always keeping to himself, reading too much, not mixing with others of his own age. Funny things could happen to children who became loners too early in life. They got to thinking too much about things they couldn't understand. It played on their nerves. That mustn't happen to Rusty. Perhaps it was the wrong decision to send him upstairs to play. He should go back down to the bottom of the garden, see for himself that there was nothing there and put his mind at rest. But not on his own. She must go with him.

'Rusty,' she opened the kitchen door and shouted.

'Yes, Mum.' His reply seemed far away. It made her realise just how big the house was.

'How about if we go out for a walk, the two of us?'

'I can't. My ankle's too painful.'

Oh, hell, she should have thought of that. She heard him coming to the top of the stairs, hobbling.

'I thought maybe we'd go down to the bottom of the garden together. Let you see that there's nothing to be afraid of.'

'Mum, I don't ever want to go down there again.'

Oh, God, she'd made it worse. She ought to have left the subject alone, let it die, given him time to forget. She was making an issue of it now.

'My ankle hurts too much anyway, Mum.'

'Perhaps I'll go on my own, just to satisfy you.'

'If you want to, but Tod . . . the boy's gone now. There'll be nobody there, nothing to see.'

She sighed. There was no point in going down there on her own because there wouldn't be anything there anyway. She'd just be highlighting her own fears.

'Don't worry, Rusty. Carry on playing with your Meccano.'

She went back into the kitchen and closed the door. There was a tightness in her stomach, a dull ache. She told herself that it was her period about to start. It wasn't due for another week yet but sometimes it arrived early. Not often.

Another fall of snow in the night meant that Rusty could not go to school on the following day. Bruce Parlane had phoned in from Bournemouth to say that he might as well stay the night and then go straight on from the south coast to conclude another deal at Hay-on-Wye. He'd be home on Friday.

Anthea was uneasy. A father was always a strong influence on his son. Stronger than a mother. She needed him there right then but she couldn't explain the situation over the telephone. Rusty might be listening in and that would make it worse for him. He'd think there really was a bogeyman in the garden.

'How's your foot?' she asked him at breakfast.

'OK. Well, a bit better. Can't walk *far* on it.' *Not as far as the bottom of the garden but I'd make it to school if I could.*

She said, 'There's nothing to go out for, anyway. We'll just have a quiet day around the house. The weather forecast says there's rain and sleet spreading from the west so maybe it'll shift the snow. You'll be able to go to school tomorrow.'

He nodded and reached out for another slice of toast. She saw the gash on his arm. The briar had left a nasty wound. Vicious. There were a lot of reasons for keeping away from that garden.

Anthea had gone out on the verandah at the front shortly after lunch. Two consecutive days within the confines of the house had brought about a feeling of claustrophobia. She needed to stand out in the open air, to breathe it in deeply, filling her lungs, holding it there, letting it out slowly. It let her know that there was a wide world outside that extended beyond four wooden walls.

It was then that she saw the snowdrop. It was peeping up out of an inch of snow that had drifted into the verandah and covered the oak tub at the far end. A pair of strap-shaped glaucous leaves, keeled at the back, flat faces opposed. The solitary flower bud, wrapped in its thin spathe, showed between the leaves.

There were two things wrong. First, it should not have been showing for at least another month. That might have been due to a freak of nature. *But why was the snow which surrounded it spotted with crimson . . . like drops of blood from a cut finger?*

She moved closer, holding her breath, suddenly afraid. It

was unnatural. Even as she watched, the snow was turning a deeper shade of claret, the spots spreading, joining into a complete jagged circle which surrounded the plant.

'Mum.'

She jumped, startled. 'Rusty! I . . . I . . . '

'What's the matter with that snowdrop, Mum?' He, too, had seen it and was coming closer to look.

'I . . . I don't know. It's very strange. I don't understand it.'

'It looks like blood.'

'It can't be.'

'What is it then?'

'It must be . . . something in the soil, some kind of mineral that only shows up against the whiteness of snow. Anyway, let's go inside and have a coffee. It's getting very cold out here. I don't think that rain and sleet is going to come after all.' Anything to go indoors again, any excuse to shut it out, whatever it was.

Anthea Parlane was trembling by the time she got back into the kitchen. She thought about the garden and what Rusty had seen. She tried hard not to believe him but in the end she found herself doing so.

Anthea's uneasiness mounted after darkness fell. It was still very cold but no more snow had fallen. She wished that Bruce had not decided to stop away for another night. In fact, she had almost decided to ask Rusty if he would like to sleep in her bed. He was twelve now, though, and it might be embarrassing for both of them. She knew that he'd been masturbating for a year or so. No, it was better that he remained in his own bed. Too bad that it had to be on the floor above. Worse, it had been Tod's room. But nothing was wrong. They were both imagining things. This house wasn't haunted, just very, very old.

She retired shortly after eleven. Bruce had promised to phone. He always kept his promises so when she hadn't heard from him by ten-thirty she had tested the telephone. It was dead, not even a dialling tone. Doubtless the snow had brought the wires down somewhere. Tomorrow she'd have to walk out to a call-box and report it.

She threw an extra blanket on the bed. The atmosphere was much colder, as though the central heating wasn't working. She unlatched one of the oak panels and felt at the radiator behind it. It was piping hot.

She slid into bed and pulled the sheets up to her face. It was too cold even to read for a while. That was a pity because she felt the need for some kind of escapism. She needed something else, too. Her body was suddenly crying out for a man, her tensions needing immediate relief. Sex. She could have managed something herself, but she doubted whether she could achieve the ultimate in satisfaction and when she failed it left her with a feeling of frustration. Sleep was the next best thing. Maybe it would come sooner than she anticipated once the light was out.

It didn't. There were too many things on her mind. The Pennants. Rusty . . . that snowdrop. She wished she had checked it again before coming up to bed, but she'd been too busy worrying about Bruce and the phone. She experienced a sense of abandonment now that it wasn't working. Cut off. Marooned. They might as well have been at the south pole. She ought to have looked at that snowdrop again. *Go down and examine it now. Why not?*

No. No . . . *no!*

Hell, her nerves were playing her up. It was stupid. She and Rusty were as safe as . . . she thought she heard something and held her breath, listening.

Somebody was crying somewhere in the house. Faint sobs that went on and on. Rusty! The events of the last two days had taken their toll of him, too. He needed her. She'd go and fetch him down. They'd sleep together after all.

She reached out and pressed the switch of the bedside lamp. It clicked but nothing happened. Damn, the bulb was dud. She pulled her housecoat on and crossed the room to the main switch by the door. The result was the same. Just blackness and a faint reflection from the snow lying on the ground outside.

She tried to think where there was a torch. Downstairs in the kitchen somewhere, she couldn't think just where. She didn't even have matches or a cigarette-lighter. That was one of the disadvantages of being a non-smoker. It was better that she went to Rusty straightaway rather than wasting time searching for the torch downstairs.

She groped her way to the stairs, found the rail and began to follow it. The sobbing had stopped. She hesitated, then came to a decision. She would never rest if she went back now.

Two more steps and she heard running footsteps on the landing above, panic-stricken movements, somebody trying doors, looking into rooms, sobbing, choking for breath.

'Richard . . . Rusty! It's me. I'm coming. Stay where you are.' A horrible vision of Tod Pennant falling down the stairwell, screaming. A thud. Oh, God! 'Stay right there, Rusty.'

Silence.

'Rusty . . . are you all right?'

Noises from further up. Wails. Cursing in a foreign tongue. Women screaming.

Anthea shrank back against the wall. If only she had light. The blackness seemed more dense, closing in on her. Colder, too.

'Rusty . . . ' No more than a whisper, afraid that she might be heard by . . . *by what?*

A thud. A boy was screaming somewhere, pleading. She dared go no further and crouched down, eyes shut, not wanting to see. Praying, jumbled words, incoherent.

The smell, just an unpleasant whiff or two at first, strengthening into a putrefying odour like the time they'd had a joint of venison and left it in the larder whilst they went away for the weekend. It had taken three days to get the stench out of the house. This was worse, stronger.

A mêlèe of some kind. It seemed to be on the top storey, maybe even in the attic. Screams, a heavy thud. Then total silence, which for Anthea was far worse. She waited, listening. An odd creak or two from various parts of the house, the usual nocturnal noises that you became used to.

She wanted to flee downstairs and out into the snow-covered countryside. Run and keep on running. But her maternal instinct prevailed. She had to go to Rusty whatever the risk.

She reached the landing, and after some fumbling found

the light-switch. It wouldn't work, of course. Waste of time trying it, but . . . the blinding 100-watt bulb dazzled her with its unexpected brightness, hurting her eyeballs, forcing her to look away until she had adjusted to the light.

'Rusty!'

She flung open the door of the end bedroom. The boy was sleeping peacefully. Even her entrance did not disturb him. She had to shake him into wakefulness.

'What . . . what's up?' He rubbed his eyes and looked at her in amazement.

'Are you OK, Rusty?'

'Sure, but . . .'

'I think you'd better come and sleep with me.'

'Whatever for? I'm OK, Mum.'

'All the same, I want you to.'

He climbed out of bed and she found his dressing-gown. Together they descended the stairs and when they reached the lower landing she tried the light. It worked perfectly, just as she knew it would.

'We're going to take a walk first thing in the morning, Richard,' she said as they snuggled down in the large divan. The four-poster was in one of the guest rooms. She didn't fancy it. You never knew who had slept in it or who had died in it.

'Not . . . not down the garden?' There was alarm in Rusty's voice.

'No,' she assured him. 'To the telephone kiosk at Newbold. I want to leave a message at Hay for Daddy. I want him to come straight home. Before nightfall.'

This time he didn't ask why. It was a waste of time trying to find out what went on in his mother's mind these days. Doubtless she had her reasons. Just so long as she didn't want him to go down to the bottom of the garden again. That boy *had* been Tod. He knew it. And it was all very frightening.

9

TOSCA

Anthea Parlane regarded the Alsatian with a certain amount of dismay. It wasn't a pure-bred, that much was certain. The head was too large, the body elongated, and it looked underfed. Mean and vicious, and not to be trusted.

The chain which secured it to one of the verandah uprights chinked as the dog moved, its small deep-set eyes regarding the three people with suspicion. It whined, cringed.

'What a horrible creature,' she muttered.

'Not pretty,' Bruce replied, 'but I wouldn't like to meet it on a dark night.'

'We're . . . not actually going to have it *loose* in the house, are we?' She glanced sideways at Rusty. He was hanging back, afraid of the dog. He didn't look well, she reflected. These last two weeks had left their mark on him. He had lost weight, too.

'It'll be quite safe,' her husband assured her, 'and so will we. If there is any hanky-panky going on I reckon this will soon put a stop to it. Tosca's her name. She'd been found wandering in Leamington. Dumped, I guess. If I hadn't taken her she'd've been put down at the end of the week.'

Tosca looked at him steadily, small beady eyes hidden in a mass of black hair. Maybe she would rather have had it that way. She didn't care for humans. Neither did she like being chained up. She growled softly in her throat, a warning.

'I don't like her,' Anthea grimaced. 'And I don't trust her with Richard.'

'He'll be in bed when we bring her in the house.' Bruce stepped forward and fondled the animal. 'I think she's OK. She's just got to get used to us.'

Rusty went back inside. He had some homework to finish.

'And . . . and what if this doesn't work?' Anthea sighed. 'I can't see a dog making any difference. These ghosts or whatever they are aren't likely to be frightened of a dog, however fierce it is.'

'We've got to give it a try.' He continued stroking the animal. 'Phase one.'

'And what's phase two?'

'We'll have the house exorcised.'

'Are you serious?'

'Of course. That would settle it once and for all, if it's necessary. There are hundreds of houses in Britain that have had spirits driven out of them by exorcism. I'd rather not, though, if it can be helped. I don't want all the publicity.'

'Wouldn't it be easier just to sell up?'

'That's defeatism. Anyway, I like the place.'

She turned away. Every night now they heard noises, always in the top storeys. It wasn't doing Richard any good. He had lost almost half a stone, and she was worried about the distraught look in his eyes. Even sleeping in their bedroom hadn't helped him.

'I just hope it works,' she muttered.

It was after eleven o'clock when Bruce Parlane went out on to the verandah to fetch Tosca inside. The dog was lying in the corner, ears erect.

'Come on, old girl.' He spoke soothingly to her. 'There's a nice warm rug in front of the stove in the kitchen for you to lie on, and you'll have the run of the whole house. You'll . . .'

The Alsatian growled and edged back against the wall.

'Don't be silly. You can't sleep out here in the cold.' He slipped the chain off the post and pulled it taut. 'Come on, now.'

Tosca stood her ground, claws scraping the wooden boards as a tug-of-war began. She slipped, lost some ground and tried to pull back. Bruce was half expecting her to attack him but she showed no signs of viciousness. Just fear. Dogs which hadn't been used to living indoors took some breaking in. He wondered if she was house-trained. That was a minor point.

Somehow he managed to drag her into the hall, kicking the door shut. Well, she was inside! Hesitantly he unfastened the chain from her collar. She watched his every move, cowering, tail firmly between her legs.

'Go on and lie in the warm.' The kitchen door was wide open and he could hear the logs crackling and spitting inside the Tiba. She went back to the front door, lying up against it, head on her paws, staring into the corner, trembling violently.

'Oh, well, please yourself.' He straightened up, annoyed with the Alsatian, his patience exhausted. 'Sleep there if you want to.'

Rusty was asleep in the single bed in the corner when Bruce came into the bedroom. Anthea was sitting in a chair, a fashion magazine open on her lap, but he knew that she had not been reading it, simply going through the motions.

'Having trouble?' She had heard his struggle with the dog downstairs.

'Not really. Just stubborn, not used to sleeping indoors. She'll be all right.'

They lay there for a long time in the darkened bedroom, not talking, each occupied with their own thoughts. Bruce couldn't get the night he'd spent with the Pennants off his mind, the way the lights had fused and then come on again when the crying had stopped. He hadn't told Anthea about it. It would only have made things worse. And Tod's death. It couldn't just have been a space-hopper. Whatever forces lurked in the house were responsible. That was why he was worried about Rusty. He should sell up before it was too late. No, not without a fight. The dog first and if that didn't solve the problem then he'd resort to exorcism. Only then would he put *La Maison des Fleurs* on the market. It would fetch a good price, he'd show a nice profit. Money wasn't everything, though.

Anthea was listening intently to every sound. Rusty's breathing was even. He was sleeping peacefully and that was a lot to be grateful for. Boards creaked, they always did. Not a sound from up above. Once, just before she drifted off to sleep, she thought she heard Tosca whimper down in the hall. But that was all. The Alsatian was bound to find her new environment strange at first.

Morning. The daylight was slow to penetrate the thick

fog which had formed overnight, grey light seeping slowly into the bedroom. It was much warmer. Probably it would rain before the day was out.

Anthea awoke first and glanced at the alarm clock on the bedside table. 7.20. It wasn't due to go off for another ten minutes. There was no hurry. Rusty would go up to his own room to dress; he was at a self-conscious age when he didn't like dressing in front of his parents.

Bruce wouldn't rise until eight. It was a kind of ritual. He always said he'd only be in the way downstairs but that was just an excuse to lie-in for an extra half-hour. She didn't mind though.

She listened hard. There was no sound from Tosca. Everything had been all right. Perhaps, she scarcely dared to hope, the presence of the Alsatian had actually deterred the spirits. She'd read somewhere that dogs were psychic. It was early days yet.

7.29. She reached out and switched off the alarm. There was no point in letting it jangle harshly. She could wake the others. Maybe . . . maybe she could persuade Bruce to get up first this morning. She didn't really like the idea of going downstairs and being confronted by a strange dog.

'Bruce.' She shook him gently. 'Bruce, wake up. It's half-past seven.'

He stirred and regarded her through half-closed eyes. 'Is it? Don't I get a cup of tea this morning, then? It's not Sunday.' He always made the tea on Sunday mornings.

'No, it's not Sunday, but . . . well, I thought that maybe with Tosca downstairs you'd like to go down first. Today, anyway.'

'All right.' He kissed her. 'I'll go down and put the big bad wolf out on the verandah. And make the tea.'

She watched as he swung himself out of bed. Naked, he always slept that way, summer or winter. His body was full but not fat. Muscular. He hadn't changed in twenty years, no different from the way he had looked on their honeymoon. It didn't seem that long . . .

He dressed in a couple of minutes, pulling on a shirt and sweater and faded jeans. He even looked spruce, a knack that few men had within so short a time from being roused from a deep sleep. Confidence, that was what did it, she decided. Confidence in himself to meet and deal with all kinds of situations. Even those in *La Maison des Fleurs.*

'I'll wake Rusty when I come back,' he whispered and let himself out on to the landing.

There was just enough light to see by and he didn't put on the light as he went downstairs. Now where was that dog? Probably it had decided that the kitchen was the best place after all.

'Tosca,' he called softly. 'Come on, old girl.'

Nothing moved. In all probability the Alsatian was comfortably curled up in front of the Tiba and was going to show as much reluctance to go out as she had to being brought inside the previous night.

'Tosca.'

Bruce Parlane halted at the foot of the wide oak stairs. His early morning exuberance began to wane, and in its place came a sense of uneasiness. Something was wrong. He could see in through the kitchen door. There was no sign of Tosca.

'Tosca . . . Tosca.'

Suddenly he saw the dog, only a yard or so from where he was standing, still in the same place, up against the front door, where she had settled down when they had gone up to bed. She was stretched out on her side, all four legs pressed tightly to her body, gaping jaws showing the full extent of the massive canine teeth.

Bruce Parlane stiffened, let out a low whistle through pursed lips. He knew only too well that the dog was not merely asleep. *Tosca was dead.*

Only when he switched on the hall light did he witness the full extent of the horror. Those small eyes which had been hidden beneath the coarse fur were protruding, bulging. Their inflation alone reflected the terror which the animal had experienced prior death. The jaws, frozen with rigor mortis, depicted cringing fear, whining and whimpering rather than a ferocious growl.

There had been signs of eczema in the coat when Bruce had collected Tosca, patches of hairless skin on the flanks and joints. Now there were weals, a series of gashes across the body, deep cuts that had bled into the hair and congealed.

'Christ!' Parlane was on his knees, touching Tosca, finding her stiff and unyielding. *'She's been thrashed to death!'*

Opening the front door he dragged the dead animal outside and into the furthermost corner of the verandah, where he found an old hessian sack to drape over her still form.

He lit a cigarette and stood there in the greyness of a winter's morning, inhaling the smoke, attempting to steady his nerves. Compassion at first, a mistiness in his eyes that was only natural in the bereavement of a pet, then fear. His lips tightened and his hands clenched. Anger came last. And stayed. Whoever or whatever these devils were, they were going to pay the penalty.

In the end, there was nothing left but exorcism.

The Reverend Herbert Pinchbeck enjoyed an unparalleled status, not only in his own extensive parish but throughout the diocese. In fact, he constantly reminded himself, it elevated him beyond even the bishop. Exorcism was a gift bestowed upon the chosen few by God himself. In a way it was like water-divining. You could either do it or you couldn't. There was no in between. And if you could, then you commanded an envied respect.

At fifty-five Herbert Pinchbeck still had hopes of promotion within his calling. A canon perhaps. It was all a matter of time. Patience. There were older men than himself above him and they had to retire some time. Or die. Of course, the bishop was jealous. That house at Snitterfield, the one that had been plagued by a poltergeist for years. The bishop had gone there personally to rid the occupants of their unwanted spirit. He had failed. A month later Pinchbeck had succeeded. A triumph, but it had not done him any good. His future had been jeopardised; a country parish, well out of the way, a sort of retirement, in fact.

Now he sipped his brandy with relish, comfortably satisfied by the excellent cuisine of Mrs Parlane. His thinning grey hair was damp with sweat. He always sweated at exorcisms; one had to put everything one had into it. Just reciting the printed words was not sufficient. His usual ruddy complexion *was* somewhat paler. Well, it *was* rather frightening, a personal battle with the forces of evil. You could feel their presence, their malevolence, striving to defeat you, but if you had faith you won in the end.

He accepted the cigarette which Bruce Parlane offered him. A moderate smoker, the clergyman had already consumed his quota of ten a day but on this occasion he would permit himself a small bonus. After all, he had earned it. It had been hard work tonight, harder than he had ever known before. Whoever these spirits were they were exceedingly powerful. They raged and fought, defied him until the bitter end, but finally they had faded. He had beaten them.

'You think we're OK now, vicar?' Bruce Parlane asked.

Anthea fidgeted, stirring her coffee. She, too, had sensed the evil presence. Now she ought to be relaxing, but it was impossible. She was taut, more highly strung than ever before. If only she knew, one way or the other.

'I should sincerely hope so.' Pinchbeck rarely committed himself. 'I shall pray in church tomorrow that I have rid this exceedingly beautiful house of its evil spirits. I have yet to be called back a second time after an exorcism.'

'We'll pray, too,' Bruce said.

Pinchbeck inhaled deeply and blew a cloud of smoke up to the ceiling. He felt exhausted. They had been very, very powerful, but he was confident of victory. The boy had slept through it all upstairs, that was a blessing. The less one so pure and young knew about these matters, the better.

Anthea was the first to notice the door opening, swinging back on its hinges slowly as though caught by a draught.

'Look' – she spilled some coffee into her saucer – 'the door . . .'

The other two turned and saw the empty hall beyond. A movement, a soft thud. The vicar's black coat, suspended from a peg on the hallstand, suddenly fell, opening out to its full extent, arms splayed, lying full length on the floor like a man suddenly struck down.

'Oh!' Anthea Parlane clutched at her throat.

Bruce half-rose from his seat. Pinchbeck flinched and showered cigarette ash into his lap. He stared and cleared his throat. 'My . . . coat needed a . . . a new tab.'

It sounded weak. An excuse. He wished, the moment he had uttered the words, that he had kept silent.

Three people sat transfixed. The door bumped against its stop, vibrated and then began to close again. Herbert Pinchbeck drew hard on his cigarette. Suddenly he knew, knew that *they* were back again, revitalised and angry, their wounds licked and ready for the fray. They wanted revenge.

'We . . . must try again.' The clergyman fumbled in his pockets. He didn't need the printed form of service though he always used it. He knew every word by heart, and began mumbling some beneath his breath, garbled, knowing it was a race against time, a losing battle.

The lights flickered. On, off, on . . . and then stayed off. The whole house was plunged into darkness. Bruce's hand groped for Anthea and pulled her close. He noted how she trembled. Or was it himself?

'Richard . . . ' she whispered.

'Stay here, I'll . . . '

Whatever his plans, Bruce Parlane had no chance to put them into action. All three of them felt the coldness, the heaviness and menace of the evil in the atmosphere. They fell back, cowering beneath the table. Crockery and glassware rattled. A tearing gale converged on the room, gusting the curtains, lashing those who cringed before it.

A second? A minute? An hour? They seemed caught up in a timeless void where winds howled and tortured souls screamed and cursed.

Then it was all over, as suddenly as it had begun. Lights flickered and came on, flooding the house with their brightness, showing every stark detail: the prone coat, the open curtains, paper serviettes strewn across the floor of the dining-room.

Three people had taken refuge beneath the table. Only two emerged. Anthea jerked her head away. She did not want to look. One glimpse of Herbert Pinchbeck's face had told her all she needed to know. The contortions, pain both physical and mental, the terrible encounter which had forced the veins to stand out like blue cord; then defeat, forced to yield, the lips muttering a final prayer for help just as the end came. Death in its most horrible form.

She shuddered and buried her face against Bruce's chest.

'I . . . I think he's had a heart attack,' Parlane muttered 'I'll . . . phone for an ambulance.'

Anthea wanted to yell, *he's dead, dead. You're wasting your time.* But she followed him to the phone, clutching at his sleeve, afraid to let him out of her sight.

Even as he began to dial, Bruce Parlane knew that he was beaten. His two aces had failed miserably to beat the pack. All that remained was his promise to Anthea. They would be leaving *La Maison des Fleurs for good.* This house of hell would be going up for sale, and may God protect whoever bought it.

10

VOICES AGAIN

> Country residence, situated in its own grounds in the heart of Warwickshire, built by Swiss craftsman. 12 bedrooms, 3 bathrooms, extensive kitchens and dining-rooms, lounge. An exceptional dwelling with potential for hotel business. Offers are invited in the region of £750,000.

Bruce Parlane studied the quarter-page advertisement in the latest edition of the *Coventry Evening Telegraph* and the photograph, a somewhat blurred view of *La Maison des Fleurs* taken from the front drive. Why the hell didn't these estate agents use a decent camera? You could not make out the floral decorations, they just looked like vague blobs. He'd deduct something off their fees when he got the bill.

Overland Grange had cost him a hundred thousand on overdraft at seventeen per cent. In many ways it was fortunate that this large black-and-white gabled mansion, less than a mile from *La Maison des Fleurs,* had come on the market.

Not that the Parlanes were going to stay there indefinitely, but it would serve its purpose until the Swiss house had been sold.

A week, and no takers. It had been advertised in *Country Life* last Thursday. That was always a good source for this type of property. Again, not a single enquiry. Of course, the dailies hadn't helped. That business of the exorcism and Pinchbeck's death had made the front page of two of the more sensational ones. Reporters had been snooping round. It had been featured on the main television news. It could have helped, some wealthy crank seizing the opportunity to buy himself a few ghosts. It appeared to have had the opposite effect.

'No takers?' Anthea came through into the hall just as he had finished on the telephone.

'No,' he shook his head. 'The agents say they can't understand it. It would appear that all the adverse publicity is to blame.'

'It'll sell,' she smiled encouragingly.

'Sure. One day. And in the meantime the bank is fleecing us for this place. On top of that my capital is all tied up. There's a likely looking place for sale up in Scotland, a bargain. We just don't have the ready to buy it.'

'Richard seems a lot better.' She changed the subject. 'He's put most of that weight he lost back on. He's more himself, too.'

'Good.' Parlane nodded. 'Well, all we can do is sit tight.'

'A holiday would do us all good.'

'Maybe, but I can't get away. I need to be here just on the off-chance of a purchaser. Of course, it's a bad time for selling. Even the most enthusiastic house purchasers are disinclined to get off their backsides in winter.' He was kidding himself. *La Maison des Fleurs* should have been snapped up at any time.

Rusty felt more at ease in his new surroundings. The house was big, not as big as the previous one, but it had a friendly atmosphere. He had no fear of the darkness now and was glad to be sleeping in a bedroom of his own once more. The bicycle which his parents had bought him for Christmas meant that he was able to cycle into Stratford on

Saturday mornings and join his schoolmates. All the same, he would be glad when his father had sold *La Maison des Fleurs.* It was the one cloud on their horizon, as though fate decreed that they were not to be rid of it for all time.

Rusty never cycled along the lanes close to his old home, and on one occasion when he had topped a rise and seen the house standing out starkly against a late winter landscape he had turned round and pedalled hard in the opposite direction. Grim and forbidding, it had seemed to beckon him. *Come back, boy, we have not done with you yet!*

Spring came early, warm sunshine and showers in the first week of March. Buds showed on trees and bushes, and the fields took on a deeper green.

No matter how hard he tried, Rusty could not get the Reichenbach place off his mind. Some nights he dreamed about it; he was back there in his old room, hearing the noises, the screeching of angry banshees, the man with the decayed face standing at the foot of his bed.

And the boy, the one he'd seen in the garden that snowy morning, he was there too. Sorrowful, pleading. *We need you, Rusty, why have you deserted us? Come back, come back, don't leave us.*

The dreams became more frequent, stronger. Mostly now they featured the fair-haired boy. It *was* Tod Pennant. Rusty recognised him, the features older and shrunken, cheeks hollowed with pain and suffering. No longer was Tod silent. He pleaded constantly. *Come back, Rusty. The more there are of us the less harm he can do us. We are becoming stronger all the time. One day we will overthrow him. We need you. Come back to the house, I have something to tell you.*

Something to tell you . . . something to tell you . . . come back . . . The words hammered into Rusty's brain day after day. He couldn't concentrate at school and became listless, losing weight again.

'You're not still scared, are you?' Anthea asked him, a worried frown on her face. 'I know that we went through a terrible time, all of us. But it's over now. They can't hurt us here.'

'I wish Dad would hurry up and sell the house.' Rusty

stared down at his untouched food. 'I keep dreaming about it.'

'But they're only *dreams.* They'll fade altogether in due course. Would you like to come and sleep in our room for a while?'

'No,' he shook his head slowly, 'I'll be OK, Mum.'

'I've no doubt the house will be sold any day now. Winter's always a bad time for selling property' – she knew that wasn't true – 'Mr Kinnerton, the agent, phoned again this morning. They're going to increase the advertising, put it in a lot more magazines. Somewhere there's somebody who wants it.'

No, that's not true. Nobody wants it because once you've bought it they'll *never let you alone. You'll never get rid of* them.

The dream again. So vivid it brought Rusty out of his troubled slumber. He hadn't really been asleep, just lying tossing and turning in the darkness. Tod Pennant stood in the doorway. The door was wide open. He was beckoning. *Come on, Rusty. Come with me. Don't be afraid, we only want to talk to you. We won't keep you there, we'll let you go outside.*

Rusty tried to hold back. It was a feeble effort. His limbs moved, obeying commands that came not from his own brain but from the boy who called him. He got out of bed, swayed, almost fell, then found his balance.

He walked down the stairs, across the hall. The front door was wide open. The night was chilly. He should have dressed first but there hadn't been time. No time even to pick up his dressing gown. Tod wouldn't wait.

He hurried, running at times to keep up with Tod, who forged on ahead not once looking back, knowing that Rusty followed. Along the deserted lanes, the stone chippings dug into the soles of his bare feet. Silence, not even a gust of wind.

La Maison des Fleurs. Lights were showing in the windows and he could hear the sound of voices.

Up the wooden steps, holding on to the rail, into the hallway. Rusty should have been afraid, terrified. He wasn't. It couldn't be happening. It was just another dream like all the others. Any moment he'd wake up. He would be lying in his own bed, his body damp with sweat. He was curious, though. This time it was different. *Go with Tod, see what they want, listen to them. They won't keep you. They'll let you go again, Tod promised.*

As he stepped inside the house a familiar odour met him. Decay, matter that should have rotted away to nothing yet had survived. Constant putrefaction that would go on and on without ending.

It was then that Rusty knew that it was no dream. It was all happening. He wasn't safe in his bed at Overland Grange. He was in *La Maison des Fleurs.*

His complacency and curiosity vanished, immediately to be replaced by stark terror. A scream was beginning in his throat. He turned, starting to run.

The front door was closed, the heavy bolt securely in place.

And somewhere in the darkness of the large hallway Tod was laughing, mocking him.

It took Anthea Parlane some minutes to realise that Rusty was actually missing from the house. She had banged on his bedroom door as usual on her way downstairs at 7.30. Rusty generally put in an appearance in the kitchen by a quarter to eight.

At ten minutes to eight she went back upstairs to call him again. There was no response to her knock as she opened the door. Even then, as she stared into the empty room, her first thought was that he must still be in the bathroom.

Three minutes later she was frantically shaking Bruce awake. 'Bruce, Richard's not here . . . *he's gone*!'

'Gone!' He sat up, throwing back the bedclothes. 'What d'you mean, gone?'

'He's not around, not in his room, nor the bathroom.'

'He can't be far away.' Bruce was already pulling on some clothes. 'Don't panic. Perhaps he's gone out into the garden.'

Anthea followed her husband down the stairs and noticed for the first time that the front door was ajar, a draught moving it slightly as though to draw their attention to it.

'Look . . . he must have gone outside,' she whispered.

'As I said, nothing to worry about,' he replied. 'I expect he's playing in the garden. No reason why he shouldn't.'

No, no reason at all, but she could not share Bruce's confidence. They went outside. The sun was shining, the air smelled fragrant. Peaceful. Nothing could have happened to Rusty. It was impossible. He was around somewhere. Any minute they would see him. But they didn't.

A grey squirrel looked up, ears erect, a morsel from the bird-table on the rear lawn clutched in its paws. It regarded them for a few seconds, then departed in a series of bounds, making for the nearest shrubbery. Bruce Parlane licked his lips. Rusty certainly hadn't been this way; if he had, the creature would not still have been around. He turned back.

There was nowhere at the front of the house where the boy could be hiding. Spacious lawns, flower-beds, low privet hedges. Not even the squirrel could have hidden there. Where on earth was Rusty? He tried to come up with a few possibilities, mainly for Anthea's benefit.

'Maybe he didn't finish his homework and went to school early to get it done, something to look up in the library. Or he could've gone for a bike ride.'

'His bike's still in the porch.' Her voice sounded far away, as though it were coming from somewhere else, like stereo playing softly on an upper storey. 'And I know he'd finished his homework.'

'Let's look in the house again. It might be a joke he's playing on us.'

'Richard has never played practical jokes.'

Running out of possibilities fast. Thank God this wasn't *La Maison des Fleurs*. Nothing could happen to him here, though always supposing that he was here ...

Every room was the same, silent and empty, seeming to mock them. *He's not here. He's gone. You won't find him.*

Anthea felt physically sick. She wanted to scream, go into hysterics, collapse on the floor. *Oh, find him, Bruce. Find him for me before I go mad.*

'Well, he's not here.' A note of resignation in Bruce Parlane's tone. He was trying to think of something else, but failing.

'He hadn't even dressed.' Anthea wrung her fingers together. 'Just got up out of bed and . . . and went.'

'There has to be some explanation.'

Of course there has. That's what I'm frightened of. After all that had happened at the other house. 'We'd better ring the police,' she said.

'Let's not be too hasty.'

'We can't afford to be apathetic. He might be in serious trouble.'

'We'll check once more.'

She followed him up to the top of the house, then down again, looking in each room. Nothing in the rear garden. There was no sign of the squirrel; it had retired for the day now that humans were abroad. Back at the front door, staring at the lawns and flowerbeds as though Rusty might suddenly put in an appearance. Despair was creeping in.

'I'll ring the police,' Bruce sighed.

She waited outside, not wanting to hear him say 'My son's missing'. She wanted to yell 'Rusty . . . Rusty . . . *Rusty*'. Or to go and search again. Anything. Doing nothing was the worst part.

'Somebody will be with us in a few minutes.' Bruce appeared in the doorway. 'I'll make some coffee. We could both do with it.'

Coffee! Why, when something serious happened did everybody have to start thinking about tea or coffee? Because it calmed the nerves. Rubbish! It was something to do rather than look at each other whilst futility and despair rubbed off until they became neurotics.

It was a kind of wide-awake dream sitting in the kitchen sipping instant coffee. Anthea thought it tasted like liquorice. Maybe they were putting liquorice in the granules nowadays. It didn't really matter what it tasted like. Nothing mattered except Richard.

Two policemen arrived half an hour later. Plain-clothes men in a Bedford van. They didn't hurry. She watched them sauntering up to the door. *Oh, God, don't you realise my poor baby's gone missing?* Of course they did. Somebody, somewhere, went missing every day. It was routine, certain questions to be asked, various steps to be taken.

'What time did he go to bed?'

'Nine o'clock.'

'Did you hear any unusual sounds in the night?'

'No.'

'Has anything been troubling him lately? Any worries?'

'No.'

'Have you checked with his school?'

'No.'

Raising eyebrows, the two CID men exchanged glances.

'We'd better do that right away.'

It's a waste of time, she wanted to yell. Instead she bit her lower lip. They'd check, anyway. They didn't look concerned. That was because it wasn't their son.

She sat there in the kitchen, hearing the tall one speaking on the telephone. 'You're *sure* he's not there? I see. Well would you mind checking again. Thank you.'

A long pause. Somebody had gone to check the classroom and the playground. Another waste of time. Bruce was looking out of the window. Several blackbirds and thrushes were clustered on the bird-table outside. Others were searching amidst the long grass for twigs and flying off with them. A new cycle was beginning. Nesting, then breeding. Some would rear their young. Others would lose them. It was all a gamble. Fate decreed.

'Well, Richard's not at school.' Detective-sergeant Repton came back into the room, stooping so that he did not catch his head on the low centre beam. He had a notepad in his hand. Anthea wondered what he'd written. Whatever it was, it hadn't come up with the right answer. Yet. *Be patient.* It was difficult. 'We'll radio for a tracker-dog. Just in case he's still in the immediate locality.'

Anthea Parlane clutched at her throat. She thought at first she was going to faint. 'Still in the locality' . . . the words punched themselves at her. That meant close at hand. And if Rusty was close then he wasn't able to let them know. Because . . .

'You don't think he's *dead*, do you?' She couldn't stop herself from asking the question. The words just seemed to spill out.

'Don't alarm yourself, ma'am,' the smaller of the detectives, a constable, answered as he lit a cigarette. She couldn't see his eyes, perhaps it was as well. 'Lots of kids go missing, cause a scare. They usually turn up. Just been playing truant.'

'My son's never played truant. He loves school.'

'Never can tell, ma'am. A lot o' kids tell their parents they do when they don't. Is there a pool of any kind in the area?'

A pool! Oh, my God!

'Yes,' her voice was shaking. 'Across the field behind. Why?'

'Might've gone fishing.'

'He's never been interested in fishing. He doesn't have any gear.'

'Fishing rods are easily made. A stick, a piece of string and a bent pin. Used to do it myself when I was a kid.'

'Bert'll be here with the dog in a few minutes.' Repton returned from radioing and picked up a mug of coffee. 'Could you find us a piece of your boy's clothing, Mrs Parlane? Anything will do.'

'Of course.'

It took courage to go back upstairs to Rusty's bedroom. Bruce should have gone but he was too busy answering some more of Repton's routine questions. On the stairs she heard the policeman asking about a pool again. She swayed and had to hold on to the rail. Warning lights flashed in her brain, newspaper headlines she'd skipped over, not really interested in them – 'FOUND DROWNED' . . . 'CHILD'S BODY DISCOVERED IN POOL' . . . 'SEARCH FOR MISSING BOY GOES ON'.

Oh, Lord, it was worse in the room. Clothes neatly folded, the way she'd taught him, as though they were discarded, abandoned; he wasn't coming back. Bedclothes rumpled, still damp from Rusty's sweat. He'd had another nightmare. She picked up a shoe and almost ran back downstairs. Even as she crossed the hall she saw through the open front door a navy-blue van with the word POLICE on the sides coming up the drive. There was a grille of some kind immediately behind the front seats. A dog, an Alsatian, was in the back, dark-coloured . . . like *Tosca*!

'Here.' She thrust the shoe into Repton's hands. She could not meet his gaze, once more afraid of what she might read in his expression. *He's dead, you know, Mrs Parlane.*

A conference took place outside; the dog-handler, a short, stocky uniformed man in his mid-thirties, square-jawed, determined. Repton was pointing back behind the house. The pool? Bruce Parlane kept his distance, for once unsure of himself.

'Right, Bert, let's make a start,' Repton said, and the other walked round the back, Rusty's shoe in his hand, to let the dog out.

Anthea watched the animal, a lithe creature, keen but not over-excited. It was sniffing the shoe, taking its time as though deriving some kind of pleasure from the scent. Its master had it on a short leash. Repton and the constable were pulling on wellington boots. The pool...

'If I can help . . . ' Bruce spoke nervously. His usual confidence had evaporated, his features were pale and haggard.

'Thank you, sir, but we'd prefer to work on our own.' As Repton spoke the dog was already pulling away, not in the direction of the fields behind the house but towards the road. 'You hang on here, sir. We'll be back presently.'

Slowly Bruce Parlane walked back to where Anthea stood in the porch. His arm came around her, pulling her close.

'Do . . . do you think . . . ?' She didn't know what she wanted him to think.

'They're going down the lane,' he pointed. The three men were walking quickly, the dog screened by the straggling hedgerows. 'Not towards the pool.'

Oh, thank God! But where could Rusty have gone to? The school lay in the opposite direction. Across there, there was nothing, a fcw scattered farms and cottages . . . one large wooden mansion supported by stilts. *Le Maison des Fleurs.*

Anthea Parlane saw it in her imagination, exquisite, sinister, starkly outlined against the distant hills. Standing, waiting. Her breathing almost stopped, then started again, shallow, frightened.

She clung to Bruce, trembling. She could almost smell the

foul odours of the Reichenbach dwelling. Yet, and she prayed to God that she was right, Rusty wouldn't go *there*. He was terrified of the place. Nothing could persuade him to go inside it again.

Or could it?

11

ANCIENT EVIL

Tod had mocked, and beckoned again. Rusty moved forward, forced to follow. There was no going back, the front door was barred.

Past the stairs, through the kitchen and out into the grounds behind. The night was black and cold. He couldn't make out any details, just the boy in front walking quickly, not even looking back because he knew that the other would be following.

Bramble thorns ripped at Rusty's legs. His feet were already bleeding. He wanted to stop, to rest, but he could not. The garden had not changed, winter had merely checked its wild growth.

They came to the fence at the bottom. Somehow Tod was already on the other side. Rusty scrambled over, fell, then picked himself up again. He was sobbing softly. *Oh, please, please let me go home.*

This is your home!

Down a slope and across the wide stream, the icy rushing torrent cooling his scratches. On again. A half moon had emerged from behind a bank of clouds, flooding the landscape with its faint silvery light. He had never come this far before. Indeed, the bottom of the garden was the furthest he'd ever been.

A long wood stood in the hollow below, an ancient coppice of fully matured oak and beech, their bare limbs reaching upwards as though paying homage to the moon above. The covert itself was bathed in shadow, dark and mysterious. Somewhere beyond a dog-fox barked. A warning?

Rusty knew that they were going in there. Tod was half-running, gripped with a sudden urgency, glancing back. *Hurry, hurry. We are late.*

Late for what? Rusty did not know, he did not want to guess.

Beneath the trees it was cold and damp, his feet sinking into the soft earth, black and squelching up between his toes. An unpleasant aroma assailed his nostrils as they followed a narrow winding track beneath the boughs of the massive trees, a rancid odour that reminded him of *La Maison des Fleurs.* He knew that it came from a kind of fungus known as stinkhorn. They'd studied it at school. A wood like this would be full of it.

He sensed that they were making some kind of detour, treading a narrow track which wound its way through an area of thick dead bracken, brambles clutching as though trying to hinder their progress. Rusty cried out aloud as the thorns raked his skin and Tod turned. There was no pity in his expression, just cursing because they had slowed up. *Hurry.*

Eventually the path widened and they emerged into the centre of the wood, a large clearing that had once been a quarry, the far side a high mound of slate and rock, weeds growing on it, knitting it together.

Tod had stopped, moved to one side so that his companion could see. Dark shadow was broken up by sections of feeble moonlight like some carelessly stitched piece of patchwork. The breeze soughed softly in the branches, almost apologetically, and then died away.

Tod had gone. Rusty glanced around to the hostile blackness behind; the path which they had followed was swallowed up. The worst part of all was the silence. Even the wind appeared to have halted because the powers of darkness had commanded it to be still.

Rusty swallowed and wondered how long it was until

dawn. And then he was aware of movements in the open space before him.

Subconsciously he tried to reason why he had not seen them before; they must have been there all along. He watched, transfixed, terror rendering him motionless. A huge black mass swaying, dividing, becoming separate entities. It was some moments before he realised that they were people, all dressed alike in flowing black robes and cowls so that they were difficult to discern in the semi-darkness.

It was becoming lighter, too. Not the moon, nor the advent of dawn. A kind of faint greyness merging with the night, allowing one to see silhouettes yet masking the details. A dozen or so figures, he did not count them, grouping into a circle around a taller one, covering their faces with their hands as though they were afraid to look upon this individual. Low moans broke the silence, wails of terror.

A yellow light, spreading, growing, throwing out flickering beams. Fire. It burned beneath some huge cauldron, the flames licking up hungrily, silently, not even crackling as they devoured the dry kindling wood.

The tall figure turned, and as Rusty saw the features in the glow of the fire he cringed. He wanted to turn away, to cast his eyes where they would not see. But he could not. He was forced to watch.

The wails grew. More people cowered beyond the blaze, only now visible in its light, three naked men, a woman and a boy, their hands bound behind their backs. Rusty started. The boy was Tod, the blond hair, the way he stood. For some reason his features were discernible, searching the surrounding darkness, pleading desperately, looking for . . . *Rusty*!

Help us.

Rusty's brain could not cope with the situation. A few seconds earlier Tod had been by his side. Now he was a prisoner in the hands of . . . of what?

The smell, a faint vileness wafting on the night air, and this time Tod knew that it was not stinkhorn. The tall man was facing him, seeing him with hollow orbless eyes, black voids that saw and transmitted their malevolence across the clearing. The face was the same as before, the peeling flesh, ribbons of rotten human meat, the thin lips moving silently, speaking without an audible voice. Death itself in human shape. *Reichenbach!*

Two of the robed figures were carrying one of the prisoners by his hands and feet, oblivious of the screams and struggles, and only then did Rusty realise what was happening. It was a baptism of evil, the lords of darkness submerging their victims in scalding water!

It was over in seconds, the prisoner thrown to lie on the ground nearby, huge blisters growing like air-bubbles on his skin, filling and bulging, some bursting. The man was still alive, kicking feebly but not able to scream through a scalded throat.

Two more men, then the woman, her breasts blistered so that the nipples were indistinguishable beneath the cancerous-looking mounds of tortured skin. Now the boy, looking for Rusty, silently beseeching him to . . . to what? There was nothing Rusty could do except watch helplessly.

Tod lay jerking in agony amongst the other four. And then the perpetrator of this vile inhumanity turned once more towards Rusty. The others were watching, too, faces hidden beneath their cowls. The smell of decay was heavy in the atmosphere, not just of rotting flesh but of decomposing vegetation. Even the air itself smelled dank and stale, as though it had suddenly been released from a pit where it had been imprisoned for centuries.

These are but a few of those who have offended. Over the years there have been many, many more. And still there will be others. You and your kind have defiled our home.

Rusty nodded dumbly. An admission of guilt. He sensed the power of the other, the sheer force of the evil. Judgement would be pronounced. Tod had already paid the penalty. Now it was his turn. Fear, like pain, had its own barrier. Beyond it there was nothing but numbness. Rusty knew that he had passed into that state.

Return us to our rightful place.

He nodded again.

The boy called Tod was commanded to do so. He failed. You have witnessed his fate. The same will befall you if you fail.

The scene in front of Rusty was lighter. Possibly the fire had blazed up or else the moon had come out from behind the thick bank of cloud. He didn't know. His mind could not reason clearly, only accept that which it saw.

The gathering was hushed, the evil minions of the putrid man bowed and humble, the scalded victims still, not even a groan escaping their blistered mouths and lips.

The ground was clearly visible now, a mass of tiny white flowers giving the effect of a light snowfall, reflecting the hideousness of everything in that clearing. White on red. Each plant was ringed with crimson, the soil wet and glistening.

The boy recognised the species even in the midst of his terror. They were *snowdrops*! Identical to the one which had flowered and gushed its scarlet fluid in the oak tub on the verandah of *La Maison des Fleurs.* And he knew without a doubt that somehow they formed an integral part of this evil!

The man who was undoubtedly Reichenbach was no longer watching him. Instead he had turned and was crouching on one knee, staring into the blackness beyond, arms outspread as though calling upon the powers that controlled him, muttering incantations in a foreign tongue.

Rusty found that he could move. His limbs ached but they no longer held him in this awful place. He turned, stumbled and began to run. He fell, picked himself up again and groped his way blindly back in the direction from which he had come.

Somehow, miraculously, he was on the path again, following its winding course through the deep woods and dense undergrowth. Trailing briars scratched him but no longer seemed to curl their spiked tentacles around his legs as though trying to hinder his escape. *Begone, boy, whilst you can.*

A long dark journey. Exhausted but still managing to make progress, Rusty was afraid of becoming lost but somehow always found the track.

Finally he was in the open, a dim moonlit landscape, undulating grass fields leading down to the rushing stream. He crossed it, the cold water reviving him somewhat. Over the fence and into the wilderness of a garden, terrified of the place but knowing no other way to reach Overland Grange.

The darkness rolled back again as intense as ever, obscuring every landmark, every detail. Suddenly he realised that once again he was being led, not by Tod but by some invisible force that drew him as surely as a Pied Piper; trying to hold back, powerless, legs moving in an ungainly fashion. He fell, and felt the hardness of wood beneath him; he was at the steps leading up to the house. He gripped the rail and tried to stop himself, but already his feet were starting to climb. Seconds later he gave up the struggle. It was no good trying to fight against these things.

Inside, groping along the walls, not knowing where he was going, he lost all sense of direction. A room; it was damp and cold. He shrank back, knowing that he was not alone. Silence, and yet he could feel the presence of others; that same decomposing smell again. Festering flesh.

Gradually the scene was revealed to him. Although once again he had no idea where the faint light was coming from, it was just enough for him to be able to make out his surroundings. The walls were of rough stone, dripping with condensation, a big square room with a flight of steps leading up to a grille-door above him. He did not recognise the place. It was a dungeon of some sort. Yet *La Maison des Fleurs* had no dungeons! It was impossible because it was raised on stilts above ground level.

Nevertheless it was some kind of underground room, terrible to behold. It had no right to exist in this day and age. From a line of manacles secured to the walls hung human beings, suspended by their wrists, feet just brushing the uneven floor. A dozen, maybe more. Men, women and children. Some faced the wall, others were turned inwards, their bodies scarcely recognisable as belonging to humans. Bloody faces, much of the flesh gone, revealing damaged bone structures. Three of the men were hairless, their craniums raw and bleeding where their scalps had been removed. Another had a gaping groin wound. Rusty jerked his gaze away and retched. He couldn't vomit, probably because his stomach was empty. That made it worse.

Tod was there, too, right at the end of the line. He still had enough strength left to enable him to moan, his eyes searching out Rusty, pleading mutely. *Save us from this fiend.*

Hell, the very place itself, the ultimate in suffering and grief, death barred from its portals. Every one of them still lived, even the woman with slashed breasts whose one leg kicked feebly. The other lay on the floor beneath, amputated, sinews trailing.

That was not all. A steel rack had stretched one body so that legs and arms had been pulled from their sockets. A blanket covered the lower half of the victim, soaked with blood. Rusty could not tell whether the sufferer was male or female, it was so mutilated. Some terrible act of torture had been performed beneath the saturated covering.

Something else, a steel frame that was constricted by means of a series of screws, crushing whatever it held; a ball of stinking flesh and bone still oozing blood – and still living!

These were the victims. The tormentors were standing back against the opposite wall, watching, gloating.

Rusty's eyes were drawn from face to face, the only similarity was their expression of cruelty and bodily decomposition. Leering skulls, only remnants of flesh left on the bone. Uniforms of a dark coloured material that was also rotting away, exposing the wasted frames beneath. Peaked caps pulled down over the hollow eye sockets. And, of course, in the centre was the tall man with the thin lips who was Reichenbach. Rusty knew that he would be there.

Something showed white in the gloom behind this bunch of torturers, a contrast that could not go unnoticed. The boy stared and made out the shape of the small flower, its squatness, six stamens opening at the tips, the large green ovary at the base. *The snowdrop again.* It sprouted up out of the earth between two cracked flagstones, vivacious and commanding attention.

Reichenbach's harsh tones whipped into Rusty's brain, lashing it with the force of a bullwhip.

The war is not over. These people are the enemies of the Führer and must pay the price for their folly. As must you and your kind.

Rusty swallowed. He tried to figure out how Reichenbach had got back from the wood, changed out of his robes and brought these poor people with him, all in a matter of minutes. He gave it up. They defied the laws of logic. The unseen powers of evil performed their own black miracles.

Their bodies will remain here for all time, their souls condemned to wander the house and its grounds, their agonies prolonged forever. That is my fate, too. My officers are being withdrawn as our Master has use of them. Only I will remain. So it must be. And unless we are returned to our homeland whence you brought us then you, too, will share this communal grave where bodies rot and souls are imprisoned.

Rusty knew that the others were fading and tried to figure out how. His limbs were static. It was as though the scene before him was being drawn away by some inexplicable means, becoming smaller and smaller, the blackness rolling back, the curtain falling slowly at the end of a macabre theatre performance. Just one white dot showing starkly, then blurring into nothingness. The snowdrop.

The snowdrop must be returned.

He was lying on smooth wooden boards somewhere, a layer of dust that rose in clouds every time he moved choking him. He knew that he was in *La Maison des Fleurs* but he wasn't sure which room. It didn't matter, anyway. His body felt weak, and he doubted whether he had the strength to stand up. There was no urgency. The danger was past. They would not be returning at present.

His head ached, so he rested it on his folded arms behind him. He needed time to think. It wasn't easy; a jumble of incidents all rolled into one, the wizards of a bygone era and the Gestapo. He recognised the latter from pictures he'd seen in war comics. The link was Reichenbach. No, not entirely; the snowdrop. A kind of symbol, an embodiment of evil that lived and breathed, withered, died and came back to life again. Without it the others could not exist. Somehow it absorbed them and brought about some kind of astral projection. The blood which it contained must have seeped into its bulb out of the earth in that communal grave in Switzerland, probably even before then, a living entity that retained the evil and kept it alive.

Maybe it wasn't just one snowdrop, there had been scores

of them in the wood. The seeds would be distributed by insects, by the wind.

Return us whence we came.

That was all they wanted, Rusty concluded. *Send them all back to the Reichenbach Falls and we'll be free.* But how? He couldn't do it alone. And his father would put it all down to another nightmare. But unless the house was returned . . . he shuddered at their fate. Everlasting damnation, pain that was ceaseless. They'd done it to Tod Pennant; they would not hesitate to take their revenge upon himself!

It was becoming lighter. Dawn battled to penetrate the dirt-stained mullioned windows and Rusty saw that he was in the lounge of *La Maison des Fleurs.* He tried to struggle up. He couldn't move; his legs refused to respond, as though they were gripped by some form of paralysis.

Fear began to flood back over him. He opened his mouth, attempted to shout. A hoarse whisper was the most he could manage. Reichenbach had already exacted his revenge, not waiting for his demands to be carried out . . . *condemned forever in this communal grave where bodies rot and souls are imprisoned.*

The atmosphere was flat and stale. Rusty felt its sourness, its mustiness in his lungs.

He was cold, as cold as he had been in the wood and in that hellish cellar. He shivered. Maybe he could crawl to the door and . . . he couldn't.

He wanted to cry. No tears came. He could move his head and arms a little. The effort weakened him. Why didn't his father come and rescue him? Because nobody had any idea he was here. It was the last place they would think of looking.

Time passed. The sun rose. Some sunlight managed to penetrate the room, emblazoning the opposite wall. He found himself watching the shadows of moving clouds, some of them forming into grotesque shapes. Once he thought he could make out the outline of a snowdrop but it had merged and disappeared before he could be certain. Another time it was a twisted, writhing human body being slowly pulped up into a mangled ball.

The sun was still shining, but not directly into the room.

That meant that it had moved past its zenith. He tried to work out how long it was until dark. Five or six hours. There was no real way of checking the passing of time except by the sun. When that went down dusk would form, then blend into darkness. The night . . . oh, God, he couldn't stand the thought. He'd go mad. Maybe he already was mad.

He wasn't going anywhere. Not ever. He was resigned to his fate. He'd remain there forever. With *them.* And the snowdrop, of course. None of them could exist without the snowdrop. It was the source of life itself. Life after death.

A noise. He listened intently. Scratching. Rats. There had always been rats around *La Maison des Fleurs.* Probably more colonies had moved in during the winter months whilst it had been unoccupied, and bred. Rusty shivered. Previously he had not been unduly worried about the creatures but it was different now. He was helpless, with no way of defending himself. They would crawl over him, biting, gnawing through his bones, and he would not even be able to defend himself. Filth and disease, fleas. He might finish up like Reichenbach, *ugh*!

Something was scratching at the door, panting, whining. It sounded big, too big for a rat. He closed his eyes and for the first time in his life he wanted to die.

The door was opening. Footsteps, muffled voices. Rusty cringed. They were back already. Reichenbach and his torturers had not waited for nightfall. It had all been a game, like a cat toying with a mouse. They had only pretended to set him free, knowing that he had not the strength to leave the house. Now they were going to take him back down to that torture-chamber, suspend him alongside the other poor creatures and perform unspeakable acts of sadism. After that he would be one of them.

'Hey, he's here!'

Of course, I'm here. You knew I couldn't get away. He kept his eyes closed tightly so that he would not have to look upon their devilish countenances.

'It's him, all right. Hey, kid, we found you.'

It was a dog, he didn't need to look to know that much. Human voices that spoke aloud, not somehow transmitting their message into his brain.

'Wake up, lad.' Somebody knelt by his side, hands feeling at his body, examining him.

Rusty's eyes flickered open. It took him some moments to take in the scene, the uniformed policeman with the Alsatian. It looked just like Tosca. In this place anything could happen. The others, they had to be policemen, too. Plain-clothes men. Detectives.

He opened his mouth. He wanted to say 'I'm all right, take me home, please.' Instead, all he managed was a kind of gurgle, his lips moving but no sound coming out.

'What's the matter with him?' the dog-handler asked, pulling the Alsatian back.

'Shock. Maybe exposure as well.' The taller of the detectives felt Rusty's pulse. 'A night in here in only your pyjamas wouldn't do you any good either, Bert. He's in a filthy state, as if he'd been on a cross-country run and failed the water-jump at the end. Call up an ambulance. The sooner this kid gets some attention, the better.'

Rusty made another futile attempt to speak. *No, don't call an ambulance. Just take me home to my Mum and Dad. I want to tell my Dad about the snowdrop. It's urgent. Vital.*

His vocal chords failed again.

'Don't you try to talk, son. We'll soon have you safe and sound and you'll forget all about what's happened to you.'

Forget! Never, not if he lived to be ninety would Rusty Parlane be able to get this night of terror out of his memory. He had to warn his father. They didn't realise where the danger lay. The snowdrop. It had to be taken back to its original resting place up on the Reichenbach Falls. At once.

He felt his senses slipping from him, the blackness closing in again. He could *smell* them, hear them. They were angry with him. They would punish him for failing them. They were lurking in the darkness waiting for him.

12

CANNIBALISM

It was strange, Rusty reflected, that *they* were absent. Blackness, total and peaceful. Sometimes it seemed that people were moving about around him, they even leaned over him and touched him. They were gentle, almost as if they cared. The smell had gone, too; the decomposing odour, anyway. In its place was a sharp clean smell that seemed to purify. He couldn't place it although it was vaguely familiar and reminded him of something . . . like a visit to the dentist.

It took him some time to figure out where he was even after he had come round. A small room, brilliantly lit with strip-lighting that hurt his eyes if he kept them open for too long, women in white overalls, sometimes a man. Rusty knew that his brain wasn't functioning as it should. Everything was hazy, realisation was a gradual process.

It was not until he opened his eyes and saw his mother and father sitting by the side of the bed, watching him anxiously, that everything clicked into place. Of course, hospital. But not like the one where he had had his appendix out. That had been huge, rows and rows of beds. This was just a small room.

'Richard.' There was relief on Anthea's face. 'Thank goodness. You've had a fever, pneumonia. You've been tossing and turning for almost a week, not able to recognise anybody.'

She reached across and felt his forehead. It was much cooler. Almost normal, in fact. She didn't tell him that only twenty-four hours ago he had been fighting for his life. It had been touch and go. But, thankfully, the crisis was past now. They could tell him about it another time.

'I . . . I have to tell you something, Dad.'

'What is it, Richard?' Bruce Parlane bent close to his son.

'They . . . it's the snowdrop that . . .'

'Don't you go thinking about snowdrops, Richard. You're safe here and . . .'

'That's just it, Dad. None of us are safe. Do you know why they killed Tod and what they did to him afterwards?'

'Richard' – there was a mild reprimand in Anthea's tone – 'it's all been one terrible nightmare. It played on your nerves so much that you went sleep-walking.'

'I didn't sleepwalk,' Rusty snapped. 'Tod came and fetched me because *they* wanted me.'

'Now look,' she interrupted him, but Bruce's hand squeezed her arm in a gentle warning.

'I think we'd best let Richard have his say,' he murmured, 'and get it all off his mind once and for all.'

'Dad,' Rusty hesitated, 'you know as well as I do what was going on in our old house. They aren't just ordinary spooks that give you a scare. *They're dangerous.* Reichenbach existed in the days of the Druids and he's still around because for some reason a snowdrop absorbed his remains from his grave and reincarnated him time and time again. Worse still, his victims have lived on with him. But he's angry because the house was taken from Switzerland. I don't know what would have happened if the snowdrop had stayed there. Maybe they would have remained behind. But they're here now, in England. They demand to be returned to the Reichenbach Falls. You can't fight them. They're too powerful even for exorcism. Look at what happened to the vicar. They'll punish us if we don't obey their orders. Oh, Dad, please get the house shipped back to Switzerland!'

Bruce and Anthea exchanged glances. It was unbelievable, the kind of ramblings one would expect to hear from a boy who had survived an acute dose of pneumonia. Weird fantasy. Yet they had seen it all for themselves: the blood around the snowdrop in the tub, the sheer force of the evil which had struck down the clergyman, the Alsatian lashed to death without a sound. And what Rusty told them was no more unbelievable.

'I think the boy's hit on the solution to our problem.' Bruce gripped Anthea's arm so firmly that she knew he was serious.

She stared at him blankly, wishing that somehow they could change the subject.

'We can't find a buyer in England for *La Maison des Fleurs,*' Parlane said, 'so we'll have to sell it abroad. And why not to the Swiss? They object to wealthy Americans running off with their old houses so perhaps they'd like to buy one back.'

'It's an idea,' she admitted. God, the house could not stand much more transportation. It would fall to pieces, surely.

'I'll phone Kinnerton first thing in the morning,' Bruce grinned with the delight of a schoolboy of average intelligence who has just hit upon the solution to a complicated algebra problem within minutes of the finish of an 'O' level examination. 'I'll get him to cancel those new *Country Life* advertisements, withdraw the sale, and then I'll wire Gilda in Geneva. He's the best agent on the continent. He'll find a buyer before the week's out. Strewth, why didn't I think of it before? It'll probably find itself erected on the shores of Lake Geneva by the end of the autumn.'

'But Dad,' there was desperation in Rusty's voice, 'that's no good. It's *got* to go back to its original site on the falls.'

'Hmm.' Parlane wondered whether or not to humour the boy. There were limits even when psychic forces set out their demands. 'I see. Well, that should be no problem. Costly, but the gnomes of Zürich won't worry on that score. We still own the plot of land on the Reichenbach Falls so we could sell it on site. There's just one snag. With my capital tied up as it is I can't ship it out there before we find a buyer. If by any chance there's nobody to leap at the offer then the damned house will have to stay where it is whatever our nasty tenants might have to say.'

'But he won't wait, Dad.'

'He'll have to. Maybe he's got a better idea seeing as he's so clever.'

'Bruce' – Anthea's eyes flamed angrily – 'Richard's ill. He can't stand . . . '

'Yes I can,' Rusty almost screamed. 'You've got to find a buyer, Dad.'

'Don't worry. I'll do my best, I promise.'

Rusty watched them as they left the small hospital room half an hour later, and he breathed a faint sigh of relief. At least they had taken him seriously. Unless it was all pretence. He didn't think so. Their lives, their very souls depended upon the appeasement of Reichenbach. His victims wanted to go back to Switzerland also. They knew there was no escape for them whatever; they just craved to go home.

Rusty fell into a fitful slumber, grateful for the dim light which shone in his room throughout the night, comforted by the knowledge that the night-sister would look in frequently. Not that she was any defence against the powerful psychic forces which *La Maison des Fleurs* harboured. But he had tried, done his best. They would give him a little time, surely.

It was cold and damp, the mist which seeped up from the marshy ground penetrated Rusty's bones until they ached. He was just standing there alone, not even Tod was with him this time.

He glanced around him. Visibility was restricted to a few yards, the landscape beyond invisible. There was no way of knowing even what country this was.

The mist had an unpleasant stale odour, one that was vaguely familiar. He had smelled it somewhere before. He tried to remember where. That wood, that was it. He shuddered; the stench of bygone centuries.

He had no idea how he had come to that place. It was as though unseen forces had whisked him there whilst he slept and abandoned him in the midst of some vile bogland.

Mud gurgled and squelched. Quicksands, bottomless mires, rumbled because they were hungry for a victim, sucking loudly in anticipation, scenting a human being. He glanced down at himself. His clothing was unfamiliar, hand-stitched ragged garments that reeked of an unwashed body, urine-stained trousers. His body felt more muscular, more powerful than usual. And then he knew. *It wasn't his own body but a casing of flesh and bone which he was inside!* It frightened him. He didn't understand. Furthermore, he knew that comprehension was beyond him.

He wondered what he was going to do. He could not

remain here indefinitely, yet if he wandered far he was likely to blunder into one of the sucking bogs.

Then he noticed the winding track, cloven hoofmarks clearly visible in the black mud. Sheep or wild goats, it did not matter which. Where they had trodden safely so could he. Cautiously he set off.

The mist swirled around him, thickening, thinning, thickening again. Yet there was no wind. Rusty kept his eyes on the path in front of him, stepping carefully, noting how it turned back on itself, made seemingly pointless detours. Of course, the animals which used this knew the quagmires; they had discovered them by trial and error, seen a fellow creature struggling helplessly in a patch of apparently safe lush green grass and learned to avoid that place. It had probably taken years before a safe crossing was finally established and many creatures had perished in the quest. Even now, the odd one made a mistake and paid the penalty.

Every few yards Rusty halted and attempted to peer ahead, screwing up his eyes until they hurt. Nothing but an opaque grey vapour. He wondered what time of day it was. The prospect of nightfall was formidable. How extensive was this marsh? Might it not have been wiser to have retraced his steps? There was no way of knowing what lay beyond or behind. He licked his lips. They were dry and cracked and there was an unpleasant taste in his mouth. A dull ache in his stomach told him that he was hungry. Tired, too, but this was no place to rest.

The bog had its own odours, gases released from the thick mud as it shifted, hanging in the still atmosphere. He wrinkled his nose in disgust.

Time passed; he had no way of determining it without sight of the sun. He doubted whether the sun ever shone there, it was that kind of place. Gloomy. Evil.

Something loomed up in the mist ahead and a few yards further on he saw that it was a house. A large place, towering, its upper storeys hidden by the fog, disguising its true size. He quickened his step, then halted suddenly, a feeling of dismay creeping over him. Its outline was familiar: heavy wooden stilts protruding out of the mud, supporting it above the marsh, a flight of wooden steps going up to a ground floor verandah. He knew without a doubt that it was *La Maison des Fleurs.* The timbers looked new, unseasoned, condensation dripping from every beam.

It seemed to stare balefully at him, mullioned windows watching him unblinkingly. Drip . . . drip . . . drip . . . the mist melted on its gables and dripped loudly, almost deafeningly in the silence.

Rusty tensed and stepped back a pace. The path which he had been following led right up to the foot of the front steps, hoofprints merging into an unidentifiable morass of black mud, as though the creatures from this land of mist converged there for shelter, spending the nocturnal hours beneath the elevated flooring.

Beyond the building there was no continuation of the path, only mud and slime gurgling in anticipation of another victim. The terminus, *La Maison des Fleurs,* the house of the Reichenbachs!

The boy looked behind him, his thoughts already turning to flight. The mist had thickened, darkened. The atmosphere was much colder. He shivered. Nightfall was not far off. There would be no dusk in this place. The light was fading fast. No longer would he be able to find his way; the animal track was obliterated and he had no means of seeing his route. One mistake . . . there would be no second chance.

He heard the sound of a door opening and slow dragging footsteps scraping on wooden boards. He turned, fearful, his lips forming into a cry of terror. A man was standing on the verandah, holding on to the balustrade, the yellow light from the hallway illuminating him plainly.

No, not you, the fiend with the festering putrid features, the one who . . . But it wasn't. Tall, similar in build, the same stance, but the flesh on the aquiline face was complete. He was old, the skin wrinkled like dried fruit, but the eyes were sharp and penetrating, questioning.

'You have lost your way, boy.' A statement, not a question. 'It is lucky for you that you found your way here instead of into the bog.'

Rusty nodded his head like a string puppet.

'From where have you travelled, boy?'

'I . . . don't know.'

'It does not matter.' The mouth widened into what was supposed to be a smile. 'You are hungry and tired. I have a meal in preparation. Come inside and rest awhile.'

Don't go. Rusty's feet moved forward slowly, one after the other. *Run, flee.* He mounted the first step, gripping the rail to pull himself up. *Turn back.* Up on the verandah, his breathing was shallow, a lump in his dry throat. The man had turned, walking back inside, stooping, shoulders hunched. Through the doorway, the door swung closed on its hinges, thudding, the latch falling into place. *Too late, you were warned!*

The hallway was bare, unfurnished, smelling of unmatured wood recently hewn from felled oaks. The kitchen was large, with a scrubbed table and two chairs, a huge blackened open range in the corner, flames crackling and spitting as they devoured the dry kindling wood.

Rusty sat on one of the chairs watching the other busying himself preparing the food. The stranger's mode of dress intrigued him. The material was much the same as his own, crudely fashioned animal skins held together with leather thongs, bulky in places, too tight in others.

Wooden plates were placed in readiness by the oven, and some kind of vegetable stew was ladled on to them from an iron pot above the fire. The oven doors were opened. Rusty felt the heat searing his face but his host did not appear to notice it.

The meat was laid out in chunks on a large dish, submerged in thick brown gravy, reddish tints from the blood of whatever beast it was. The aroma was appetising, allaying the boy's fears somewhat and making him realise just how hungry he was. He could not remember when he had last eaten. Indeed, his memory went back no further than a few hours except for odd flashes of things that had happened a long time ago.

The meal ready, they faced each other across the table, a spoon for the vegetables and to slurp the gravy, a sharp-bladed knife with which to spear the meat. The latter was remarkably tender, its flavour vaguely familiar, similar to pork yet much more palatable. Tangy.

Rusty ate ravenously, finishing long before his companion,

then staring nervously at his plate. His hunger appeased, the fear was returning, a terror that increased steadily. He could feel his limbs shaking and dropped his hands into his lap so that the other should not notice them. He had to get away from here, leave this place as soon as possible, take his chance out on the marshes.

'Of course it would be foolish to attempt to cross the marsh at night.' The old man looked at him steadily, pale blue eyes unblinking as though he was aware of his visitor's every thought. 'It is dangerous enough by day here.'

Rusty nodded dumbly. Somewhere a shutter rattled. A low long drawn out moan came from the upper regions of the house. The wind was getting up. He tried to convince himself that it was the wind. It had to be. Perhaps it would blow away the mist and then he would be able to find his way back to safety.

'The marsh has claimed many lives.' The other was still looking at him. 'Mostly animals. Very few humans venture here.'

It was cold in the room in spite of the roaring fire. The temperature seemed to have dropped several degrees.

'You are tired, boy. Let me show you to your quarters and then in the morning we can talk again.'

I will be gone as soon as it is light. You will never leave here. The old man is kind but does not understand. He is dangerous. It is the same man before his flesh rotted. It can't be. It is.

Rusty rose and followed in the other's footsteps. Across the kitchen, out through an adjoining door, down an unlit corridor, his host a shambling shape in the gloom in front of him, wheezing for breath.

They paused before a large iron-studded door. The tall man produced a key from the pocket of his jacket and unlocked it. It creaked open, showing a long narrow room with an oil-lamp burning, casting eerie shadows. A hand closed over Rusty's arm, fingers that gripped with unbelievable strength, pulling him inside. Eerie shadows, yet they could not hide the familiar surroundings, nor the grisly scene which met the boy's eyes. He knew the room, he'd been there before, a long time ago, watching the sunlight come slanting in through the dirt-stained glass panes reflecting the passing clouds and moulding them into strange shapes. Now there was no sun, just total blackness outside, shutting in the horrors, away from the outside world.

Rusty would have fallen had not his companion been holding him. He saw it all, every detail, grotesque proof of man's inhumanity to man.

The only recognisable human bodies were those hanging by their necks from the hooks on the wall, blood-covered, freshly killed, skewered. A couple dropped maggots. The rest were jointed on a stone table beneath the window, neatly severed legs and arms in a row. A pile of heads was heaped against the wall, the lower ones already rotted to bare skulls, staring sightlessly, mouths open mutely echoing their death screams. A pile of offal stank.

The stench was overpowering. Rusty retched, pulled away from the vile perpetrator of these mutilations and almost fainted. He fell to the floor, turning his head away in an attempt to shut out the nightmarish scene. It could not be. It was impossible.

He heard the man go back outside. The door slammed shut and the lock turned, shuffling footsteps fading into an awful silence.

The house. The man. *The beginning of it all.*

The lamp burned steadily. Something forced him to turn round and look again. One empty hook at the end of the row . . . waiting.

Carnage. Senseless killings. Sadism.

The flavour of his repast still lingered on his palate: highly spiced vegetables, the roast with its sharp, not wholly unpleasant tang . . . Realisation was slow. He tried to push it away. No! *Yes!* No! *Yes!*

He was vomiting even as he blacked out, the stench of the room coming at him in nauseating waves.

'They're going to keep him in for another couple of days.' Bruce Parlane came back from the telephone and spread the morning newspaper so that it hid his unfinished breakfast and also screened him from Anthea's searching look. A frail defence.

'Why?' she asked anxiously. 'They said last night he'd probably be allowed out today.'

'He had a bad night. He's also been sick. Just delayed reaction.'

'*Delayed* reaction! He's been nearly out of his mind since that awful night.'

'He'll be OK. He'll be home on Wednesday.' *Play it down. For Christ's sake we don't want you in there as well.* 'They said we can go and see him later.'

A moment's silence, suddenly shattered by the bleeping of the phone in the hall.

'I'll get it.' Anthea was half way there by the time Bruce had lowered his paper. She was back in a few seconds. 'For you. Personal call from Geneva. Gilda.'

'Right.' He pushed past her with the nervous haste of a college student opening his examination results. 'That was quick. He wouldn't have rung unless it was urgent. Some prospective buyer is jumping in with both feet.'

Anthea stood there listening. Her husband's 'Oh, I see,' and 'hell, they can't do that,' sent her hopes plummeting. *La Maison des Fleurs* was not sold. A quick buyer suddenly backing down? Surely Gilda wouldn't have rung just to tell them that. It was early days. It would sell. Even Kinnerton, the London agent, said it was best to put it up for sale in Switzerland and he had the most to lose. Almost as though he didn't want to handle it any more.

Bruce Parlane came back into the room tight-lipped, anger and disappointment in his expression, tossing his newspaper on to the floor and sinking down into the chair as though he was exhausted. She waited nervously, not asking. He'd tell her when he'd gathered his thoughts together.

'You won't believe this.' He lit a cigarette with fingers that shook slightly. 'Oh, Jesus Christ, you just won't believe it!'

'Some wealthy speculator has offered over the odds and then found he's been declared bankrupt?'

'I wish to God it was,' he laughed harshly, trying to get something out of his system. 'I even wish the little gnomes had been queuing up and then all backed down. At least that way we'd still be in with a chance.'

'Whatever do you mean?'

'Just this. Gilda put some adverts in the Swiss dailies. His telephone never stopped ringing. Then came the killer punch. A government environmental control minister with an embargo. *Not only is the bloody house not to be put up for sale in Switzerland but they've also vetoed its reimportation.* In other words, thanks for taking it off our hands but no way are we having it back!'

Anthea blanched, muttered 'Oh, my God!' and thought about Rusty.

13

THE POWER OF THE SNOWDROP

'What . . . what are we going to tell Richard?' Anthea Parlane poured some more coffee. It was cold, bitter, but it gave her something to do. She grimaced as she tasted it.

'I'll think of something,' he replied. 'He needn't know the truth.'

'These . . . these forces that inhabit the house will know. You can't lie to them.'

'Maybe Rusty can if the truth's kept from him.'

'I doubt it. They're too dangerous to fool with, Bruce. We can't take any more chances where Rusty is concerned. Perhaps if we moved again, bought another house as far away as possible, even abroad.'

'I've told you before, all my capital's tied up in this deal. It would take too long, anyway, and they'd do something before we got clear. No, I've got to do something positive. Quickly.'

'Like what?'

'Hell, I don't know. Give me a chance to think. I'll come up with something.'

'We're going to see Richard this afternoon. What if he asks? He's almost bound to.'

'Then we'll tell him. In fact, I think he's in a better position to negotiate with these devils than we are. He'll have to tell them we're doing our best. We can't do any more.'

'I just pray that they'll leave him alone.' She pushed her coffee cup away. 'God, they've done enough to him already, haven't they?'

By the time they went to see Rusty in hospital that afternoon Bruce had already come to a decision. It was so simple really but neither his wife nor his son must know about it, not for a long time anyway. He hoped it would do the trick, that he had the courage to see it through. *La Maison des Fleurs must be destroyed by fire!* The place was built almost entirely of timber and once it was blazing nothing could save it. A heap of ashes at the finish, just a few nails and screws remaining. Even that vile snowdrop would be incinerated.

And, as a bonus, Bruce would have a pay-off from the insurance company. No need even to try to sell the place now. *Burn it, pick up the insurance. You've earned it, done everybody a favour.* He lit another cigarette and drew on it with newly-found satisfaction. The job would have to be done next Friday night. He had to go to Banbury to meet Kinnerton. He tried to work out whether it would be best to carry out his act of arson on the way there or coming back. The outward trip gave him the most scope. Just a slight detour, a crumpled newspaper and a match, the work of a few minutes. It'd blaze all right. He'd be with Kinnerton in Banbury by the time the alarm was raised. A perfect alibi, not that he needed one. Nobody would ever suspect. But one had to be careful.

'You're suddenly feeling very pleased with yourself, aren't you?' Anthea glanced at her husband seated in the driving-seat beside her, a half-smile playing about his lips. She knew the signs, the same silent jubilation as when he'd just about got a property deal through. Self-satisfaction. It even showed in the way he gripped the wheel; enthusiasm.

He did not take his eyes off the road ahead, changing down and slowing to negotiate a roundabout.

'All right,' she murmured, 'you think you've hit on the solution but you're not going to tell me in case it turns out to be another flop. I know you too well, Bruce.' She forced herself to laugh, to make light of it, in an attempt to cover up her anxiety. 'Carry on, but for God's sake watch what you're doing. They killed Pinchbeck because he tried to drive them out. They won't hesitate to do the same to either of us. Or Rusty.'

'I'll be careful,' he promised.

The subject was dropped. Ten minutes later they arrived at the hospital and made their way inside the wide glass doors. It was hot and stuffy, the smell of disinfectant almost overpowering. The middle-aged sister was seated at her desk. The door of her office wide open, and she glanced out as though she was awaiting somebody. The moment she saw Bruce and Anthea she got up and came towards them.

'Good afternoon,' she smiled, a deliberate attempt at reassurance, a façade she had perfected over the years. One never showed one's true feelings but put relatives at their ease before the patient's condition was discussed. 'Before you go into your son, Dr Perry would like a word with you.'

Anthea tensed, her stomach starting to churn. 'Why . . . how is Richard?' Something was wrong. It was like the time she'd called to visit her mother. The sister had smiled, somewhat sadly admittedly, and then told her that her mother had passed away a few minutes ago.

'The doctor will give you a complete run-down on his condition, Mrs Parlane.' The short dumpy woman turned, already leading the way towards the door at the end of the corridor, the plastic plate denoting that it was the office of DOCTOR PERRY.

The doctor looked up from his desk as they entered, a small wiry man of indeterminable age; he could have been as young as forty or as old as fifty. Rimless glasses, pensive, almost an effort to turn on a kindly front. Vague.

'Oh . . . yes, thank you, sister.' He motioned to two vacant chairs. 'Sit down, please, Mr and Mrs Parlane.'

They sat down, stiff and upright, tense. Dr Perry took his time folding up the file and putting it in a drawer. 'Oh, yes . . . Richard. I have just completed a thorough examination of the boy. Physically, there's nothing wrong with him apart from weakness after his illness. In fact, I think it would be preferable if you took him home. He'd probably be more settled.'

'Then what *is* wrong with him, doctor?' Anthea Parlane leaned forward, her fists clenched until the knuckles whitened.

'It's hard to say.' Dr Perry, fingertips together, looked up at the ceiling as though seeking an inspiration, stalling because he did not know the answer. 'He woke up in the night, screaming, then vomited. He hasn't eaten at all today. Won't look at food. I'm sure the trouble is psychological. Nightmares are common in young people, you know. Fortunately, I know the case history, all he's been through. I think it'll take time to wear off. In the meantime I'm prescribing some mild sleeping tablets and hopefully they should help to get him through the night hours. I think, though, the best thing for him would be a complete change of environment. A holiday, perhaps a week or two staying with friends or relatives.'

'As a matter of fact,' Bruce smiled, 'I was thinking the same thing myself. Maybe next week. A break would do us all good.' *After Friday, after I've destroyed* La Maison des Fleurs.

'Good.' The doctor relaxed, another problem solved, or at least the responsibility for a patient shifted. Any further trouble and it would be the GP's pigeon. 'I'm sure Richard's ailment is only temporary. A good rest in the right surroundings should put him right. Now, perhaps you'd like to go along and collect him.'

Rusty was sitting on his bed fully clothed, a small zipped holdall by his side. He looked weak and pale, the smile an effort. Fear had left its stamp on his freckled features.

'You're coming home with us.' Anthea kissed him, helped him to his feet and slipped an arm around him.

'Have you sold the house, Dad?' The question was direct, blurted out with the urgency of life or death.

'Er . . . well, not exactly . . . not yet,' Parlane stammered, averting his gaze. 'I'm sure that before long . . .'

'Something's gone wrong.' Rusty fixed his father with an accusing stare. 'I can tell. You're not going to sell. You're trying to keep it.'

'No, no,' Bruce snapped, then sighed. 'We'll sell. Only . . . only the Swiss government have refused to allow the house back into the country.'

Rusty closed his eyes and clutched Anthea's hand.

'Let's get back home,' she said softly, pulling him close to her.

There was an awkward silence throughout the journey. Rusty sat in the back of the Volvo, his head resting against Anthea's shoulder. She was aware of his tension, the way he breathed, the tightness of his grip on her hand. Damn the Swiss government! She wondered if there was any likelihood of an appeal. It would take weeks, months. Bruce had something up his sleeve, he'd said as much. She just prayed that it was feasible, that it might work.

'It happened again last night,' Rusty said later, ignoring the mug of tea which she had placed on the hearth by his side. 'Different. Worse.'

'Try and forget it. Don't talk about it.'

'I must, Mum. I have to tell you. You have to know.'

'All right, go ahead. But it was only a dream.'

'A dream, but real. As if . . . as if they came and took me out of myself, left my body in the hospital bed and took me to . . . a swamp of some sort. I've no idea where it was. The mist was thick, but the house was there, almost the same as it is today, only newer. It was built on those stilts to stop it from sinking into the bog. And *he* was there, not like he is now. His face hadn't started to rot. He . . . he had a room full of people he'd killed. And . . . and . . .'

'Easy.' She knelt by his side, pulling him close, afraid.

'He . . . ate human flesh, Mum. *And so did I,* but I didn't know until afterwards, then I was more sick than I'd ever been before. *I can still taste it in my mouth!*'

'Calm yourself.' She wished that Bruce hadn't gone out. 'I know it's vivid. Awful. But your father's got a plan to end it once and for all.'

'What's he going to do?' There was alarm in Rusty's eyes. 'He says the house can't go back to Switzerland. There's nothing else that will appease them. They'll wreak their revenge on us if we try anything . . . anything like exorcism again. And going away's no good. Wherever we go they'll follow us.'

'I don't know what he's going to do.' She tried to smile, attempting to show a confidence which she did not feel. 'He wouldn't tell me. But you know your father, he doesn't do rash things. He plans everything carefully beforehand.'

Her mouth was dry. Even Bruce Parlane was no match for Reichenbach.

Friday evening was cool with a slight drizzle in the wind. Teatime had been an ordeal for all of them, especially Bruce Parlane. Nobody spoke much. Both Anthea and Rusty were searching him out in mute interrogation. *You're going to do whatever it is you're going to do tonight, aren't you? Something stupid that'll backfire and bring their wrath down on us. Don't do it, Dad. Don't Bruce, for God's sake.*

Going away wouldn't solve anything. He pushed his plate away and lit a cigarette. The box rattled in his hand as though the matches inside knew and were eager to get started. Just one match. There had been a tobacco advert bearing those three words years ago. 'Just one match will light a pipeful of pleasure.' Funny how little things like that stuck firmly in the memory. It only needed one to create the necessary inferno, to raze *La Maison des Fleurs* to the ground and end the reign of the Reichenbach reincarnates.

It was too early to start out yet. Hell, he'd give anything to get out of the house, to be doing something. Waiting was the worst part.

He went through to the study, sat at his desk and pretended to do some work, shuffling papers, opening and closing drawers. It didn't really fool anybody. They were sitting there in silence in the adjoining room, listening to him. There wasn't any work to do these days. All buying and selling had come to a halt thanks to this latest deal with Al Pennant. He wondered what had happened to Al. The American was right off the scene these days. It was no wonder after all that had happened.

8.30. He slammed the drawers shut for the last time. Loudly, so Anthea and Rusty would hear. He picked up a file, everything appertaining to the cursed house. Kinnerton could hold it. Shortly the insurance brokers would want to see it. They were bloody well welcome to it. All of them.

'I'll be back later.' He picked a light overcoat off the hook, gave them a cursory glance, taking care that he did not meet their gazes directly. 'I should be back by eleven. Unless . . . ' (*anything goes wrong*) . . . 'I get held up.'

Outside. Freedom. The car started first time. He felt in his pocket for his cigarettes. The box of matches rattled again, a sound that stuck in his mind all the way down the lane until the powerful headlights picked out the gateway to *La Maison des Fleurs.* A void, gaping blackness beyond like the crossing place on the River Styx, the ferryman lurking in the shadows.

Parlane pulled the car into the drive and with some difficulty turned it round so that it was facing back towards the road. It wouldn't be seen here by passers-by, not that there was likely to be anybody about. He couldn't take chances on anybody seeing it.

He got out, closed the door quietly and began to walk in the direction of the house. The matchbox in his hand rattled again.

Rusty was tense and afraid. He knew that his father had gone to do whatever he was going to do. He also knew that he would fail. Anthea was busying herself in the kitchen, doing chores that didn't really need doing and pretending to do others. Everybody was trying to fool everybody else. Unsuccessfully. You couldn't fool *them*, though.

He went up to his room wondering how to pass the time. The Meccano had lost its appeal lately. Reading was difficult when your concentration was gone. It'd have to be a book, though. *Sit there with it open and pretend; as everybody else was doing.*

Come back. We need you. Now.

Rusty started, cringed. He'd had no warning that anybody was present, no inkling of their coming. So soon, too, not even waiting until the household was still.

It was Tod, features pallid, body emaciated, patches of bare scalp showing amidst the blond hair. He was standing over by the window, but Rusty knew he had not climbed in that way. He didn't need to.

You must come quickly. Your father has gone on a mission of foolishness to La Maison des Fleurs. *He must be stopped before it is too late, before the others know.*

Rusty's initial fear at seeing Tod again was being replaced by a greater one – that his father's mission was doomed to failure. It couldn't possibly succeed, not against *them.*

I knew he had gone to the house but I had no idea of his plans. I could not have stopped him, anyway.

He plans to burn the house, believing that by doing so he will destroy us. I cannot stay. You must go alone and stop him before it is too late.

Rusty was alone again. Afraid. Shocked. Perhaps he was already too late. There was no time to be lost. He crept down the stairs, pausing half-way to look and listen. His mother was still in the kitchen. A shaft of light cut through the partly open door. Saucepans jangled.

He hastened, half-running on tip-toe, opening the front door and going outside. It was dark and beginning to rain more persistently. He should have brought a coat but to go back for one would be a waste of valuable time.

He kept to the grass verge until he was clear of the gravel drive, glancing behind him, relieved when he reached the lane. Ten minutes, maybe quarter of an hour. Perhaps something would delay his father: a last look around the house by torchlight, a bizarre farewell. It wasn't likely. Bruce Parlane would not be inclined to linger there longer than necessary.

Running until he could not run any more, Rusty was reduced to a fast walk, the weakness left by his illness making every step an effort. *You might already be too late!*

Somehow he found the drive entrance in the pitch darkness and almost walked into the parked Volvo. Relief flooded over him. The night sky was not yet lit up by shooting flames and showering sparks. And then, still some fifty yards away, he spied the beam of a torch. His father was on the verandah above the wooden steps. There might still be time.

Bruce Parlane resisted the temptation to use his torch as

he climbed the flight of steps. Any light might be seen from a distance. Before long this ancient wooden structure would be a beacon seen for miles around.

The pulses in his forehead pounded and the palms of his hands were clammy with sweat. A scuttling noise somewhere inside made him jump. It was only a rat. The place would be full of them; they'd be burned with it, squealing as they sizzled, trapped, the fur burning on their backs.

He'd have to go inside to start the fire. It would spread more easily behind closed doors and also it was unlikely to be noticed before it had got a hold. The last thing he wanted was the fire brigade there within minutes of the blaze starting.

He was feeling for his key when something diverted his attention. A patch of white in the darkness, glowing like a night-light, commanding him to stop and look.

'*The snowdrop!*' he muttered.

He had forgotten all about it recently. It was stupid of him. It was the link, the controlling factor, the generator of evil.

He stood looking at it for some moments, a tiny flower that bloomed in the darkness. So beautiful. The ultimate in evil.

Thoughts and ideas were jumbling in his brain, striving for cohesion. Without the snowdrop Reichenbach and his torture victims were nothing. This was the heart that pumped life into them. Kill it and they died with it, rip it from the soil, crush it, pound it into dust, obliterate it. There was no need to burn the house after all.

Parlane took a step forward. It seemed to be mocking him, erect, defiant. He could almost feel its willpower but that was ridiculous.

Something fell and rattled at his feet. The matchbox. He ignored it. Another step. The atmosphere was cold, as though it was freezing, the night pitch black. Even his torch beam seemed to be dimming, or was the flower becoming brighter and giving forth some mysterious radiance?

Fighting. Determined. He dropped the torch, hearing it clatter and roll, its light extinguished. He didn't need it anymore, he could see everything that was necessary.

'I will destroy you as you destroyed the Pennants and

others,' he shouted, his words whipped away by a sudden gust of icy wind.

'Stop!'

Parlane halted and half-turned, realising that the shout came from behind him yet unwilling to take his eyes off the evil flower. A boy's voice, angry, high-pitched. If it was the spirits gathering then he had to destroy the snowdrop at once. They could not exist without it.

His hands were outstretched. The oak tub was less than a yard away, the snowdrop within seconds of being torn asunder. It couldn't escape him now. Nothing could save it.

His fingertips touched the leaves. They were cold, as though coated with frost, as hard as the vegetation on a yucca plant. *Dig deep, pull up the bulb.* He began to scrape at the soil with his fingers.

'Stop!'

A hand clutched at Bruce Parlane's arm, dragging it away, pulling frantically. He staggered back and got a grip on his adversary.

'Dad, don't. You don't know what you're doing.'

'Rusty!'

Parlane stared at his son, recognising him in the faint luminous glow. The boy was frantic, angry, bathed in sweat.

'What the hell are you doing here?' Bruce snarled. 'You're ill. You should be at home in bed. I've a good mind to give you the thrashing of your life.'

'I don't care what you do to me.' Rusty was struggling to speak, sobbing for breath. 'If you touch that snowdrop or attempt to burn the house down they'll strike us dead just like they did Mr Pinchbeck.'

'You stupid young fool. Without the snowdrop they're nothing. When it dies, they die.'

He turned back, hands outstretched. *Rip it out. Now!*

Rusty hit him with a force that knocked the breath from his body, a shoulder charge that knocked him off balance and sent him staggering back against the wooden wall. The impact jarred him, shocked him. Then, without warning, it unleashed his anger. Nobody was going to stand in his way, not even his own son. The boy was ill, obsessed with his nightmares. Maybe even under *their* control.

Parlane lashed out, felt the back of his hand slap across Rusty's face and heard him cry out. Oh, God, he'd never hit the boy in his life before. One brief moment of shame.

Rusty swayed but he did not go down. Instead he squared up, crouching like a wild beast about to spring, blood trickling from his mouth. 'I warned you, Dad.'

Parlane's attention was distracted for a moment; the snowdrop appeared to glow brighter. He was too late to throw up a defending arm to ward off the clenched fist that started somewhere around Rusty's thigh and finished in the pit of his own stomach. Bruce grunted and was thrown forward. Another blow to the jaw sent him reeling back, sprawling.

Rusty leaped on his father, kicking, punching, biting. Bruce was at a disadvantage, afraid of injuring his son, attempting to grapple rather than fight.

The boy neither expected nor gave any mercy. His father was struggling to his knees, warding him off. Once he regained his feet the advantage would be with Bruce Parlane. Rusty summoned every ounce of his remaining strength and used it to drive a short punch and felt it sink into his father's face, throwing him backwards.

Parlane felt himself hurtling back and braced himself for the fall. A resounding blow on the back of his skull; he knew he'd hit that damned brass plate that was screwed to the wall by the front door. Amidst a blinding red haze in front of his eyes he saw the words plainly, taunting him; *The dance of death, All that go to and fro* . . . it was fading, he felt the blackness rushing at him, the coldness. Then oblivion.

Breathing heavily, Rusty stared down at the crumpled form of his father. The boy's anger was gone, replaced by a terrible remorse, fear of what he might have done. That sharp crack had sounded like splintering bone. No movement came from Bruce Parlane.

You have done well, but only just in time.

Tod's voice but there was no sign of him, as though he was calling from afar, almost a fearful whispered message.

Now go. Quickly.

The darkness had rolled back. Rusty glanced about him.

There was no sign of the snowdrop, not even a faint glow.

He stood there. A dilemma. His father was unconscious, perhaps even . . . *no! He couldn't be!* He needed help. Quickly.

The boy staggered down the steps, fell, crawled and picked himself up. Shambling, exhausted, crying, not knowing if he was heading in the right direction. Bruce Parlane needed help. He had to get it, fast. *He might already be dead. No! He's lying there at their mercy. He'll be all right. They won't harm him now. If he's still alive they'll kill him just like they did Pinchbeck. You might already have killed him!*

Whispered words on the night air stabbed into his tortured brain; a poem he'd remember for the rest of his life, one he'd felt compelled by some strange force to read over and over again, every time he'd gone out on to that verandah.

The dance of death.
All that go to and fro must look upon it,
Mindful of what they shall be; while beneath,
Among the wooden piles, the turbulent river
Rushes impetuous as the river of Life.

He felt the hardness of the tarmac beneath his feet. Wind and rain lashed his tortured body. Far off he heard the pounding of a waterfall, coming closer. Closer. Deafening. He screamed and fell forward on his face, lying motionless in the middle of the deserted lane.

14

AMNESIA

The same room, the small one with the dazzling strip-lighting. People dressed all in white, hushed voices, a sharp smell of cleanliness, almost to the point of unpleasantness.

Rusty stirred, tried to open his eyes, then closed them

again. His head hurt, throbbing as though the top were lifting up and dropping back down again. Breathing wasn't easy, a distinct effort. Sometimes his body was boiling hot; other times it was cold, making him shiver. He tried to work it all out and in the end gave it up. They could do what they liked with him, any of them. He had not the strength to fight any more.

People came and went. There was no break between day and night, always artificial light, sleeping, half-waking, sleeping again.

The headache subsided. He found he could open his eyes without experiencing the shooting pains that went right the way through to his brain. The middle-aged dumpy woman in the dark uniform was kind in every way, patiently feeding him, mostly broth, helping him to and from the toilet. The grey-haired man with rimless spectacles and a long white coat came to see him at frequent intervals, sounding and listening to his chest, checking a chart that hung on the bottom of the bed. Frowning. Nodding. After a few days he even managed a faint smile.

Rusty recognised his mother, of course. He wondered where his father was but he didn't ask. Probably away on business.

Anthea sat for long periods by the side of Rusty's bed, holding his hand, pale and drawn, not talking much. He had been ill, of course. Very ill. He did not want to think about it. Whatever had been wrong with him, he was getting better now, that was all that mattered.

His memory was playing strange tricks. There were a lot of things he could remember clearly; some were just vague flashes that disappeared before he could grasp them. But there was an awful lot that didn't come back at all.

The house. *La Maison des Fleurs.* They'd had to leave because of things that lived there, happenings beyond their control. That was a long time ago. He had been very frightened at the time but it was all over now. Better not to think about it.

Another sleep, a long one, then waking beneath that same fluorescent lighting. Night or day, it didn't matter. Two people by his bed; his mother sitting anxiously watching him, the grey-haired man consulting the chart and writing something down on it.

'Richard.' Anthea's fingers squeezed his own. 'You're looking better.

'I'm OK.' He closed his eyes briefly, then opened them again. 'Where's Dad? He hasn't been to see me lately.'

Anthea Parlane and Dr Perry exchanged glances. The latter shook his head slowly. *Don't tell him, it wouldn't be advisable.*

'He'll be coming to see you soon,' she smiled, her lower lip quivering. 'But not just yet. He's very busy.'

Rusty screwed up his face. There was something he wanted to ask her, something to do with the house. In the end he couldn't remember what it was so he gave up.

They just sat there looking at each other. Dr Perry mumbled something to Anthea, and when Rusty glanced towards the foot of the bed again the doctor had disappeared.

Rusty's eyelids felt heavy. They kept closing, and at length he could not hold them open any longer. A long sleep this time, total oblivion. When finally he awoke the room was empty.

Anthea Parlane was virtually living at the hospital. She alternated between the room on the ground floor where Rusty lay and a larger one, a private ward, on the second storey.

Bruce was waiting for her eagerly when she walked in. He looked more alert beneath the bandages which swathed his head than he had done during the past two weeks.

'How's Rusty?'

'OK. A lot better, in fact.'

'God, I wish I could remember what happened that night,' he groaned.

'Relax.' She leaned over and kissed him, her eyes misty. 'It doesn't matter what happened so long as you both make a complete recovery.'

'It does,' he said. 'I can remember everything clearly up to the time I left home. I was going up . . . *there* . . . to . . . to set fire to the place. Something happened, I don't know what.'

'They found you lying unconscious on the verandah with a fractured skull . . . after a passing motorist had discovered Richard in the road. It brought the pneumonia back. He must've lain for a couple of hours in the cold and pouring rain. Dr Perry warned me a week ago yesterday that he probably wouldn't make it through the night. Somehow he rallied round and after that the recovery was slow. He'll be all right now, though. Apart from this amnesia. His is far worse than yours. He can't even remember going up to the house at all.'

'A blessing in disguise. It's wiped out some of the horrors. Jesus, I can't wait to get out of this place!'

'Well, you won't be coming out just yet' – a firmness in her voice. No arguments. He wasn't in any position to argue.

'We'll see.' He managed a smile. 'The doc says that in a day or two they'll take me down to see Rusty. You never know, seeing me might jog his memory a bit.'

She sighed. Perhaps it was better if Rusty didn't remember. Let them both get well and forget that night when . . . when *something* had happened to them.

'I'll come and see you again tomorrow.' She smiled as she left about half an hour later. On the way out she checked on Rusty again. He was sleeping soundly. The rest would do him good.

Her fears that either Bruce or Rusty, or both, might not make it had lessened considerably. In their wake they left a depression, a feeling of hopelessness. Trapped. All three of them were trapped, governed by forces beyond their control that emanated from *La Maison des Fleurs.* She knew it wasn't over yet. A lull, and then it would all start again. And there was nothing whatever they could do about it.

Rusty heard his name being called over and over again.

Rusty. Rusty. Can you hear me?

He stirred restlessly in his bed. *I'm tired. Let me sleep.*

Rusty. Rusty.

Yes. What is it? A determined effort, the voice seeming to drag him from the depths of his slumber, commanding. It could not be ignored.

Rusty we need you. He is becoming impatient, angry. We must be returned to our native land. We cannot wait much longer.

Who are you? Where do you want to go to?

You do not know? You do not remember?

No. I remember . . . some things. Before . . . whatever it was.

Before you stopped your father from destroying the snowdrop. But that is not enough. We must be returned. Soon.

I will ask . . . my father.

Your father is very ill. You hurt him when you saved the snowdrop.

Me? I don't remember. I hurt him?

Yes. Now you must persuade your mother to return us. Or else you will all die!

Fading. The voice still there, but fainter. Rusty felt himself slipping back into unconsciousness, groaning with mental anguish, knowing that there was something he had to do, but not what or how.

Mel Barnes had been keeping *La Maison des Fleurs* under observation for the past fortnight, ever since his discharge from Winson Green prison; three months deducted from his twelve-month sentence for good conduct. He blamed himself for getting sent down this time; his own fault because he had been stupid enough to think that big house in Moseley was a cinch. He ought to have known that a guy with a place like that would have had burglar alarms installed. It was careless of him, over-confident. You didn't get gaoled for breaking and entering – you went to prison because you were foolish enough to get caught.

Small and wiry, a growth of stubble on his angular chin, he crouched in the bushes which bordered the drive leading up to *La Maison des Fleurs*, the collar of his overcoat buttoned up to keep out the chill wind which somehow found its way through the foliage.

This was another one which looked too good to be true. Nobody had been near the place for two weeks. Windows that you could force with a penknife; and it wasn't as though the place was even empty! He'd had a look through the dirty windows. A lot of stuff that was out of his class, items that a fence would shy at, like that long room with all those iron things fixed to the wall. Antiques, real collectors' items, gave you the bloody creeps. Torture instruments. Worth a bomb if you liked those sort of things. Mel Barnes didn't. But there would be other loot. Three more storeys to be examined. He thought about it, what he might find there, the risks involved.

Mel Barnes licked his dry lips. It would be dark in another hour. He had to come to a decision, something which he never found easy. It was too soon to be back in business. Usually after a stretch inside he left it a month or two, let things settle. The cops always had their eye on you, knew your style, pulled you in for questioning.

Yet, the temptation was too great. Whoever owned this place might take up residence again shortly and that would make things much more difficult. It was now or never.

Once it was dark he made his move, slinking furtively along the shrubbery, each step carefully deliberated, dodging back into the foliage when a car passed along the lane fifty yards away and only emerging when the sound of its engine had died away. It would be just his luck if the owner came back tonight.

Funny sort of place, he reflected, stood up like that on pillars of wood. You could park a fleet of cars underneath. Maybe that was the idea. These eccentric rich bleeders chucked their money about on all sorts of queer things whilst chaps like himself had to struggle just to make a living, and they played lights out if you helped yourself to something that they could well afford to do without. Sod 'em, their houses ought to catch fire, but even that wouldn't trouble 'em too much. Just a slight inconvenience. The insurance pay-out would more than set 'em up again. Time for a real change of government, somebody who really shifted wealth instead of just talking about it. That big house would make an ideal hostel for the homeless, for folks like Mel Barnes to live in, between prison sentences.

He approached the house, gazing up the flight of wooden

steps, then mounting them one at a time, still listening intently. A quick flash of the torch.

The dance of death.

'Strewth!' he recoiled, almost dropped the torch. 'Morbid bleeders. A right nut-house this one.'

He tried the door and made sure it was locked. On no account would he have gone inside if it had not been. It did not take him long to fix the ageing lock, even though his fingers were trembling throughout. Creepy bloody place!

He stepped inside, and with some reluctance closed the door behind him. It smelled stale and musty, as though nobody had been here for years. Under normal circumstances that would have been a reassurance . . . He was sweating, shining the sliver of light up and down the dark oak panels, almost deciding to abandon his mission. Then he thought about what might lie up above. It wouldn't take long. A quick grab.

Barnes had gained the first landing by the time he realised that something was seriously wrong. Nothing that he could be positive about . . . just that the blackness around him seemed alive, closing in on him with cold damp fingers, touching him. So cold, like a winter's night with all the doors and windows open. A draught. Maybe there was a window open somewhere.

A door stood ajar and he pushed it open a few inches and shone his torch inside. A bedroom. A single bed with a carved oak headboard, the covers crumpled around a form that moved as it breathed.

'*God Almighty!*' He stared. *There was somebody in the bed, stirring, sitting up!*

Mel Barnes wanted to run, to rush headlong down those stairs out into the open air, to keep on running until he reached the road. But his feet would not move. His shaking fingers held the torch focused on the bed as though paralysed.

It was a boy. He had long fair hair and wore green and white striped pyjamas. He rubbed his eyes sleepily, staring back at the intruder, apparently not dazzled by the beam of light.

'Hallo,' the voice was soft, almost musical, with a strong American accent.

Barnes gulped. What was a boy doing all alone in a house like this?

He was climbing out of bed, coming towards Mel.

'I . . . I better be going,' Mel gulped. 'I . . . '

'Come with me. I've got something to show you.'

The tone was commanding. You heard it and you didn't think of doing anything except obeying. The burglar stood back, letting the other pass by him, a cold draught fanning his face.

The boy reached the foot of the next flight of stairs and glanced back. The man was following him so he proceeded to mount the wide steps. Barnes shivered. What the hell was going on? This kid was acting as if everything was quite normal, not even scared at meeting up with a burglar. It wasn't natural.

It was even colder now. The boy didn't appear to notice though he was barefooted.

The fourth storey. There was nowhere else they could go except the attic. The burglar noticed with some amazement that his torch had gone out but that he was still able to see all around him. It was strange, indeed. Weird.

'Er . . . I'll have to be going,' he said. It sounded trite.

'Look.' The boy was standing by the rail, pointing down into the stairwell. 'That's where I fell. Down there.'

'Eh? You must be kidding.'

'All the way down to the hall.'

'And . . . it didn't hurt you?'

'Oh, yes, it did. I broke my neck and my back. *It killed me.*'

Barnes felt the beads of sweat standing out coldly on his forehead, as though they might turn into stalactites at any moment. He wanted to yell 'liar' but he couldn't get the word out.

'*They* killed me.' There was a wistful expression on the young features, no trace of malice. 'At least it was quick. Not like some of the others.'

The others! Mel Barnes stepped back and glanced around. Somebody was coming. He knew that there was somebody standing on the flight of stairs below. Watching. Waiting.

'I . . . I'd better be going,' he whispered again, or thought he did. Maybe the words had never materialised, were still in his brain.

'You won't get back that way,' the boy was smiling, almost sadly. 'They're coming now. Just like they did before. There's only one way. Down *there*!'

No! Not down the stairwell. It yawned blackly, a grave ready to receive its corpse.

'It won't hurt much, I promise.'

Get away, leave me alone. Small hands gripped the terrified intruder, and the moment he began to struggle he realised how much he had underestimated their strength. They encircled his waist and lifted him clear of the floor. Kicking. Struggling. His shins banged against the woodwork but the pain went unnoticed. Screaming. Pleading. Words that died before they were born. A cloying nauseating smell.

'Quickly, they are here now!'

Hands came out of the darkness behind, grabbing at him, icy fingers that only found the loose-fitting coat. Slipping, jumping. Shouts of rage, curses following him down. Headlong, turning. Something struck him, knocking the remaining breath from his body. Upturned, he looked back for a split second before the gathering momentum of his hurtling body twisted him in another direction. He saw a gallery of horrific faces, features that were a blasphemy in their very existence, partially decomposed corpses that still lived and carried with them the odour of the grave whence they had come.

The final impact; stout floorboards, the immovable object repelled the moving one, throwing it back up. It bounced, then came to rest in a twisted heap that did not stir.

Up above, the boy struggled and fought, a token resistance before he was finally pushed out into space. He knew the fall, every turn, and winced in anticipation of an obstructing balustrade, the crack of a breaking leg, falling faster . . . and faster. Only this time the landing was softer, a broken human body instead of hard oak boards rolling him over.

He laughed to himself, momentary defiance which turned

to a whimper of fear as he heard them coming down the stairs. They would be angry with him for what he had done. The man, whoever he was, was safe. He was dead. They could do no more to him. It was far worse for those to whom death came a thousand times and still they did not die. Death was easy. It was the prelude which was the worst part. A rehearsal that went on and on in Tod's case, a scenario that would never come to fruition. Die today. Die tomorrow. Die forever more. Then live!

'My God, how awful!' Anthea Parlane stared in shocked horror and disbelief at the impassive features of Detective-Sergeant Repton. Disbelief because she wanted it that way. But she knew it was true.

'I'm sorry to trouble you, Mrs Parlane,' he sighed and wished that they didn't always send him on these errands. If somebody died at their work it was always a case of *Send Repton to tell the widow. He's got the right manner. Understanding, sympathetic.* That was because nobody else wanted to do it. OK, so she didn't know this guy Barnes, had probably never even heard of him, but she had to be told because it was her husband's house and Parlane was in no fit state to take it. 'I know you've got a lot on your plate at present, what with your son and your husband in hospital, but the inspector wants a full investigation into the cause of death. Of course, on the face of it, it was just an accident, a burglar falling down the stairs and . . .'

'From the fourth storey?'

'Yes.' Surprise registered on his lean features, turning to faint suspicion. 'How did you know that?'

'I didn't but . . . but the son of the previous owner met his death in exactly the same way . . . when the house was in America.'

'Oh . . . I see. Maybe there's a dangerous fault on that landing, something that you trip over, or . . . ' – it sounded silly, he couldn't find the right words. The landing was safe enough, he'd examined it himself. It was more like suicide, but Mel Barnes wasn't the type. He didn't have the courage. 'Anyway, we won't trouble you any more than we have to. We'll keep the key for a few days.'

'Please do. Keep it as long as you like, sergeant.' *Keep it for good. I don't want it back. Ever.*

Another thing worried her. The hospital was sending Rusty home the next day. She'd suggested to Dr Perry that it might be better if he had another week under their supervision. 'No, not at all, Mrs Parlane. There's nothing wrong with him. *Physically.* Just shock. His memory will come back gradually, I'm sure. He'll be better in his own environment.'

But it wasn't his own environment. Nor Bruce's. Nor hers. Not with that hellish house squatting like a brooding spider less than a mile away, waiting for its victims to get caught in its web. The forces within it ruled all their lives.

She went back into the kitchen to finish drying the dishes. Dr Perry had said something else, too. Bruce would be home in a week or so. *Take them both away on a holiday. You need a rest, too.* That wouldn't solve anything.

A plate slipped from between her fingers and crashed to the floor, smashing into fragments. She stared at it for a few seconds whilst her emotions adjusted, built up to a peak. Then came hysteria, the uncontrollable sobbing, the weakness that collapsed her into the chair, the depression which took over her whole body like a physical illness.

She knew then that she was cracking up. She couldn't go on much longer.

PART THREE:

TOD AND RUSTY

15

THE RAVENS FEED

Bruce Parlane knew that he was back in Switzerland. Furthermore, he was aware that he was somewhere in the region of the Reichenbach Falls because he could hear the constant rushing and pounding of the water in the deep gorge. It couldn't be any other falls, he knew the sound of these too well, had listened to them night after night. They always seemed louder after dark. And it was dark now.

He was alone, on foot. Puzzled and frightened. He couldn't remember the journey out here, the flight from Heathrow. Or the steep climb in the funicular. But that wasn't surprising because his memory had been playing funny tricks lately. Dr Perry had assured him that it would come right in the end. Bruce had his doubts and it worried him. God, what *was* he doing here?

Voices. They seemed to be coming from somewhere up ahead of him. He walked on, following the narrow track, feeling his way carefully, afraid that he might make a mistake and fall to his death down some precipice.

He saw them as he topped a rise and shrank back against an outcrop of rock, fearful that they might see him. He presumed that they were human: two arms, two legs, standing upright. There the similarity ended. Dwarf-like caricatures, naked shrivelled bodies, heads that seemed too large and heavy for their shoulders, wizened and shrunken. A gathering, illuminated by the flames of a fire that burned on the rocky ground, jabbering excitedly, angrily. In the centre lay a taller man, propped up on one elbow, a look of terror on his aquiline face. He was much larger than the others, naked also, his body wasted almost to the point of emaciation. Dried blood caked his features. His mouth, a thin narrow line, twisted into words. Evil evocations. The others shrank back, looking at one another as though seeking to draw courage from their numbers.

They were shouting, screeching and pointing at the one in their midst. A conflict of curses.

Bruce Parlane wanted to run, to get away from this place, but he was held there as if by some invisible powerful force. *Stay and watch!* Oh, God, it was awful, the figments of some nightmare that could not possibly be real. Yet it had to be. He felt the coldness, the penetrating black atmosphere.

Beyond the circle of light he caught briefly the vague silhouette of stunted trees when the fire burned up, stark twisted limbs like victims of lightning, dead and warped, seeming to lean forward as though they, too, were commanded to be spectators.

He tried to work out what was happening. These shrunken creatures were obviously bent on harming the one in their midst. Their malevolence was apparent and so too was their fear, a party of hunting pygmies that had happened upon a wounded lion, terrified, yet determined to slay it by their sheer weight of numbers.

The one who appeared to be their leader had a long bladed knife in his hand. It glinted faintly as he brandished it, pointing with it at their victim.

The man on the ground struggled up to a sitting position, tried to stand, leering with bloodied lips as the group fell back once more with wails of terror, then surged forward again when it was apparent that he had tested the very limits of his draining strength. Cursing, eyes uplifted as though beseeching some unknown power to come to his aid.

Something else caught Bruce's attention: a small dab of whiteness on the ground which had until now been shielded by the man's body. Parlane stiffened and caught his breath as he recognised the crushed petals, flattened by the weight which had lain on them. *A snowdrop!* Even now the petals seemed to be springing back into shape, slowly reverting to a vertical position.

The group had hunched together. Bruce counted them. Eleven, including the one with the knife. The others were clustered around him, jabbering, pointing. It was all too clear, no interpreter was needed to translate their harsh shrieks of rage. *Finish him now! Kill him!*

A sudden rush, and the leader was propelled like a frond which had snapped off and fallen into a swift torrent, knife upraised, one of the others gripping his arm as though to add impetus to the death blow.

A huddle of bodies. Bruce Parlane clapped his cold clammy hands to his eyes but discovered that he could not shut out the scene. He found himself peeping through splayed fingers, even moving his head from side to side as though trying to make out the details amidst the writhing mass of bodies.

The knife rose and fell, going deep into the abdomen of the helpless victim, spearing him like a blood-red cherry on a cocktail stick. The blade stuck and it took two of them to wrench it free; finally it came away in a gushing fountain of scarlet fluid.

The man on the ground tried to stem the flow with long thin fingers clutching at the gaping wound, somehow finding the strength to strike a blow with his other hand. One of his attackers dropped to the ground and lay there, wide eyes dilated in features that might have belonged to a stone gargoyle.

Kill, before it is too late!

The knife was stabbing frenziedly, slicing through flesh, grinding on bone, ripping and hacking, sinews and ribbons of flesh clinging to the blade. The courage of the small men grew and reached a peak as vile insults and curses were hurled at the one on the ground.

Bruce could see that the victim was dead; the long abdominal wound went right up to the throat, meeting in a T-junction, a river and its tributary, the one flowing into the other, filling it to capacity, bursting its banks.

Legs and arms were hacked at the joints but the blade had not been heavy enough to sever them totally from the mutilated body. The eyes were gone, gouged from their sockets and tossed away, a tasty morsel for the ravens at first light. Others tore at the hanging flesh with their hands, ripping it away.

Bruce Parlane felt the bile rising into his throat. Nausea.

Oh, Jesus Christ it was vile! Their bloodied lips. They couldn't be. It was impossible. No creatures barely resembling human shape could do *that!*

The Dance of Death.

A maniacal frenzy. Their foe was dead but their revenge seemed insatiable. Only when the first rays of dawn lightened the eastern sky did they relent, huddled together once more, their shrill piping voices becoming awed whispers as though they feared the daylight.

A sudden decision. They flitted away, shambling, glancing fearfully back over their hunched shoulders, and then they were gone. Silence, terrible in the gloom of a mountain dawn.

Parlane saw the remains of the corpse, a pile of twisted broken bones and offal. He smelled it, the stench of death and . . . *but it couldn't be decomposing so quickly! It was!* Flesh and entrails moved, alive with maggots which spilled on to the ground, a sudden rush of blood from somewhere pouring out, forming into a dark puddle, the hard ground unwilling to be saturated; a jagged circle with a white centre, a hideous rosette, the thick fluid building up around the solitary snowdrop, slowly seeping away beneath its leaves until all that remained of the blood was a dark stain on the ground.

Daylight was grey and slow to come, as though it feared to expose the true horror of the carnage that had taken place. Parlane crouched low as he heard the slow wingbeats, the deep *cronk-cronk*, the harsh nasal corvine calling. Ravens. Two circling, closing their wings and alighting by the remnants of the murdered man, stabbing with powerful black beaks, crooning softly to themselves as they sampled the unexpected offering.

More birds came with full daylight, another half dozen, belligerently insulting the first arrivals, noisily joining in the repast. Beaks clicked on bone, picking off the flesh. Talons tore at the offal as though desperate to devour it before the maggots completed their meal. A sickening banquet that had Bruce Parlane retching, still unable to take his eyes off the scene.

Mid-day. Silence, except for the distant sound of the

waterfalls. The ravens had gone, leaving in their wake bones to be whitened and dried by the sun, the smell of putrefaction dying away, the fresh mountain breeze strengthening and cleansing.

Bruce found that he could move. He should have turned and fled from this place. Instead he walked forward, picking his way carefully across the rock-strewn plateau until he stood beneath the stunted firs and dead trees.

The skull faced upwards, the neck well broken and hacked, the mouth wide, frozen in its last cursing, calling upon dark forces to come to its aid. The black prayer had gone unheeded.

The snowdrop bloomed, radiantly beautiful, a flower of death that had drunk its fill. A faint scent, like lilies on a newly filled-in grave, poignant, mocking the solitary watcher, the warm sun fast drying the blood-soaked soil.

Parlane sank down and stretched himself out on the ground, the desire to sleep too strong to resist. Every limb, every muscle quivered with exhaustion. His eyelids flickered and closed and he saw again the face of the victim, somehow vaguely familiar.

It seemed an eternity before Bruce Parlane awakened, realisation slowly flooding back. He kept his eyes tightly closed, afraid to open them, terrified that he would have to look once again upon the voluptuous flower. He could still smell its fragrance, the stench of death that had been artificially sweetened in an attempt to disguise it.

'Bruce. Bruce. Dr Perry is here to see you.'

He struggled into waking, forcing his eyes open, blinking in the brightness of full daylight. The mountainside had gone. He no longer lay stretched out on rocky ground. Beneath him was the springy comfort of a divan. The room, so familiar: the stone inglenook fireplace with its adornment of bronze horseriders, the fire unlit, the woven hearthrug. Anthea, blue eyes narrowed in concern, the doctor peering thoughtfully through his rimless spectacles.

'Are you feeling all right, Bruce?' Anthea asked.

'Yes. Yes, I am.' He noted that he was trembling, and he felt slightly sick. That smell; sweet, almost overpowering. It came from a vase of newly picked daffodils and tulips. 'I've been asleep.'

'You've been asleep since breakfast,' she smiled. 'It's now just after mid-day.'

'Must've been tired. This sitting about doing nothing is inclined to make you feel that way, isn't it, doctor.'

'And you've still got a lot of it to do,' Perry argued. 'You've had a rough time. It'll take weeks to get you back to normal, Mr Parlane. And I'll bet you haven't done a thing about fixing that holiday I advised.'

'No, not really, although I was going to phone the travel agents this afternoon.'

'Well, see that you do,' the doctor grunted, and began to give his patient a brief examination. 'Hmm, you're making an improvement. Pulse a little fast.'

My God, Parlane thought, *it's been racing like a turbo engine this last . . . how long?*

'And where are you planning to take us?' Anthea came back into the room from seeing Dr Perry out. 'The last time I mentioned a holiday you said "we'll have to see".'

'Switzerland.' He dropped his gaze.

'No. Anywhere but. It wouldn't do you or Richard any good.'

'We're going to Switzerland.' He stood up and crossed to the window, gazing out on to the spacious lawn where Rusty was playing with an old croquet set which he had found in the attic. 'Or maybe I'd better go alone.'

'Over my dead body.' She whirled on him angrily. 'Bruce, I'm not letting you out of my sight. Now, what's on your mind? Come on, let's have it. I'm not having you going off on any more wild escapades and ending up in hospital. Or worse!'

'OK.' He sat down. His head was beginning to ache again. It had throbbed abominably these last few days since he had returned home. 'Let's take a cold hard look at our situation.'

'We've been doing that for ages and still not come up with anything.'

'Agreed, but we've been too concerned with trying to get *La Maison des Fleurs* back to Switzerland. We must now face up to the fact that that is no longer a possibility. So we must do the next best thing.'

'Which is?'

'Take the snowdrop back and plant it in its original setting.'

'It's crazy,' she said. 'As if that's going to make any difference.'

'It might. On the other hand it might not. But we've got nothing to lose.'

'I don't want Richard to go back up there, not up the falls, anyway.'

'Maybe you're right. But in any case I'd go the last part alone, from Meiringen, anyway. You and Richard could stay in the hotel at Interlaken. I could take a day-trip with these sightseers who flock up to the Reichenbach Falls to see the place where their hero supposedly died. I don't have to go at night or anything like that. Neither do I have to dig the snowdrop up at night. The morning we leave will do fine.'

'All right,' she sighed, 'we'll give it a try. I won't be happy till it's over, though.'

'Tell you what,' he laughed – his headache had subsided considerably. It was probably caused by nervous tension, anyway – 'Once I've planted the bulb we'll get out of Switzerland. A week in Paris. How's that?'

'I'll hold you to it. In fact . . . ' she broke off. The telephone in the hall was bleeping. 'You stay right there. I'll get it.'

She was back in a few seconds. 'For you. It's Kinnerton. He wouldn't leave a message.'

Bruce Parlane crossed the room, aware that his legs were weak. There was a tight feeling in his stomach. There didn't have to be. All nerves. Just the weekly routine call to say that there had been no offers. There weren't likely to be. So why hadn't he just left word with Anthea?

'Mr Parlane, you won't believe this,' Kinnerton's voice was harsh on a crackling line, excited.

'I'll believe anything. You've had an offer from the Youth Hostels Association?'

'I'm serious. A syndicate has made an offer through a West German agency. I gather, reading between the lines, that they regard it as some kind of wartime relic. That's nonsense, of course, but who are we to dispute it? Herr Schaffer has agreed to the asking price without any haggling.'

'Well?'

Bruce knew that Anthea had been listening. Almost a flicker of hope in her eyes. Not daring to hope.

'We have a buyer.' His voice was slightly unsteady. 'A West German by the name of Schaffer. I've never heard of him. Certainly he isn't well-known in the trade. In fact, I don't think he's a dealer at all. No matter, we've got our price if the deal doesn't fall through in the meantime.'

'I can't believe it.' She stepped forward, her eyes misting up. 'I just can't believe it. Not only will we get rid of the accursed place, but we don't need to go to Switzerland now to . . .'

'Oh, yes we do,' Parlane's smile vanished. 'The snowdrop has to go back to its original site.'

'But for God's sake why?'

'I don't know, but it does.' He turned away. He didn't want to tell her about the dream. There was no point. But one thing he knew for certain. The snowdrop had to be returned to that patch of bloodstained soil, the very place where the first Reichenbach, the ancestor at the root of an ancient tree of evil, had laid and cursed as the blood drained from his body. Evil had to be reunited with evil if the Parlanes were ever to be left in peace. Their very souls depended upon it.

16

EVIL TO EVIL

La Maison des Fleurs looked almost friendly as Bruce and Anthea walked up the weed-covered driveway. The early morning sun slanted on to the windows; the grime had been washed off by a recent heavy thunderstorm. One could almost believe that somebody lived there, Anthea thought, and then shivered. Well, they did! She was glad that Rusty had agreed to remain in the car. This errand wouldn't do any of them any good.

They mounted the steps. She glanced at the front door. A man had died inside there only a matter of weeks ago. The coroner's court had given a unanimous verdict of 'death from accidental causes'. They couldn't logically come to any other conclusion. As in the case of Tod Pennant.

Bruce led the way across the verandah. The oak tub stood there at the end. Weeds were sprouting out of the soil: some groundsel and a sprig of bugle. A tiny puddle of water was still trying to sink into the damp soil where the rain had driven into the front of the house. There was no sign of the snowdrop, not even a dead leaf.

'It'll have died off by now,' Bruce was trying to convince his wife as well as himself. 'Couldn't expect to find it still in bloom. Too late in the season.'

She passed him the trowel and held the small polythene bag in readiness. *Oh, please God, let it still be here!*

'Got to be here somewhere.' Bruce delved with the trowel, scooping weeds and soil to one side, sifting through them. 'Ah!' Relief. For both of them.

Anthea stared at the bulb cradled in the palm of her husband's left hand. So tiny, no different in appearance from the kind one bought by the pound in the autumn from Woolworths. Yet more deadly than any other plant, an embodiment of sheer evil, a tiny pear-shaped tuber which was capable of destroying all of them.

She closed her eyes, held the bag wide and heard it plop into the bottom. Her fingers shook with terror and urgency as she closed the neck and twisted the tie. She handed it back to Bruce and saw him slip it into the pocket of his jacket. *Ugh*, it was horrible.

They walked back towards the car, neither of them speaking, each experiencing the same feeling and not wishing to confess it to the other – a sensation of being watched, eyes peering from behind mullioned windows, hatred directed at the two people who had intruded upon an ancient domain. She was glad Rusty had stayed in the car.

Interlaken. The holiday season had barely started and many of the tourist shops were still closed. An air of desolation, hibernation that was still in the last stages and unwilling to be jerked into wakefulness.

The Parlanes had booked in at the Touriste. Dinner, bed and breakfast. By the following afternoon they hoped to be on their way.

'I still think I ought to come with you tomorrow,' Anthea said as they sipped whiskies in the residents' bar after dinner. Rusty was upstairs in bed in the single room at the end of their floor.

'No,' Bruce shook his head. 'I'd sooner you stopped here with Richard. We can't leave him on his own. And, anyway, there won't be any danger. It'll be full daylight and there'll be loads of tourists up there. The "Baker Street Brigade" don't just stick to the summer season, you know.'

'I suppose so.' She looked thoughtful. 'But I won't rest until you're back here.'

'Look, take Richard on a cruise around Lake Thun. The trips started this week. And when you get back I'll be here. Then it'll all be over. We can forget it. And if there's any further funny business in *La Maison des Fleurs* then it'll be Herr Schaffer's problem. He'll be able to discuss it with a fellow countryman by the name of Herr Reichenbach.'

'Don't joke about it, Bruce, please.' She was on edge. Upstairs in their bedroom, tucked in the corner of an unpacked suitcase, was the snowdrop bulb. It was like carrying a time-bomb around, not knowing from one moment to the next when it might explode. Most of all she dreaded the night hours. She could almost feel its presence.

The funicular was crowded on the upward journey. Bruce Parlane huddled in the far corner, glancing over his travelling companions, attempting to keep his mind away from his own mission. His head ached slightly, nothing to worry about. He envied every one of them. They lived in their own world of fantasy; of villainous deeds, murder, even a hero who had never existed in reality. They wanted it that way. They wore their tweed deerstalker hats and Norfolk jackets, smoked their bent pipes and wove their own imaginary mesh of evil over the Reichenbach Falls. Even the sensational press reports on the happenings to the Pennants had not evoked a spark of interest. These people were only interested in one place up there, a narrow shelf of rock with a tourist safety rail separating them from the sheer drop down to the jagged rocks and foaming water below. Maybe some of them had even fantasised about leaping over, welcoming the mode of death, the epitaph, identifying themselves with the sleuth who had gone over the drop, locked in the grip of a madman. But he hadn't gone over, that was the irony of it all; he had taken the opportunity to fake his death. After all, then, there would not be much glory in the contemplated suicide. So none of them leaped into the falls.

Bruce Parlane walked with them from the cable-car, a straggling line, a few hurrying, unable to believe that their long journey was nearly at an end. A few hundred yards further on he took a path that veered off to the right. Several glanced after him. *Hey, that isn't the way. Maybe he's just going for a pee.* Brief astonishment that one should stray, then back to their mutual fantasy.

He felt the bulb, its tiny shape firm inside the flimsy covering, then almost snatched his hand away, like a shoplifter who suddenly supposed that the man behind him was a store detective.

A matter of minutes now. Then he'd go straight back and wait for the car to come up again. Simple.

He emerged from the trees and stared at the flat area of rock and soil; a barren wasteland. Few traces of the original garden remained. Scrubland that went unnoticed; the site of the house had grassed over so that it blended with the surrounding terrain. Nothing was left of the borders or flower-beds.

He walked across, gazing at the wildness of it all, wondering where the bulb should be planted, a shopper faced with scores of cut-price offers and not knowing which one to take. *Sit down, look around, pick your spot. There's no hurry. The last car doesn't go down until five o'clock. Plenty of time. Your old home. Beautiful.*

He sat down on a boulder and lit a cigarette. Spring was merging into summer. It was warm for the time of year. He should have brought Anthea and Rusty, after all. They would have enjoyed it. There was nothing to be frightened of here.

He tossed the butt of his cigarette away but still he did not move. He felt his headache coming back again. There had been a nagging pain behind his eyes ever since he had awoken that morning, the kind that never goes away until it becomes worse. Those whiskies last night hadn't helped. They never did.

He leaned back against the rock behind him and closed his eyes. It was then that he felt the first fluttering pains in his chest. He grunted. Indigestion. He didn't suffer from it very often. Mostly it was due to fried food; he could usually trace the cause. Hell, that was strange. He hadn't had a fry-up for breakfast. Rolls, butter and black cherry jam. The black coffee had been strong. He'd had it that way in an attempt to clear his head but it hadn't worked. Perhaps it had upset his digestive system.

Take it steady, Bruce. Rest, relax and it'll ease up. It didn't. A few minutes later he knew for certain that it wasn't indigestion. It was something much more serious, something which frightened him almost as much as the snowdrop in his pocket.

He forced his eyes open. Blinding sunlight through a red haze of pain. He was sweating, too. *Oh, God, please don't let me die!* Agony. Writhing. A kind of fluttering inside his chest, as if a bird were trapped in there and desperately trying to get out.

After a few minutes the pounding subsided a little. He breathed a sigh of relief. His brain worked more clearly. What the hell was the matter with him? The hairline fracture in his skull could not have brought this about. The steep climb on foot from the funicular was probably to blame. It had been an effort but that was only to be expected after all that he had been through. He hadn't been breathing easily during that last hundred yards or so, there'd been a constricting feeling as though steel bands were encircling his chest and being tightened all the time. Once he reached the summit it had eased off. Just out of condition, that was all it was.

Bruce Parlane sat up. The sun was very low in the west but he couldn't have been there all that long. An hour at the most. Nevertheless, in sickness or in health, there was a job to be done. The snowdrop had to be returned to its last resting place; evil to evil.

He stood up, holding on to the rock for support, swaying, looking around him. The piece of land which had once been the Pennant's garden had reverted to the wild. It was scarcely recognisable. The lawns and borders were a jungle of weeds. Somewhere amidst the docks and nettles was a square inch of ground that had been the grave of a succession of Reichenbachs, their evil absorbed in the snowdrop bulb, flowering and dying, season after season. The exhumed tuber had to be reburied in that same ground.

He worked out his directions. The house had stood on his left, facing towards him. That meant that the border in question was somewhere on his right, about thirty yards away at an angle of approximately thirty degrees.

He took a step, almost overbalanced, then tried another. Waves of dizziness swept over him; his arms were outstretched trying to keep his balance. There was open ground all around him, nothing to hold on to.

Sheer determination. *Got to keep going. Take your time. You're not ill, just tired after your journey.*

Five yards. Ten. Each step now a mammoth effort, a dull ache across his chest that was sapping his strength fast. Stumbling, trying to hurry, his breath rasping in his throat.

Only a short distance to go. He tottered, shading his eyes with his hand. God, it was hot! There, slightly to the left, was a stunted laurel. That was the border for sure. He made out a straight line, almost obscured, where loose soil merged into thicker grass, the edge of what had once been the lawn. This was the place.

He lowered himself into a crouching position, his vision blurring. For one awful moment he thought that he was going to black out. The sensation passed. He waited a few seconds, scarcely daring to move.

Slowly Bruce Parlane withdrew the small polythene bag from his pocket, glancing down at it. He saw the bulb, tiny, insignificant, smaller than a hazel nut, lying amidst the dried soil. He fumbled with the tie. It wasn't easy; the wire inside its paper casing had tangled. He didn't seem to have the strength to undo it, cursing, pulling at it. At length, somehow, the strands parted and the neck of the bag opened.

Bruce thought that he was going to be sick; a sudden rush of nausea that started the juddering in his chest again.

Quickly, there isn't much time.

The soil was caked hard amidst the mass of weeds. He scratched at it with his hand, broke a fingernail, but made no impression. Hell, he should have brought a trowel or some other sharp instrument. Even a penknife. He didn't have anything.

His brain was working slowly. He saw the jagged piece of rock on which he had scraped his nail. Of course, the ideal instrument. He picked it up, grasped it like a dagger and gouged at the earth. It sank in half an inch or so. He began to scratch with it, dislodging some weeds, throwing up a tiny pile of soil until he had made a hole about an inch deep. That was enough. It would do.

He lay on his side, shaking the bulb from the bag. It fell on to the ground, rolled, stopped just short of the tiny hole as though reluctant to be returned to the earth.

Bruce Parlane grunted. His chest was reverberating as though a series of miniature explosions were being detonated inside it, each one causing him to wince. He groaned, closed his eyes, forced them open again. The bulb, it had to be buried. In the open it might be carried away by small rodents or birds. Not that that mattered. Wouldn't it have been just as easy to destroy it? He didn't know. It might not finish Reichenbach and the others as he had once supposed, but instead bring their wrath upon Anthea and Rusty. *Do as they commanded – bury the bulb in the soil.*

He could not see. His sight was gone, just a blaze of red with black shimmering spots. Groping blindly, fingers closing over a round object; too heavy, too hard. A stone. Cursing. Something lighter, softer. He scraped the bulb along the ground and pressed it hard into the indentation, piling soil over it. Done. Finished. *Please God, I don't want to die!*

Parlane rolled over on to his back, staring sightlessly up at the sky. Every muscle in his body was tautening as though with acute cramp, the pain now constant, increasing. He wished that he had allowed Anthea and Rusty to accompany him. It was too late now, though. He didn't know the time, could not even see the sun to hazard a guess. But it was colder, the temperature several degrees lower than when he had first rested against the rock before the pain came. Night was not far off.

He had prayed not to die, now he wanted to end it all. He could not stand much more. Oblivion threatened, then receded. Even the pain eased a little and changed down to a dull throbbing. Worst of all now was the loneliness, the knowledge that he was the only living mortal above the funicular station. Helpless and dying. No way was he going to make it through to morning.

Jumbled thoughts. Rusty. The boy would be OK. So would Anthea now that the threat was lifted from their lives. Months of hell and as soon as it was all over he had to go and die. They'd cope without him, there was enough money to last them for the rest of their lives. *La Maison des Fleurs* was as good as sold. Funny it had to go to a German. Schaffer. Just a name, a guy he'd never meet, didn't particularly want to.

Try and get some sleep. You'll never wake up. Nothing you can do about it. Stop panicking, it might not be as bad as all that. It's a coronary. You're going to die!

Slipping into unconsciousness; floating, suspended in a black void, painless and restful. Waking slowly, stirring, trying to remember . . .

The pain was gone, not even a dull ache remained as a reminder of those long hours of agony. No headache either.

He opened his eyes. No longer was he lying on the rough stony ground. Instead he was in some kind of room, a gloomy place with rough stone walls, condensation dripping to the uneven floor. Faint grey light shafted in through a grille high in the wall.

A movement attracted Bruce Parlane's attention. He stared, trying to focus his gaze. It was a man, sitting with his back to the opposite wall, head slumped forward into his hands. It was impossible to make out details except that he was tall and frail.

Bruce coughed. The man's head was raised slowly. A long pale face, the mouth seeming out of proportion, unnaturally wide like a comic cartoon character. The head was either bald or shaven . . . no, it was neither. The flesh covering the top of the skull was rough and uneven, hideously scarred. With a start Parlane realised that the man had had his scalp removed.

'Where are we?' Parlane asked, hardly recognising the hoarseness of his own voice.

'Where else?' The tall man spoke with a lisp, a foreign accent, too, choosing his words carefully as though unaccustomed to speaking English. '*La Maison des Fleurs.* Gestapo headquarters since the cessation of hostilities.'

La Maison des Fleurs! It was impossible. The house was in England, in Warwickshire. And this room had never been a part of it.

'Never!'

'I assure you, my friend, that is where we are. Allow me to introduce myself. I am Pierre Lautrec, once a member of the French Resistance during the occupation of France. Forty years, and still it is not over. I killed him once, *mon ami.*'

'Who?'

'Reichenbach. The monster. And still he lives.'

'Why are we here?'

'To answer for our crimes against the Führer.'

'But I wasn't even in the war.'

'My friend' – the Frenchman's lips parted in a grotesque attempt at a smile – 'One does not have to fight a war to offend *them*. Nevertheless, you have done something, otherwise you would not be here. All the others are dead. They have been taken out and executed.'

'What others?' Parlane felt his skin prickling and tried to move but could not. It was as though he was paralysed.

'The boy. The women. The other men. They are leaving us until last, allowing us to suffer. It is the end, and yet it is not. Soon it will start all over again. The long period of captivity, tortured daily until you pray for death. Then execution. Myself, I shall be beheaded. I do not know how they will kill you because I am always killed before you.'

You're mad, Parlane thought, *stark raving mad. And so shall I be if this goes on much longer. Where the hell am I?* He tried to recall the events leading up to his imprisonment in this foul stinking dungeon. Of course, the snowdrop. Bizarre. Maybe Lautrec knew something about it.

'I brought the snowdrop back,' Bruce whispered. 'Buried it . . . in the ground that used to be the garden of *La Maison des Fleurs.*'

'Ah, that explains it.'

'Explains what?'

'Why the imprisonment has been so prolonged this time. Why the execution has been delayed. He had to wait until we came back to Switzerland.'

'Who?'

'Reichenbach. Schaffer is back, too. He has been absent for a long time.'

'And who . . . who is Schaffer?' Parlane felt his senses reeling.

'Another Nazi bastard. Reichenbach's lieutenant. One that escaped us. I killed Reichenbach but it made no difference. You can't fight them, dead or alive. When did they kill you?'

Bruce Parlane shook his head. 'I can't remember dying.' It was the truth. He must have died. This couldn't be real. And yet he did not feel any different. Just weak, but the pain had gone.

He fell into a fitful doze, aware that Pierre Lautrec still talked on. He wished he had the strength to listen. So much that he ought to know, explanations concerning all that had taken place in *La Maison des Fleurs.* Most of all he worried about Anthea and Rusty. What had happened to them? At least they were not imprisoned in this foul place. Were they still in Interlaken? God, he hoped they would not come looking for him up on the Reichenbach Falls. But he wasn't on the falls. He couldn't be because he was in the Reichenbach house and that was back in England. So how had he got back there? It was all too much for him.

The sound of booted feet, bolts being withdrawn. Parlane was jerked into wakefulness, staring in amazement at the two men who entered the dungeon. *Jesus Christ, nothing like that had any right to exist on earth!*

The tall one, Reichenbach, his flesh almost gone, a uniformed skeleton that stank like some vile cesspit, remnants of skin still clinging to the skull and hands, eyes still living in those deep sockets. Hating, seeking revenge. The other, short and squat, was in the early stages of decay, with mouldering skin that festered and rotted, heavy lips and a jowl that was peeling down on to his tunic like a paper party beard.

'Lautrec.' Reichenbach stood with his back to Parlane, looking down on the Frenchman, 'You have much to answer for. My patience is exhausted and it is time for you to die. Schaffer . . . '

The other hastened to obey, a schoolboy scurrying to do his teacher's bidding, eager to please. With surprising strength he hoisted the prisoner to his feet, turning him round so that he faced the wall, fastening the gaunt wasted wrists into rusty manacles which protruded out of the rough stone. Lautrec hung there in silence, head bowed. The Nazi reached across, gripped the victim's shirt collar and tugged downwards. A loud ripping sound, the cloth shredding, rotting as it was torn asunder, exposing the wasted back, the rib-cage visible beneath a wafer of flesh.

'He is ready, Herr Reichenbach.'

'Good.'

The tall German took up his position a yard or so behind the Frenchman, cracking the short whip in his hand. Parlane winced. The tip of the thong was embedded in a sliver of steel!

Bruce wanted to close his eyes but he could not. Some strange force was compelling him to watch. Unable to take his eyes off the scene before him, he counted the lashes, watching the Frenchman's back being lacerated, the wounds deep, filling with blood and trickling downwards.

. . . thirteen . . . fourteen . . . Oh, God, no living being could survive such a flogging. An occasional whimper, then silence. It was over but the brute did not let up.

. . . twenty . . . twenty-one . . .

The German's fury was building up to a crescendo, the

whip a blur in his hand, the individual strokes now impossible to count. Lautrec's back was a raw morass, the lash spotting blood on the walls and floor.

Finally Reichenbach eased up, gasping for breath. 'Finish him, Schaffer.'

The other stepped over. Parlane wanted to yell, 'he's dead. You're wasting your time. You can't hurt him anymore.'

His lips moved but no sound came out. Schaffer had an axe in his hand, the heavy blade shining where it had been sharpened, the handle worn smooth with use. He raised it above his head, eyes fixed on the Frenchman's neck. The blow was heavy, the whole of Schaffer's strength behind it, the blade biting deep, cutting through skin and bone, not quite severing the neck. Almost, but not quite. The head lurched to one side, lying at right angles across the shoulders, held in place by a single bloody sinew.

Schaffer swung the axe again, the second blow even greater than the first. This time there was no mistake. The sinew snapped like a length of taut elastic. The head moved slowly, gathering momentum, then crashed to the floor in a crimson shower, rolled, then came to a halt, gazing up at its tormentors. The eyes still seemed to live, retaining the agony and the hate; the slitting mouth was open as though pouring forth abuse. Reichenbach kicked out savagely, sending the skull spinning. It hit the wall and came to rest beneath the dangling legs of Lautrec, as if unwilling to be parted from the body which it had known in life.

Suddenly Parlane was aware that the two Germans were standing over him. He cringed and looked up fearfully, dismissing any idea of mercy. There would be none.

'Schaffer,' Reichenbach's breathing was heavy, his bowed shoulders revealing his exhaustion, 'kill this one. He is not important. I cannot waste any more time.'

'Ja, Herr Reichenbach.'

Bruce Parlane wanted to close his eyes and shut it all out but the lids refused to move. He was forced to watch like a helpless rabbit before a stoat, knowing that death was inevitable, praying for it to be quick.

Schaffer was taking his time, easing the heavy .45 revolver

out of the holster on his belt. Tarnished leather and metal, age and disuse, hammer creaking under the strain as it was cocked, the barrel rust-streaked.

'Now, Herr Reichenbach?'

'Now! This one is of no importance to us. Just a nuisance.'

The barrel was only inches from Bruce Parlane's face. Cross-eyed he looked into it. Disbelief. Unreality. Wanting to say something, brain and vocal chords desperately trying to co-ordinate. Failing. *Don't shoot. I've returned the snowdrop. It's buried . . . somewhere. You're all right now. Don't . . .*

Too late! A flash that brought instant oblivion, throwing him back. Deafening reports like one continuous detonation, heavy slugs ploughing into his throat and chest, one after another until the hammer was clicking on an empty chamber.

17

THE DANCE OF DEATH

Lake Thun in a thunderstorm is a spectacle not to be missed, a memory that will linger on, a reminder of the dark side of nature, her power and anger in a brief display before she relents and becomes tranquil once more.

The storm clouds appeared to hit the mountains and bounce back, lightning sparking from the impact, changing direction. Lower and lower, almost touching the water, then exploding with full venom. Lashing rain and wind, the sunlight obscured, white-tipped waves driving across the lake and catching the small steamer in their swell. A moment of fear for those on board as they recalled stories of shipwrecked mariners, crafts capsizing, the last wails of the drowning, frantically clinging to pieces of flotsam.

Then it was all over, the storm passing with unbelievable speed, bright sunlight following in its wake and scintillating on the water. A rainbow in the sky above marked its passage.

The passengers on the steamer emerged from beneath the canvas covering on to the deck, laughing gaily now, watching the heavy clouds begin to rise as they approached another mountain range, struggling to gain height, lightning flashing as jagged peaks scraped the fluffy undercarriage.

'Some storm,' Anthea Parlane commented.

Rusty did not answer her. He was staring away in the opposite direction towards the four turrets of Zähringen Castle. His whole body was tense, his fists clenched, lips pressed tightly together.

'Rusty?'

'Mum.' He spoke almost inaudibly and there was no mistaking the expression of fear on his features. 'Dad's in trouble. I know it.'

'How . . . how could you possibly know?' she was uneasy, nevertheless.

'I . . . just *know*. We've got to get up to the falls and help him.'

She glanced at her watch. It was just 2.30. 'In all probability he's on the way back now. We'd probably pass him en route and then he'd worry himself sick wondering where we'd got to.'

'No. We must go. *Something's happened to him!*'

'All right.' She felt for his hand and he did not resist. 'The boat's on the way in now. We'll catch a train or a bus to Meiringen. Maybe they'll know at the funicular whether he's come back down.'

Anthea Parlane's uneasiness grew as they stepped ashore. Now she had the feeling; maybe it had rubbed off from Rusty. Like the time her teenage brother had been killed in a motor-cycle accident. She'd *known* he was dead before the police had come to the house.

She tried not to break into a run as they headed towards the station. Somehow she had to remain calm for Rusty's sake. The hand clasped in hers was trembling violently.

It was four o'clock by the time they arrived at the cable-car station outside Meiringen. The car had just pulled away, climbing steeply, seeming to groan under the strain, faces pressed against the windows, all staring upwards, eagerly.

For many it was the culmination of a lifetime of fantasy. For the two people left behind it was a matter of life or death.

'Parlez-vous anglais?' Anthea approached the only occupant of the platform, a dark-haired youth in jeans and an open-necked shirt, a roll of red tickets in his hands. Probably a student doing holiday work, she thought.

He shook his head. She had the impression that he did speak English but he didn't want to be bothered. She tried to describe Bruce to him but he merely shrugged his shoulders. He wasn't interested in who came and went.

It was half an hour before the car returned, some half dozen passengers emerging. Anthea and Rusty took their seats in silence. The cab was hot; their damp clothing clung to their bodies.

The driver had disappeared somewhere, probably in search of a cooling drink before the next trip. It was all a boring routine to him. He wouldn't hurry.

More people were arriving. An elderly grey-haired man smoking a huge curved meerschaum pipe sat opposite Anthea. He looked as though he wished to engage in conversation so she turned her head and looked out of the window. She had that feeling all right now. Something *had* happened to Bruce. There was no doubt in her mind.

When they reached the upper landing stage she found herself pushing her way down the gangway, still clinging to Rusty, cursing beneath her breath. *Get out of my way you stupid bastards, my husband's up here somewhere. In trouble. We've got to find him.*

'Last car down five o'clock,' the driver shouted after them.

Anthea hurried on, breaking into a run, Rusty close behind her. It was slightly cooler up here, and they felt the sudden chill of their damp clothes. The path led off to the right, going sharply uphill, slippery with its powder-dry surface. The boy fell once, picked himself up and hurried on after his mother. He was close to crying.

The ground levelled out to a small plateau screened by tall trees. Anthea pulled up, suddenly very afraid. Beyond lay the place where *La Maison des Fleurs* had once stood, hell's own acre. It was here that Bruce had come; here where he might still be. They knew that he was.

Moving on, hesitantly, pulses thumping, and looking around. Wilderness. A raven took off from one of the trees on the far side of the clearing, cronking its disapproval at the disturbance.

'Let's look around,' she whispered. 'Stay close to me.'

Aimless searching, parting the branches of saplings and bushes, sighs of relief at finding nothing. Perhaps they had been wrong and Bruce was already on his way back to Interlaken. Or else . . . They came to a laurel, green leaves paling and yellowing as though some disease was draining the life from it. Drooping. Dying.

At that moment Anthea saw Bruce. He lay on his back amidst the tall grass, knees drawn up rigidly, hands clutching at his chest, an expression of excruciating agony on his pallid features.

'Oh, my God!' She stepped back, stifling a scream.

Rusty clung to her, unable to take his eyes off the inert form of his father. There was no doubt in either of their minds that Bruce Parlane was dead. And that his death had been one of a terrible nature.

Mother and son clung to each other, sobbing their grief. They had known all along. This was merely a confirmation of their fears, the worst part of all.

'We shall have to get help,' she said at length. 'Maybe if . . . no we'll go together. Summon those people on the falls, get them to go back and . . . fetch somebody.'

Somebody . . . an undertaker, riding up on the funicular with a coffin to fetch the body down. Oh, God, it was awful! Reichenbach had had his revenge in the end.

They headed back in the direction of the falls, stumbling, sobbing. The first person they saw was the elderly man with the meerschaum pipe, standing aside from a group of tourists, staring out across the cascading torrent as if meditating on the drama which he had read over and over again.

'Please,' Anthea blurted out.

'Madam.' He lifted the peak of his deerstalker hat and bowed slightly, 'I trust that you and your son have . . . '

'My husband' – she pointed back behind her – 'he's dead, up there. We need help.'

'Dead! But . . .'

'Please. Would you go down on the next car and telephone the police?'

He stared at her blankly and began to tremble. He preferred fiction to fact. He didn't want to believe her.

'I assure you, I'm telling the truth. I can take you and show you.'

'No, madam. No, indeed. I believe you. The next car down will be leaving in a few minutes. I'll get word to the police.'

'Thank you.' They watched him leave, walking quickly, glancing back over his shoulder every so often. Then he was lost to sight.

'We'd better go back up there,' she said, 'and wait. We can stay by the first clump of trees. I'll have to show the police where . . . where to go.'

They settled themselves down on a slab of flat rock at the base of some tall firs and fell into an uneasy silence. There was nothing to say; they could share their grief without words.

Time passed and the shadows lengthened. In the distance they heard the cable-car rumbling up and down, the voices of its passengers as they alighted.

But there was no sign of the police, nor of the man with the big pipe.

'We'll have to do something soon.' Anthea looked at Rusty. Their tears had dried. The real grief was starting now. 'Perhaps that man forgot, or else he didn't believe us.'

'I wish I could get my own back on those spirits.' There was defiance in Rusty's eyes, adolescent anger and frustration, an attempt to build a façade.

'Ssh!' she slipped an arm around him. Why had nobody come?

'We'll have to go down ourselves,' she said at length and stood up. 'Come on.'

They hastened down the track and arrived at the station a few minutes later. The silence, the deserted atmosphere told its own story, confirmed by a clock on the wall. 5.15.

The last car had gone. They were the only two people left up on the Reichenbach Falls! Abandoned.

'Oh!' She let out a deep sigh and could have sunk down in despair. 'We'll have to try and find our way down on foot. There's sure to be a track. Tourists were coming up here before the funicular was built.'

'I reckon it would be beyond . . . beyond where the house used to stand.'

She shuddered. They'd have to pass by Bruce again.

The sun had dipped behind the distant peaks. Another hour and it would be dark.

'We'd better hurry,' she muttered. 'Maybe the path is easy to find. God, I hope so.'

Through the dense weeds, they deliberately skirted the place where Bruce Parlane lay dead. Circling the perimeter of the clearing, following the line of trees, looking for a well-used track and finding none. Twenty minutes later they arrived back at the place where they had started.

Anthea tried to conceal her rising panic. It was no good, there was no way down to Meiringen on foot from here. They were marooned in this dreadful place as surely as if they had found themselves on another planet in outer space.

'What . . . what are we going to do?' Rusty asked.

'We'll have to try again.' She tried to sound confident. 'We must have missed the opening. Let's go round again in the opposite direction.'

They started off, walking side-by-side, huddling together in their mounting fear and loneliness, glancing apprehensively towards the shadows cast by the tall pines.

Then, suddenly, they saw the boy, leaning up against a tree trunk, watching their approach, waiting for them. *And Rusty knew without any doubt that it was Tod Pennant.*

Anthea felt as though she was going to faint. She recognised Tod, he looked much the same as always; thinner, more gaunt, perhaps. Wide-eyed, dishevelled. But it was Tod.

There isn't much time. He has already killed your father and the others. What has happened to the snowdrop? I know it is here, otherwise we should not be back in Switzerland.

They heard although there was no sound, no movement of his lips. Only a flickering of his eyes. Urgency. Fear.

It is here somewhere. My father brought it.

Then let us try and find it quickly.

They followed the blond-haired boy, running at times to keep up with him, cutting into the centre of the clearing, heedless of nettles and thistles. Bruce Parlane still lay where they had left him. Anthea tried not to look but her eyes were drawn down to the body of her husband. She started. His eyes were closed, the agonised expression was gone. It was as though suddenly he was at peace.

It must be here somewhere. Find where it has been buried.

Rusty groped and scratched with his fingers; stones and hard-baked earth, then soil that was loose and powdery.

Here, I think. Yes.

He grasped the tuber, holding it tightly between forefinger and thumb, afraid that it might slip from his grasp and be lost in the weeds forever.

Let us go quickly. To the falls. It must be cast into the chasm and swept away by the torrent.

Running, Tod Pennant in the lead, Rusty close behind, Anthea bringing up the rear. Back on to the rocky path, the sound of the falls louder, calling them, urging them to hurry. Two or three hundred yards at the most.

Stop!

The command cut into their brains, slewing them to a halt instantly. Topping the rise some fifty yards behind them they saw a man. *Reichenbach!* Anthea's screams died in her throat. Tod and Rusty cowered. There was no mistaking the figure of the Gestapo torturer, his ragged uniform flapping in the late evening breeze, ribbons of flesh billowing like torn carnival streamers.

Too late! He is here!

For some seconds they stared, feeling the force of the putrid man's malevolence, the hate and the triumph.

Give the bulb to me.

Tod stepped forward, placing himself between the tall man and the other two. One glance backwards at them that said everything. *Run to the falls. I will try and gain you the precious seconds.*

It was as though Rusty's limbs had suddenly been freed

from some terrible paralysis. He turned and broke into a run, hearing Anthea follow him. *Thank God!*

Screams and curses followed them. *Don't look back. Run, and keep on running.*

Once he almost fell but somehow kept his balance. His lungs shrieked their agony, his chest pounding and heaving, legs threatening to buckle under him at any moment.

One final scream, cut off so abruptly that they realised that Tod's last stand was over. No longer could he stay the wrath of the last of the Reichenbachs.

They were at the falls now, the narrow shelf standing out over the wide chasm, the flimsy balustrade, the plaque fixed into the rock face.

The dance of death.

No, that wasn't right. Something else, words that were indecipherable, irrelevant.

Give me the snowdrop!

Anthea had shrunk back against the rocks. Rusty's arm was bent, poised, when the command hit him. He felt the paralysis, every nerve in every limb stiffening and freezing. Fingers open. The bulb rolled slowly down the palm of his hand, gathered momentum, fell, bounced. Rolling.

Give me the snowdrop!

The tiny tuber came to the brink beneath the rail, slowed, almost stopped. Then it was gone, falling into the darkness below.

The falls roared, gushed spume high into the air, deafening. Almost drowning the cry of anguish from the decaying man at the end of the platform. Almost, not quite. A shriek that never reached a crescendo, dying slowly away like a siren suddenly switched off.

Rusty found that he could move again, half turned, afraid to look but knowing he had to. His mother crouched on the ground staring wide-eyed in disbelief. Their pursuer had fallen to his knees, looking not at them but out across the darkness beyond the gorge, the remaining flesh falling from his face like the last of the autumn leaves, hands feebly moving in an attempt to stem the decay. Wilting. Fading. Moaning softly as he rolled over and lay full length, as if deliberately screening his end from the watchers; defeat after centuries of immortality.

Silence; except for the noise of the falls, loud and violent as though bent upon some act of destruction in the foaming cauldron far below. Rusty moved across to his mother, nestling his head in her lap, each seeking comfort in the other's presence, no longer afraid. Nothing would harm them now. It was all over. The suffering of the victims was at an end, too. They had been freed from their terrible bonds, a watery grave that would soothe their tortured souls and destroy him who had held power over them for so long.

It was late the following day when they finally arrived back at the Touriste in Interlaken, numbed with shock that was still keeping grief at bay. Bruce Parlane's body would not be flown back to England for another week. Autopsies took time. Nobody hurried, not in these days of refrigeration.

For Anthea and Rusty Parlane the blow still had to fall, to hit them hard. They could not yet believe that the forces which had inhabited *La Maison des Fleurs* was destroyed; that Bruce was dead. That was all still to come. And then they would have to rebuild their lives.

Routine living was done automatically, eating without tasting, going to bed without sleeping, buying newspapers and not reading them because the print was a meaningless jumble of letters that did not register in their brains.

A three-day old *Sun* lay on one of the chairs in the foyer of the Touriste, thumbed and torn, the headlines in large black lettering, propped up like some advertisement hoarding. Rusty saw the words and read them. Read them again. At the third attempt their meaning filtered through, holding him transfixed.

'What's the matter?' Anthea turned back from the large glass entrance door, wondering what had delayed him.

'That . . . ' he pointed.

'HAUNTED HOUSE DESTROYED BY FIRE'

He was already snatching it up, forcing himself to read the small print.

'Last night fire broke out in an imported timber mansion

at Stratford-on-Avon, Warwickshire. Firemen were unable to check the blaze, which destroyed the property and its contents. Police investigating the cause of the fire believe it was deliberately started, as a boy was seen leaving the blaze when the fire engines arrived. He is described as being between twelve and fourteen years of age, with long blond hair, and dressed in frayed denims. The police are anxious to interview him in connection with the fire.

'The house concerned, which has a history of hauntings, is the property of Mr Bruce Parlane, believed to be holidaying in Switzerland. All that remained of the exterior was a brass plaque on which was inscribed some verse by Longfellow. Police are endeavouring to contact Mr Parlane.'

Anthea was still holding the newspaper as they walked outside. Four nights ago. The same night. Tod. It was all over, everything erased. Total annihilation. Only a few engraved words remained to mark the funeral pyre of the Reichenbachs in England.

The dance of death.
All that go to and fro must look upon it,
Mindful of what they shall be; while beneath,
Among the wooden piles, the turbulent river
Rushes impetuous as the river of Life.

FICTION

GENERAL

☐ Stand on It	Stroker Ace	95p
☐ Chains	Justin Adams	£1.25
☐ The Master Mechanic	I. G. Broat	£1.50
☐ Wyndward Passion	Norman Daniels	£1 35
☐ Abingdon's	Michael French	£1.25
☐ The Moviola Man	Bill and Colleen Mahan	£1.25
☐ Running Scared	Gregory Mcdonald	85p
☐ Gossip	Marc Olden	£1.25
☐ The Sounds of Silence	Judith Richards	£1.00
☐ Summer Lightning	Judith Richards	£1.00
☐ The Hamptons	Charles Rigdon	£1.35
☐ The Affair of Nina B.	Simmel	95p
☐ The Berlin Connection	Simmel	£1.50
☐ The Cain Conspiracy	Simmel	£1.20
☐ Double Agent—Triple Cross	Simmel	£1.35
☐ Celestial Navigation	Anne Tyler	£1.00
☐ Earthly Possessions	Anne Tyler	95p
☐ Searching for Caleb	Anne Tyler	£1.00

WESTERN BLADE SERIES

☐ No. 1 The Indian Incident	Matt Chisholm	75p
☐ No. 2 The Tucson Conspiracy	Matt Chisholm	75p
☐ No. 3 The Laredo Assignment	Matt Chisholm	75p
☐ No. 4 The Pecos Manhunt	Matt Chisholm	75p
☐ No. 5 The Colorado Virgins	Matt Chisholm	85p
☐ No. 6 The Mexican Proposition	Matt Chisholm	75p
☐ No. 7 The Arizona Climax	Matt Chisholm	85p
☐ No. 8 The Nevada Mustang	Matt Chisholm	85p

WAR

☐ Jenny's War	Jack Stoneley	£1.25
☐ The Killing-Ground	Elleston Trevor	£1.10

NAVAL HISTORICAL

☐ The Sea of the Dragon	R. T. Aundrews	95p
☐ Ty-Shan Bay	R. T. Aundrews	95p
☐ HMS Bounty	John Maxwell	£1.00
☐ The Baltic Convoy	Showell Styles	95p
☐ Mr. Fitton's Commission	Showell Styles	85p

FILM/TV TIE-IN

☐ American Gigolo	Timothy Harris	95p
☐ Meteor	E. H. North and F. Coen	95p
☐ Driver	Clyde B. Phillips	80p

SCIENCE FICTION

☐ The Mind Thing	Fredric Brown	90p
☐ Strangers	Gardner Dozois	95p
☐ Project Barrier	Daniel F. Galouye	80p
☐ Beyond the Barrier	Damon Knight	80p
☐ Clash by Night	Henry Kuttner	95p
☐ Fury	Henry Kuttner	80p
☐ Mutant	Henry Kuttner	90p
☐ Drinking Sapphire Wine	Tanith Lee	£1.25
☐ Journey	Marta Randall	£1.00
☐ The Lion Game	James H. Schmitz	70p
☐ The Seed of Earth	Robert Silverberg	80p
☐ The Silent Invaders	Robert Silverberg	80p
☐ City of the Sun	Brian M. Stableford	85p
☐ Critical Threshold	Brian M. Stableford	75p
☐ The Florians	Brian M. Stableford	80p
☐ Wildeblood's Empire	Brian M. Stableford	80p
☐ A Touch of Strange	Theodore Sturgeon	85p

☐ Celestial Navigation	Anne Tyler	£1.00
☐ Earthly Possessions	Anne Tyler	95p
☐ Searching for Caleb	Anne Tyler	£1.00

FICTION

CRIME/ADVENTURE/SUSPENSE

☐ The Organization	David Anthony	90p
☐ Stud Game	David Anthony	95p
☐ Five Pieces of Jade	John Ball	85p
☐ Siege	Peter Cave	£1.15
☐ The Execution	Oliver Crawford	90p
☐ The Ransom Commando	James Grant	95p
☐ The Rose Medallion	James Grant	90p
☐ Barracuda	Irving A. Greenfield	95p
☐ The Halo Jump	Alistair Hamilton	£1.00
☐ The Desperate Hours	Joseph Hayes	95p
☐ A Game for the Living	Patricia Highsmith	95p
☐ The Blunderer	Patricia Highsmith	95p
☐ Those Who Walk Away	Patricia Highsmith	95p
☐ The Tremor of Forgery	Patricia Highsmith	80p
☐ The Two Faces of January	Patricia Highsmith	95p
☐ The Heir	Christopher Keane	£1.00
☐ Cranmer	Steve Knickmeyer	90p
☐ The Golden Grin	Colin Lewis	£1.00
☐ Confess, Fletch	Gregory Mcdonald	90p
☐ Fletch	Gregory Mcdonald	90p
☐ Flynn	Gregory Mcdonald	95p
☐ To Kill a Jogger	Jon Messmann	95p
☐ Pandora Man	Kerry Newcomb and Frank Schaefer	£1.25
☐ Sigmet Active	Thomas Page	£1.10
☐ The Jericho Commandment	James Patterson	£1.00
☐ Games	Bill Pronzini	85p
☐ Crash Landing	Mark Regan	95p
☐ The Mole	Dan Sherman	95p
☐ Swann	Dan Sherman	£1.00
☐ The Peking Pay-Off	Ian Stewart	90p
☐ The Seizing of Singapore	Ian Stewart	£1.00
☐ Place of the Dawn	Gordon Taylor	90p
☐ Judas Cross	Jeffrey M. Wallmann	90p
☐ Rough Deal	Walter Winward	85p
☐ The Ten-Tola Bars	Burton Wohl	90p

HISTORICAL ROMANCE/ROMANCE/SAGA

☐ Flowers of Fire	Stephanie Blake	£1.00
☐ So Wicked My Desire	Stephanie Blake	£1.50
☐ Morgana	Marie Buchanan	£1.35
☐ The Enchanted Land	Jude Deveraux	£1.50
☐ Mystic Rose	Patricia Gallagher	£1.25
☐ Alinor	Roberta Gellis	£1.20
☐ Gilliane	Roberta Gellis	£1.00
☐ Joanna	Roberta Gellis	£1.25
☐ Roselynde	Roberta Gellis	£1.20
☐ Love's Scarlet Banner	Fiona Harrowe	£1.00
☐ Lily of the Sun	Sandra Heath	95p
☐ Daneclere	Pamela Hill	£1.25
☐ Strangers' Forest	Pamela Hill	£1.00
☐ Royal Mistress	Patricia Campbell Horton	£1.50
☐ The Tall One	Barbara Jefferis	£1.00
☐ Captive Bride	Johanna Lindsey	£1.00
☐ The Flight of the Dove	Catherine MacArthur	95p
☐ The Far Side of Destiny	Dore Mullen	£1.50
☐ The Southern Moon	Jane Parkhurst	£1.25
☐ Summerblood	Anne Rudeen	£1.25
☐ The Year Growing Ancient	Irene Hunter Steiner	£1.10

HAMLYN WHODUNNITS

☐ The Worm of Death	Nicholas Blake	95p
☐ The Judas Pair	Jonathan Gash	95p
☐ There Came Both Mist and Snow	Michael Innes	95p
☐ The Siamese Twin Mystery	Ellery Queen	95p

Also in Hamlyn Paperbacks

Guy N. Smith
author of Night of the Crabs

LOCUSTS

It seems the start of a glorious summer as Alan Alton and his family settle into their new home in the Shropshire hills.

Then the insects start to appear.

First there's one . . . then hundreds . . . thousands . . . millions. A smothering tide of destruction covers the land.

LOCUSTS

As the heat-wave continues mercilessly week after week, the horde of invaders grows – a hideous, red-eyed devastation spreading across town and country.

Biting, stripping, devouring . . . and hating.

Before this onslaught the human population turns to flight. As panic grows, the death-toll also rises and the whole country is plunged into chaos. Britain is being eaten alive.

Can nothing stop the locusts?